KU-141-948

Cinematic countrysides

Edited by Robert Fish

Manchester University Press
Manchester and New York

distributed exclusively in the USA by Palgrave

Published by Manchester University Press
Oxford Road, Manchester M13 9NR, UK
and Room 400, 175 Fifth Avenue, New York, NY 10010, USA
www.manchesteruniversitypress.co.uk

Distributed exclusively in the USA by
Palgrave, 175 Fifth Avenue, New York,
NY 10010, USA

Distributed exclusively in Canada by
UBC Press, University of British Columbia, 2029 West Mall,
Vancouver, BC, Canada V6T 1Z2

British Library Cataloguing-in-Publication Data
A catalogue record for this book is available from the British Library

Library of Congress Cataloging-in-Publication Data applied for

ISBN   978 0 7190 7266 6   *hardback*

First published 2007

16 15 14 13 12 11 10 09 08 07   10 9 8 7 6 5 4 3 2 1

Typeset
by Action Publishing Technology Ltd, Gloucester
Printed in Great Britain
by Biddles Ltd, King's Lynn

Contents

Figures

Tables

Contributors

David Bell is Senior Lecturer in Critical Human Geography and leader of the Urban Cultures & Consumption research cluster in the School of Geography at the University of Leeds, UK. His main interests are cultural policy, sexualities, science and technology.

Katy Bennett is Lecturer in Human Geography at the University of Leicester. Her work has examined the impacts of economic restructuring and regeneration on rural households, gender relations and identities. Her current research includes an ESRC-funded project 'Identities and regeneration in the former coalfields of East Durham'.

Catherine Brace is Associate Professor of Historical and Cultural Geography in the Department of Geography at the University of Exeter's Cornwall Campus. Catherine's research focuses on the material and symbolic production of landscape, particularly as this relates to the formation of national and regional identities.

Robert Fish is a human geographer with research interests in contemporary countryside cultures and environments. A key focus of his recent work has been to explore the construction of English rural identities in popular lifestyle magazines, television dramas and film. He is a Research Fellow in the School of Humanities and Social Sciences at the University of Exeter.

Ian Goode teaches Film and Television at the University of Glasgow. He has published articles on British Heritage and BBC documentary, television drama and the television monologue. His current research is concerned with television documentary and the home movie in Scotland.

Tanya Krzywinska is a Professor of Screen Studies in the Department of Arts at Brunel University, UK. She has published a wide range of books and articles on different aspects of popular culture and is currently working on a book entitled *Imaginary Worlds* that addresses transmedial fantasy-genre franchises such as Warcraft and *The Lord of the Rings*. Her research into popular and cult cinemas, videogames and imagined worlds, and representations of magic and sex considers the way that engagement and representation are produced at the interface between form and context.

Janna Jones is Associate Professor of Communication and Cultural Studies at Northern Arizona University in Flagstaff. Her research focuses on cinematic culture and cultural heritage. She is the author of *The Southern Movie Palace: Rise, Fall, and Resurrection* and has published essays about filmic and archival culture and cinema-going in various journals and edited volumes.

Owain Jones is a Research Fellow in the Countryside and Community Research Institute at the University of Gloucestershire. He has research interests in the geographies of children and childhood and the geographies of society and nature. Owain's work is particularly concerned with exploring 'ecologies of place and landscape' and how other lives/geographies are lived within them.

Richard Lee is a Postgraduate Researcher in the Centre for Rural Economy, Newcastle University. His current research interests are in the sociology and politics of the agri-food system. He has previously undertaken research on participation in rural development and young people's involvement in decision-making.

Michael Leyshon is Lecturer in Human Geography in the Department of Geography at the University of Exeter's Cornwall Campus. He is a social and cultural geographer with interested in youth culture, identity and performativity. His research explores, and seeks solutions to, the ways in which young people become socially, politically and economically excluded from society.

Carol Medlicott is Assistant Professor of Geography in the Department of History and Geography at Northern Kentucky University (NKU). Her areas of research and teaching interest include historical and cultural geography and landscapes of nationalism. She is interested in the rural cultural landscapes of both Asia and early America.

Mark Neumann is Professor of Communication and Cultural Studies and Director of the School of Communication at Northern Arizona University in Flagstaff. His research focuses on visual culture, documentary studies, and tourism. He is the author of *On The Rim: Looking for the Grand Canyon* (1999), and has published essays on amateur film and cinematic culture in various journals and edited volumes.

Martin Phillips is Reader in Social and Cultural Geography in the Department of Geography, University of Leicester. His research interests span rural social and cultural geography, historical geography, society/environment relations and philosophy in geography. Much of his recent work has focused on the material and symbolic constructions of rural space, with particular regard to the social relations and identities of class and gender.

Andy C. Pratt is Reader in Urban Cultural Economy in the Department of Geography and Environment at the London School of Economics. Andy specialises in the social organisation of economic development, cities and economic space, with a particular focus on contemporary cultural industries.

Jonathan Rayner is Reader in Film and English at the University of Sheffield, School of English. He has written widely on Australasian cinema, and is the author of *The Films of Peter Weir* (1998/2003), *Contemporary Australian Cinema* (2000), *The New Zealand and American Films of Geoff Murphy* (1999) and *The Naval War Film: Genre, History, National Cinema* (2007).

Maria Rovisco is a Postdoctoral Research Fellow at the Department of Sociology, ISCTE – University of Lisbon. She has published articles on the tradition of European films of voyage and is currently co-editing the book *Cosmopolitanism in Practice*

(Ashgate). Her main research interests focus on film, cultural sociology and cosmopolitanism.

Patricia Winter is Senior Lecturer in Film in the School of Arts, Design, Media and Culture at the University of Sunderland. Her research spans interests in the construction of Englishness in new English folk music and dance, issues of gender, identity and embodiment and the representation of British military identities.

Rachel Woodward is a Reader in critical geography in the School of Geography, Politics and Sociology at the University of Newcastle upon Tyne. She has researched and published widely on the theme of military geographies, and is currently collaborating with Patricia Winter on ESRC research examining how British military personnel are portrayed and represented.

Acknowledgements

I would like to express my thanks to Mark Jancovich, whose infectious sense of enthusiasm helped me to start realising, and stop fantasising about, this project. Thanks as well to Jacob Bull, for the careful eye.

1

What are these cinematic countrysides?

Robert Fish

As we shall see, staging an encounter between cinema and country-side is to invoke a rich and diverse spatial imagery. Cinematic countrysides are the expanse of the American Great West and the restraint of the English village street; the mountain terrains of North Korea and the jungle environments of the Viet Cong. Cinematic countrysides are the iconographic backdrop to national founding myths and the broken landscapes of the border zone; the pastoral scenery to an Arcadian past and the burning fields of a post-apocalyptic future. Cinematic countrysides are affirmative engagements with nature and the non-human, and nightmare encounters with a monstrous and de-natured in-human; the site where bodies are dismantled and lost, and the place where identi-ties are reconstructed and found. Cinematic countrysides are the transformative possibilities of the wide-open road and the enchant-ed landscapes of the yellow brick road; the degenerate moralities of the outback town and the terrifying realities of the battleground.

Such is our emphasis on plurality; on cinematic *countrysides*. Programmatically, the concern of this volume is to initiate an engagement with the multidimensional occupancy and experience of rural landscapes as this produces, and is produced by, the textual and material relations of film. That is to say, *Cinematic countrysides* is designed to explore the reciprocal relationship between film and the rural: how film makes rural and rural makes film. It is energised by an intellectual landscape that in recent years has sought, somewhat frenetically, to mark out the endemic rela-tionship between cultural process and spatial form and one given shape by the collaborations of geographers, sociologists, historians and film theorists specifically seeking to engage with the relationship between cinema and space (for example Aitken and Zonn, 1994; Cresswell and Dixon, 2002). As a further exploration of this issue *Cinematic countrysides* follows Shiel (2001) in seeking to think about the spatialities of film across the whole ambit of cinematic production: inspecting not only the representational spaces of film, but the way that films are materially put together, commodified, distributed and displayed.

Anti-thesis

In pursuing these concerns *Cinematic countrysides* seeks to foreground spatialities of cinema that have tended to be buried beneath existing trajectories of inquiry, for in marking out the relationship between cinema and space it is the idea of the 'urban', and in particular the 'city', that looms large (for example Bruno, 1993; Friedburg, 1993; Clarke, 1997; Shiel and Fitzmaurice, 2001, 2003; Barber, 2002). Indeed, if cinema functions as both product and instrument of geographical experience, then such experience, it would seem, is of a decisively metropolitan cast. On the one hand, cinema encompasses systems of textual and material practice that are markedly urban in expression: industries of cinematic production have tended to gather and agglomerate in the centres and shadows of the city, as have networks of cinematic dissemination, exhibition and display (Stringer, 2001; Hubbard, 2002). In urban culture and form, filmic discourse has one of its enduring and archetypal preoccupations, from the utopian visions of documentaries and the planner (Gold and Ward, 1997) to the ambivalent visions of Sci-fi and Noir (Jarvis, 1998; Farish, 2005). On the other hand, the emergence of cinema over the last century can be read as an exercise in city 'place-making': a source of urban memory, self-expression and enchantment, and a culture industry central to its economic reproduction and material shape (Jancovich *et al.*, 2003).

Scholars ignore these entanglements at their peril, we are told, not least because 'city' and 'cinema' are ubiquitous categories of experience. For Shiel (2001: 1–2) investigating the nexus of cinema-city is about charting the 'relationship between the most important cultural form ... and the most important form of social organisation', and in so doing the ground is laid for an account of 'perennial' issues and questions. Thus, through the cinematic city it is possible to learn much about the rise of industrial capitalism and much about expressions of post-industrialism; much about the experience of modernity and much about the discontents of post-modernity; much about the shape of the material economy and much about the logic of the sign economy; much about the organi-sation of world cities and much about the uneven outcomes of globalisation; and so forth. In short, the cinematic city is designed to be both emblematic of, and paradigmatic to, our condition.

After the cinematic city

According to one reading, this rather frenetic engagement with the cinematic city – this sense in city and cinema are categories both *of* and *for* each other – carries with it the implication that country-sides are somehow 'non-cinematic' in form and experience, and, more substantively, that countrysides have little purchase on these 'perennial' concerns. In this sense the volume at hand is designed to function as something of an intervention in, and subversion of, this dominant spatial imagery. It is an effort to square the 'flickering, virtual, presence of the city' (Clarke 1997: 10) with the 'flicker of lights, sunsets, shadows, sunrises' of the countryside (Denzin, 1991: 142).

Yet it would be wrong to claim that the 'non-urban' or 'more than urban' has been entirely lost to work on cinematic geogra-phies (for example Aitken and Zonn, 1994; Kennedy, 1994; Krim, 1994; Bell, 1997; Ingram, 2000; Smith, 2002; Lukinbeal and Arreola, 2005), or that histories of film criticism – from treatments of nature and wilderness in the Western (Kitses and Rickman, 1998) to the costumed landscapes of heritage cinema (Higson, 2003) and into the liminal spaces of the road movie (Laderman, 2002) and the slasher landscapes of the horror (Hutchings, 2004) – have not dealt with a range of cinematic countrysides. In fact, while moves to chart the spatiality of film have been an attempt to do something more than simply account for the text – and therein make a quite explicit challenge to the longstanding preoccupations of film studies – it is in such histories that the idea of cinematic countrysides finds its precedents.

Moreover, the idea of countryside has not been lost to work on the city itself, since the cinematic city 'thesis' rests on a category distinction, and category distinctions not only invite speculation about alternative frames of critical reference, but are necessarily produced through them. Indeed, if it is one thing to suggest that *Cinematic countrysides* is an effort to foreground a different imagery within accounts of cinema and space, then it is quite another to claim that the relational and oppositional terms upon which cinematic cities are built have gone unrecognised, or conversely, that the cinematic countrysides we will be exploring in this volume exist outside of the orbit of the cinematic city. 'City' and 'countryside' are, of course, categories whose meanings and experiences tend to configure each other. This relationship, then, is a key way in which in we might begin to inspect the idea of cinematic countrysides.

City/countryside (i) the spaces of film

> There are few more useful structures than the historically far reaching country/city opposition for understanding the way in which cities have been represented on film. (McArthur, 1997: 40)

Colin McArthur's concern is with the cinematic city but his comment cuts both ways. The country/city opposition is a means by which *both* country and city are represented on film. In one of the most insightful and sustained treatments of this relationship to date, McArthur takes us on a journey through a range of different cinematic traditions and filmic examples to explain the way that representations of city and countryside have come to charge each other positively and negatively. For McArthur, charting the relative virtues of country/city is about expressing and making sense of deep-seated changes in the organisation and experience of society, not least the transition to modernity. This experience is wide ranging. Scotland, Italy, Mexico, South Korea, China, Taiwan all produce cinematic versions of this process, as does America, which functions as something of archetype. So for instance the country/city opposition in American life is, on the one hand, an opportunity to continually reassert and revisit deeply engrained 'anti-urban, pro-small town/agrarian/pastoral/wilderness ideologies' (McArthur, 1997: 24): from *Meet Me in St Louis* (1944) and *It's a Wonderful Life* (1946) to *Witness* (1985) and *Sleeping with the Enemy* (1991) American cinema has a long tradition of coding the rural affirmatively in relation to the values, moralities and landscapes of the city. But it is also a tradition that produces less than idyllic visions: from *Fury* (1936) and *Intruder in the Dust* (1949) to *Easy Rider* (1969) and *Blue Velvet* (1986), McArthur explains how the American small town is positioned as an 'icon of bigotry, small mindedness and explosive violence' (1997: 24).

As McArthur suggests, these oppositions rely on the coming together of different compositional registers: the invocation of country and city through uses of light and colour; the application of diegetic and non-diegetic soundscapes, as well the spatial patterning and juxtaposition of narrative events. As narrative we should note that codings of country/city find a key thematic expression in the idea of mobility: the circumstances and events that befall characters and propel them in different directions. These are flights and voyages outwards from the urban (for example *Thelma and Louise*, 1991) and inwards from the country (*Wizard of Oz*, 1939), passages between cities (*Radio On*, 1980) and return trips (*Withnail and I*, 1987), as well as wandering and drifting movements (*Paris, Texas*, 1984), and they provide the spatial architecture behind journeys of mental and bodily transformation affirmative (such as self-realisation and redemption) and ill-fated (such as degeneration and death) in kind. Where city/countryside oppositions function without some narrative of physical mobility, contrasts are often introduced in psycho-aesthetic terms. Such is the antithetical reality introduced at the close of *Brazil* (1984), where the tortured main protagonist, entrapped in a nightmare urban future, escapes to a pastoral Arcadian landscape. And such is the antithetical reality at work in *It's a Wonderful Life*, where the protagonist witnesses the idyllic small town of Bedford Falls being transformed into the urban nightmare of Potterville (Krutnik, 1997).

City/countryside (ii) films in space
These relational spaces of film must also be squared with what Shiel (2001: 5) describes as the issue of 'films in space'; that is, with the extra-textual dimensions of the country/city antinomy. Contributions to Shiel and Fitzmaurice's (2001) collection on cinema and urban societies have already demonstrated how the rise of the cinematic city is part of an economic system that re-produces geographical unevenness and how networks of the cinematic city produce their own internal hierarchies; ones reflecting wider geopolitical differences between cities on a global scale. This issue

of geographical unevenness might be argued to extend too into the concerns of this volume. If evolving forms of film production, display and consumption are understood to overwhelmingly gather and agglomerate in the 'cinema-city' then it follows that in the rural they tend otherwise. A number of issues loom large in this respect: declining numbers of cinemas in many rural areas; very few film studios and post-production facilities in countryside locations; as well as highly debatable 'legacy' issues surrounding that very material yet transient connection between cinematic city and cinematic countryside: the location shoot.

Furthermore, just as much as cinematic representations will fashion city/countryside narratives that reflect our responses to deep-seated changes in the spatial organisation and experience of society, this *material placement* of cinema in urban space arguably confirms what those narratives are partly about: that the countryside is outside of, and lost to, modernity. And like the representational spaces of the text, this materialisation of cinema as a city activity may be used to marshal and express quite different understandings of city and country. On the one hand it may produce real and imagined limits to culture, where the city – enlightened and enthralled by the spectacle of cinema – affirms the countryside as deprived at best, and backward, regressive and un-modern at worst. Alternatively, the cinematic city may be read rather pessimistically. It may be read as an expression of the discontents of modernity in which ideas of disconnection come to the fore. This is a world of disenchantment, where alienated urban masses consume disembodied experiences in the 'non-places' of the multiplex (Auge, 1995). The countryside, largely absent from this bread and circus experience, thus becomes an environment for authentic and conciliatory engagements with the world; a site for reactionary and affirmative responses.

All of this said, it is easy to slip into neat but problematic distinctions about cinema's material relationship with the urban and rural; to slip into a line of reasoning that suggests that countryside locales are essentially about the absence of a cinematic experience. Evoking the idea of cinematic countrysides is partly about building upon a tentative body of work that suggests, in both qualitative and quantitative terms, the relationship between cinema and rural society has been grossly understated. Writing on the formation of early cinema audiences in America, and in particular the casual explanatory significance assigned to the emergence of Manhattan Nickelodeons, Allen (1996) has argued, for instance, that big-city patterns of display and exhibition may have been exceptional rather than indicative, and consequently that film historians would do well to take their cues from other scales of society and landscape. The role of cinema in transforming the social relations of rural areas, not least by registering their place *within* modernity, is at least one important part of this obscured and buried history of cinema. This is a world of travelling cinema, of itinerant filmmakers, and of cinema's placement within the civic and social rituals of small-town life. It is a history that serves to remind us that the geographies of cinematic display and exhibition, and their relationship to processes of social reproduction, can never be exhausted by an account of the city.

Cinematic countrysides

At various junctures the contributions that make up this volume serve to illustrate how this co-production of country and city identities figure in different cinematic traditions and texts, as well as point to the issues and politics that underlie the material organisation of cinema itself. The volume is organised around four sections, each emphasising different thematic concerns and approaches to the idea of cinematic countrysides.

The first and principal section of this collection entitled *Nations, borders and histories* explores the idea of the nationhood – how ideas of nation are formed, expressed and questioned through different articulations of cinema and countryside – and relatedly, how cinematic countrysides frame the occupancy and experience of border zones: those rural environments that bring the relationship between state, subject and cultural identity into sharp relief. For Jonathan Rayner (Chapter 2) representations of the Australian landscape are endemic to discussions of national identity, not only playing a salient role in the formation of a national cinema but a 'crucial factor in the distillation of national identity throughout the country's history'. This distillation process is complex and contradictory not least in the way that cinematic representations of landscape can be rendered both complicit with, and critical of, colonial experience. In Chapter 3, Carol Medlicott explores a largely uncharted tradition of national cinema in her account of

North Korean film. Here the relationship between cultural production, national identity and rurality is given a less ambivalent reading. Through the representation of a densely forested and mountainous border area of the Korean peninsula within film and popular artistic form, Medlicott explains how the countryside functions as a seamless and prototypical landscape of nationalism; the spatial imagery behind the 'inculcation of political ideology'. The correspondence between cinematic countrysides and the formation of a non-porous state somewhat collapses in Maria Rovisco's account of European 'films of voyage' (Chapter 4), a cinematic tradition that, she suggests, 'articulates, both narratively and visually, representations of the countryside with questions of boundaries and cultural diversity' and crucially one that, through movement, expresses how cultural and ethnic identities come to subvert the political boundaries of the nation, whether this is a subversion of a sedentary and homogenous Portuguese landscape or the scrambled and broken territories of the Balkans.

Such a concern for challenging coherent ideas of nationhood are carried forward by the work of Tanya Krzywinska (Chapter 5) in her account of the 'pagan' landscape in British cinema. For Krzywinska the portrayal of features of ancient landscapes in film and other popular media serve, partly in spite of authorial intention, to defy and contest conventional narratives of British history and identity. While the monuments and rituals surrounding the pagan landscape have been routinely coded up as evil and morally repugnant, their transgressive appeal has not been lost on the counter-cultural movement. This body of work therefore functions as a 'literal and metaphoric terrain for conjuring up buried histories, identities and narratives that have been, or are imagined to be, suppressed by "civilisation" and the dominant order'. In the final contribution to this section, Rachel Woodward and Patricia Winter (Chapter 6) extend our concern with nation and borders into the rural as a site of war. Through their treatment of British and American cinema they explain how war films are riddled with rural representations and serve to crystallise, as they put it, 'arguments and anxieties about national identity and the morality of armed conflict'. Woodward and Winter's concern is to trace these dimensions of war, rurality and cinema around both spaces of home and spaces of foreign engagement, and, by dint of this, around identities of both self and other. Thus the rural is shown to function variously as a repository of national values and virtues through which the alien intruder can be surmounted; a site of chaos and threat in which foreign intervention is shown to be allegorically 'out of place'; and a site in which war is shown to be ultimately unknowable, even by the protagonists themselves.

The contributions that make up the second section of the volume entitled *Mobile productions and contested representations* are held together by concern for examining the wider processes of production/consumption that surround the representation of countrysides in film. Issues of nationhood are by no means absent from these accounts. One of the underlying issues at stake in this section is the role that countrysides play in mediating national self-image through globalising systems of cinematic production. So in Ian Goode's account of *Local Hero* (Chapter 7), it is the object of national cinema that is at stake in its scrambled production, representation and consumption of rural Scotland. Goode explains how the narrative of *Local Hero* sets up an encounter between the values of America and the urban with those of a Scottish fishing village, a thematic that somewhat mirrors the context in which the film was produced and how it came to be critically received. For Goode, *Local Hero* can be read as an axiomatically national film that resists conventional oppositions between the incursions of Hollywood and the possibility of national cinema, yet one that also raises tensions about what the iconography of Scottishness should encompass. Andy Pratt's insights into the geographies of filmmaking (Chapter 8) represents an important intervention into debates about the internationalisation of economic activities and the real and imagined effects that come from attracting mobile investment into rural locales. While Pratt notes a series of positive economic outcomes that may come from the placement of filmmaking activities in the rural, he is suspicious about the legacy issues of participating in an international beauty contest, not least because runaway productions tend to make the rural in their (Hollywood) image. In Phillips' (Chapter 9) account of the representations and culture industries that surround the recent *Lord of the Rings* trilogy, the economic and cultural dimensions of a big-budget production on rural space are further brought home. Phillips argues that securing New Zealand as the shooting location of this production has generated tangible effects across different sectors of the economy, including the film industry itself. But it also generates ambivalent responses around issues of national self-image. Moreover, the literary and biographical precedents that shape much of the imagery of this production are, Phillips argues, firmly rooted in the social identities of rural England: a pastoral imagery that comes to be choreographed with visions of a New Zealand 'wilderness'.

The third section of this volume, entitled *Identity, difference and otherness*, addresses a quite different scale of experience. Here it is not the meta-spaces of nation at the forefront of concern (even though they are not entirely absent), nor the transnational and global networks of production, representation and consumption that serve to scramble, confuse and undo them. Rather, the matter at stake in this section is the production of rural space as this relates to the social identities of those occupying, embodying and moving through them. In particular, two key markers of social identity and difference – 'childhood' and 'masculinity' – serve to amplify how embodied identities come to inflect, and be inflected by, the idea of rural space. In Chapter 10 Owain Jones explains the multiple and often competing meanings which cinema has assigned to countryside spaces through the idea of childhood. Drawing on a range of filmic examples from Europe and North America, Jones explains how ideas of countryside and childhood are often coded in affirmative terms in films both *for* and *about* children, and, moreover, the way that the idea of countryside can be constructed as a natural space for childhood *vis à vis* the city and the urban. Yet he also wishes to set the representation of harmonious rural childhoods against bodies of work that effectively pull down the façade of an idyll. Cinematic countrysides, he suggests, also confront the 'issue of poverty … oppression through patriarchal power, and other harsher realities of children's lives' as well as rendering visible the 'otherness' of rural childhood, an experience remote and outside 'the surveillance of adults'. In Chapter 11, counter-discourses of rurality are taken to their imaginative limit by Leyshon and Brace, who attend to an entirely bleak 'coming of age' story in their sustained treatment of *The War Zone* (1998). They explain how notions of a bucolic youthful idyll – underwritten (in part) by ideas of 'playful, innocent fumbling in a hayloft' sexual identities – are entirely undone by the abusive and incestuous sexual relations at play within the film. Furthermore, pro-rural/anti-urban discourses that often pervade the idea of childhood come to be inverted in a significant way. Here a family's relocation to the countryside from the city serves to emphasise that they are, as the authors put, 'isolated spatially and temporally from the moral structures that might contain their deviant behaviour'. In the final contribution to this section by David Bell (Chapter 12), attention turns to the gendered identities of rural space and, in particular, to exploring how cinematic countrysides serve to produce ideas of masculinity. In pursuing this concern, Bell's work offers the volume its most sustained treatment of the way that urban and rural identities come to play and configure each other. Using the American films *Hunter's Blood* (1986) and *City Slickers* (1990) as his exemplars, Bell explains how urban masculinities, constructed as 'effete and feminised', come to be emphasised/transformed through their encounter with rural males constructed in turn as either feral, savage, dirty, in-bred and animalistic or noble, enviable, civilised and wise. For Bell such cinematic imbrications of rural masculinity and their placement with the experience and transformation of urban male identities connect the representation of rural masculinities to wider debates about the crisis of masculinity.

The final two chapters of this volume form a small section entitled *Mediating experience and performing alternatives*, and they address alternative ways of interpreting and practising cinematic countrysides. They serve to illuminate Andy Pratt's suggestion in Chapter 8 that rural communities and individuals should seek to re-imagine and engage the countryside outside of conventional (urban) systems of cinematic production, and, in so doing, begin to make cinematic countrysides their own. Pratt's comments are addressed towards recent technological developments that underwrite and (somewhat) democratise the creation of film (the digital camera, the laptop), but in the first of the contributions to this section Mark Neumann and Janna Jones (Chapter 13) explain how the construction of alternative film cultures is by no means new. In their eloquent account of a series of amateur productions staged between 1915 and 1940 in the northeast of the United States, they explain how the presence of a movie camera in rural settings 'enabled people to both document and dramatise rural existence'. From the efforts of summering elites to stage an amateur theatrical production of *Snow White* to the work of a grocery-store owner roaming the landscape with a 8mm camera they argue that the rural is rendered a space and time that both 'celebrates the growing forces of modern life and progress and, at times, seeks out a fantasy of the small town and the folk as a retreat from such forces'. Not surprisingly, the relational production of rural and urban identities again features within many of these amateur narratives. *Cinematic countrysides* closes with a contemporary rendering of alternative imagery. In their account of the Amber Film and Photography Collective in the north east of England, Katy Bennett and Richard Lee (Chapter 14) take us into the former coalfields of Durham and through a body of filmic and photographic work that seeks to make sense of industrial restructuring within working-class rural communities. Crucially, this work is produced collaboratively with members of these communities, a process that makes it an unusual and iterative mix of auto-ethnography, drama and realism. The work of Amber shows how alternative systems of production can function as affective (though by no means simply affirmative) imaginings of rural locale; ones that do not simply mediate experience, but act upon it.

References

Aitken, S. and Zonn, L. (eds) (1994), *Place, Power and Spectacle: A Geography of Film* (London: Rowman and Littlefield).

Allen, R. (1996), 'Manhattan Myopia: or Oh! Iowa', *Cinema Journal* 35(3): 75–103.

Auge, M. (1995), *Non-Places: Introduction to an Anthropology of Supermodernity* (London: Verso).

Bell, D. (1997), 'Anti-idyll: rural horror', in Cloke, P. and Little, J. (eds), *Contested Countryside Cultures* (London: Routledge), pp. 94–108.

Barber. S. (2002), *Projected Cities Cinema and Urban Space* (London: Reaktion).

Bruno, G. (1993), *Streetwalking on a Ruined Map* (Princeton: Princeton University Press).

Clarke, D. (ed.) (1997), *The Cinematic City* (London: Routledge).

Cresswell, T. and Dixon, D. (2002), *Engaging Film: Geographies of Mobility and Identity* (London: Rowan and Littlefield).

Denzin, N. (1991), *Images of Postmodern Society: Social Theory and Contemporary Cinema* (London: Sage).

Farish, M. (2005), 'Cities in shade: urban geography and the uses of Noir', *Environment and Planning D: Society and Space* 23(1): 95–118.

Friedburg, A. (1993), *Window Shopping: Cinema and the Post Modern* (Berkeley: University of California Press).

Gold, J.R. and Ward, S.V. (1997), 'Of plan and planners: documentary film and the challenge of the urban future 1935–52', in Clarke, D. (ed.), *The Cinematic City* (London: Routledge), pp. 59–82.

Higson, A. (2003), *English Heritage, English Cinema: The Costume Drama in the 1980s and 1990s* (Oxford: Oxford University Press).

Hubbard, P. (2002), 'Screen-shifting: consumption, "riskless risks" and the changing geographies of cinema', *Environment and Planning A* 34: 1239–58.

Hutchings, P. (2004), *The Horror Film* (London: Pearson).

Ingram, D. (2000), *Green Screen: Environmentalism and Hollywood Cinema* (Exeter: Exeter University Press).

Jancovich, M., Faire, L. and Stubbings, S. (2003), *The Place of the Audience: Cultural Geographies Film Consumption* (London: British Film Institute).

Jarvis, B. (1998), *Postmodern Cartographies: The Geographical Imagination in Contemporary in American Culture* (London: Pluto).

Kennedy, C. (1994), 'The myth of heroism; man and desert in Lawrence of Arabia', in Aitken, S. and Zonn, L. (eds), *Place, Power and Spectacle: A Geography of Film* (London: Rowan and Littlefield), pp. 137–61.

Kitses, J. and Rickman, G. (eds) (1998), *The Western Reader* (New York: Limelight Editions).

Krim, A. (1994), 'Filming Route 66: documenting the Dust Bowl Highway', in Aitken, S. and Zonn, L. (eds), *Place, Power and Spectacle: A Geography of Film* (London: Rowan and Littlefield), pp. 183–202.

Krutnik, F. (1997), 'Something more than night: tales of the Noir city', in Clarke, D. (ed.) (1997), *The Cinematic City* (London: Routledge), pp. 83–109.

Laderman, D. (2002), *Driving Visions: Exploring the Road Movie* (Texas: University of Texas Press).

Lukinbeal, C. and Arreola, D. (eds) (2005), Special issue on cinematic landscapes, *Journal of Cultural Geography* 23(1).

McArthur, C. (1997), 'Chinese boxes and Russian dolls: tracking the elusive cinematic city', in Clarke, D. (ed.) (1997), *The Cinematic City* (London: Routledge), pp. 19–45.

Shiel, M. (2001), 'Cinema and the city in history and theory', in Shiel, M. and Fitzmaurice, T. (eds), *Cinema and the City: Film and Urban Societies in a Global Context* (Oxford: Blackwell Publishers), pp. 1–18.

Shiel, M. and Fitzmaurice, T. (eds) (2001), *Cinema and the City: Film and Urban Societies in a Global Context* (Oxford: Blackwell Publishers).

Sheil, M. and Fitzmaurice, T. (eds) (2003), *Screening the City* (London: Verso).

Smith L. (2002), 'Chips off the old block: Nanook of the North and the relocation of cultural identity', in Cresswell, T. and Dixon, D. (eds), *Engaging Film: Geographies of Mobility and Identity* (London: Rowan and Littlefield), pp. 94–122.

Stringer, J. (2001) 'Global cities and the international film festival economy', in Shiel, M. and Fitzmaurice, T. (eds), *Cinema and the City: Film and Urban Societies in a Global Context* (Oxford: Blackwell Publishers), pp. 134–44.

Part I

Nations, borders and histories

2

Far from the fatal shore: finding meaning and identity in the rural Australian landscape

Jonathan Rayner

> As an icon and a resource, the Australian landscape is increasingly vulnerable to sweeping, contradictory historical narratives of ownership, development and progress. (Brabazon, 1999: 154)

Four preliminary and expository images can be offered as illustrations of the complex and contradictory responses to the landscape embraced by Australian films: a crab clinging precariously to a sheer rock face on a coastal cliff, poised to be swept off with the next wave (*Long Weekend*; Colin Eggleston, 1979); horses in close-up and in silhouette on a mountainous horizon at dusk (*The Man from Snowy River*; George Miller, 1982); a sudden sandstorm invading a Victorian farmhouse (*My Brilliant Career*; Gillian Armstrong, 1979); a moving aerial shot, looking down vertically on a desert landscape reduced to an abstraction of textures and shadings (*Rabbit-Proof Fence*; Philip Noyce, 2002). The Australian landscape on film has been inflected, interpreted and reinterpreted in multifarious ways, since the resurgence of feature-film production in the 1970s. This chapter offers a consideration of the significance of the Australian landscape within notable features, from the revival to the present. Landscape has played a conspicuous and complex role in the concretisation of the national cinema for audiences at home and abroad, just as it has been a crucial factor in the distillation of national identity throughout the country's history, as the natural, acquired or adopted home for a disparate conglomeration of imagined communities. Early attempts to define the nation and national character via the renewed feature film industry looked back to early decades of (almost exclusively) white Australian history and settlement, constructing a politically convenient but ultimately untenable collection of narratives, which not only excluded alternative versions of the past, but also appeared ignorant of and irrelevant to modern, multicultural Australia. Consequently, part of the evolving national cinema's strength has been to rewrite or redirect this investiture of the landscape with conservative values, and to foreground its use in the elucidation of alternative Australian identities.

The uniqueness, scale and variegation of the natural environment have been acculturated within Australian art as inseparable from the definition of national character, but different habitats found across the continent have featured in particular genres, and have been endowed with discreet meanings within the national cinema. Consequently, the outback, the bush, the mountain and the coast have been recruited in the elucidation and inculcation of particular traits and facets of Australian identity, and mobilised by different groups (defined in gendered, ethnic and racial terms), in support of conservative and oppositional causes. The central importance of the landscape, the 'primary determinant of Australian ideologies' (Brabazon, 1999: 153), within this range of nationalist, nationalising and devolutionary discourses, is frequently articulated through binary oppositions, connecting and distinguishing character types, rural and urban environments, and the social values they embody. These formal and ideological characteristics prompt comparisons with the American Western, but the variety of the Australian landscape, and the diversity of values placed upon it, make for a more complex and multifaceted consideration of the acculturation of nature. The national cinema's imag(in)ing of the landscape has proved crucial to the aesthetic and narrative development of indigenous film genres – such as the period film and the Gothic – and through such conventionalisation it has been instrumental in the revision and reformulation of Australian-ness.

Landscape and validation

The most formally and politically conservative conceptualisations of the Australian landscape on film are found within male-dominated and oriented narratives, detailing a relationship with territory based superficially upon harmony, but revealing at base principles of hegemony and conquest. The narratives of these films are often based upon well-known literary and/or historical precedents, which confirms both their astute commercial crafting for the home audience, and their capitalisation upon commonly held images of nationhood. The comparatively recent histories of white colonisation, and particularly of nineteenth-century exploration and exploitation, are preferred and positioned as consensual images of Australian character and culture.

The Man From Snowy River extols the virtues and reinforces the myths of Australian national character, in a narrative derived as much from cinematic precedents (such hymns to the beauty and remoteness of the country's interior as *The Overlanders*; Harry Watt, 1946) as from literary staples (its adaptation of A.B. 'Banjo' Paterson's eponymous poem). Miller's film constructs, via the conventions of the Western and melodrama, an image in which Australian-ness becomes synonymous with white masculinity, rural self-sufficiency, and a proprietorial relationship with the land. Its central character, Jim Craig, is shown to be entirely formed and informed by his upbringing in the Snowy River region. The upland territory is exacting in its demands in terms of the skill and endurance required to survive and prosper there. Jim lives with his father on their highland farm, but precipitates the death of his parent and the loss of the family home through his ill-advised plan to catch and break a disruptive group of brumbies (wild horses), led by an untameable stallion. He is humiliated by being forced to leave the mountains and seek work with Harrison, an American cattle baron. However, through this employment his passage to manhood is completed, as his skills are shown to equal and even surpass those of Clancy, the greatest horseman and stockman. His prowess is confirmed by his rescue of Harrison's daughter Jessica when she becomes lost in the mountains, his recovery of his boss's prize colt, and the final capture of the brumbies. With Jessica as his wife and with wealth accrued from the horses, Jim is able to reclaim his family's land.

Cinematography and ideology are closely allied in this ritualistic narrative. The connection between the landscape and the horses (Jim tells Jessica that the mountains are like a 'high-spirited horse, never to be taken for granted') is matched by the equation of skill, ownership and virility in possession of horses and women (Jim bargains with Harrison for the acquisition of the brood mares from the brumby herd and for control of Jessica). This unabashed artic-ulation of male ascendancy is foregrounded by panoramic views of the unspoiled wilderness, offering a disingenuous depiction of the white male's harmonious co-existence with nature within the narrative's celebration of a mythologised male potency. (Similar connections between masculine identity, virility and kinship with the landscape and animals are stressed in another latter-day Australian Western, *Ned Kelly*; Gregor Jordan, 2003). The film's anachronisms (Harrison's diatribe against feminism, Clancy's sermon on ecology and environmental preservation) underline not simply its contemporary adaptation of a literary classic, but the appositeness of its symbolic use of the landscape to the national (and national cinematic) projects of the present:

> The 'significations' are not those of the nostalgia film. Its time is not that of a lost, irretrievable communal past, but of a present ... European settlement is registered, not as the raping of the landscape, but as a fact. Further it is *Australian* and not European ... the settlers are not fighting against the bush. They are not maintaining and retaining in a ridiculous fashion their Europeanism in a hostile, alien environment. They are quite simply there and they manifestly belong there. (O'Regan, 1985: 246–7)

This proprietorial sense of belonging (of the men to the land and vice versa) invests *The Man From Snowy River*, and comparable contemporary films of masculine endeavour, with a restrictive and retrospective national meaning, which is indicative of the composition of the imagined community defined if not created by this strand of the national cinema.

In relation to the cinema's treatment of other aspects of Australian history, such as its involvement in colonial and imperial wars, the landscape features again as a definitive, formative element in the lives of male characters engaged in heroic activities. In *Gallipoli* (Peter Weir, 1981), the Australian heroes emerge from the outback to train, bond and die in the service of the Empire, in the disastrous Dardanelles campaign of the First World War. Archie, who goes on to lay down his life to save that of his mate Frank, is first seen in the wastes of Western Australia, training to be an athlete and hoping to represent his country in the Olympics. The grand, elemental setting for his first run in the desert, poised between blue sky and red earth, imbues his efforts with a purity of purpose which carries over into his naive decision to enlist, despite being under age. Subsequently, Archie's gift is mythologised further when he races a rival on horseback, and proves he can run barefoot across the desert faster than a man can ride. Before this trial his feet are rubbed with grasses by Zack, his Aboriginal mate, and afterwards his injuries are tended with biblical reverence by his uncle Jack. The insistence of these associations with both indigenous culture via Zack, and an older generation of heroic adventurers through Jack, glorifies Archie as a representative national, and quasi-spiritual, symbol.

After their first encounter at a country town race meeting, Frank and Archie run for fun and as part of their military service in the desert landscapes of Egypt and Turkey. This graphic continuity in setting adds to the sense of their integration in the landscape, but also to the aura of inevitability to their destiny. When they stow away on the wrong train on their way to join up, Archie and Frank find themselves marooned in the outback. As they cross the desert to Perth, the full breadth of the wide-screen frame is used, in emulation of *Lawrence of Arabia* (David Lean, 1965), to ennoble their figures against the immensity and blankness of the land. Overcoming this obstacle is important not only in solidifying their friendship, but also in defining their motivations to fight. Archie's belief in the Empire, and in his duty to it, which are foreign to Frank's urban immigrant upbringing, are betrayed on the battlefield by British arrogance, but Frank survives to carry home the lesson: that the qualities epitomised by the 'best' outback Australians must be elevated for the definition of the nation, rather than remaining subservient to the Empire. In this resolution, *Gallipoli* reiterates the myths of Anzac already enshrined in the official war history. The perception that a generation of perfect, doomed Western Australian youth, arising from an unsullied landscape, comes to define the nation because of its needless sacrifice to the Empire is reasserted imagistically and symbolically in Archie's odyssey from Australian to African to Eurasian deserts. The stereotype of the white male from the outback, despite being an increasingly unrepresentative national image, persists as the stock-in-trade of the first decade of film revival, delivered to the overwhelmingly urban Australian population by a national cinema recycling literary precedents and popular myths.

Landscape and fabrication

The conservative landscape cinema, portraying historical male endeavours, depicts the white male Australian's relationship with the land as defined by a genetic connection with, and the righteous conquest of, the natural environment. The expanse of the land embodies potential for freedom of movement, and the honing and recognition of skills within a single-sex peer group, without social constraints. By contrast, contemporary films which explore the relationship between white female Australians and the same natural landscape are often ambiguous: beyond the secure boundaries of culture, nature can seem uncanny and threatening, or can offer opportunities for freedom of expression, and release from societal inhibition. Male heroes appear assimilated within and in control of the land (not least because Australian locations often stand in for overseas settings[1]), even when the narratives in which they are engaged emphasise their powerlessness within wider currents of history. Archie and Frank are at home in every desert, and Harry 'Breaker' Morant and his Australian comrades command the South African Veldt, despite their subjugation and victimisation by British authorities. It might be assumed that the untamed landscape dominated by males may be construed as a threat to female protagonists, who would gravitate towards socialised and urban environments in compensation: in fact, the role of the natural landscape within female-oriented period films spans numerous meanings, incorporating its anti-cultural and anti-social associations in order to facilitate individual empowerment.

The connection of women to symbols of civilisation within settler culture suggests an overcoming or overlooking of nature, in the creation and consolidation of human society in newly acquired wilderness. Again, the American Western provides precedents in *mise-en-scène*, in the form of the homestead, the chapel and the school house, inhabited by women and families but protected against outlaws and indigenous peoples by males as symbols of civilisation. Such examples exist as paradoxes within the ideology and action of the Western: on the frontier, these embryonic societies represent aspirational ideals and indefensible incongruities, which can appear out of step with the lone, masculine activities which both secure them and transgress them. Such environmental incongruity registers forcefully in Australian period dramas, where

Victorian sensibilities and cultural icons are juxtaposed with inhospitable rural realities.

The opening of *The Getting of Wisdom* (Bruce Beresford, 1977)
sees the precocious heroine Laura composing aloud a romantic
story for her younger sister. They sit in the arid countryside, near to
the country postal office run by their mother, waiting for the coach
that will take Laura away to school in the city. The inappropriate-
ness of their Victorian dress to the landscape is exacerbated by the
incongruity of Laura's imaginative story: as she describes her
European heroine beset in a dark, Gothic forest, she pushes aside
the dry, dead branches of the fallen trees. The girl's imagination,
informed by a culture of the Northern Hemisphere, strives to overcome the inadequacy and recalcitrance of a Southern Hemisphere
environment. Laura's eagerness for education and departure from
her lower-class rural backwater seem to exalt imported culture
over nature, but the pretensions and prejudices she encounters at
her all-female college prompt her to re-evaluate the society she is so
anxious to join. In overcoming social and personal disadvantages,
Laura mimics the non-conformity of the land in her desire for self-
expression. Her gained 'wisdom' resides in achieving a
compromise between individuality and social expectation, encapsulated in her un-ladylike run through a nearby park (an
acceptable, acculturated form of nature) on the day she leaves
college to take up a music scholarship in Europe. This recalls, but
reverses, her imposition of culture upon nature from the opening
sequence. Where her story represented a victory of valorised,
imported culture over indigenous nature (the land's as well as her
own), her final run symbolises a refusal to conform entirely to
outmoded, external controls.

The heroine of *My Brilliant Career* engages in a more openly
antagonistic relationship with the rural landscape. The first
sequence sees Sybylla also composing aloud, except her work is the
prophetic autobiography suggested by the title, rather than a
cliched mimicry of an established style. She wanders around her
family's farmhouse, past the accoutrements of Victorian, domestic
respectability, before settling down to write. Outside, a gathering
dust storm hampers the efforts of male workers and lashes the
clothes on the washing line. Dust begins to invade the house via
open windows before Sybylla's mother rouses her to work and
protect the home. This sequence offers a summary of the film's

characterisation and action, which subsequent events confirm. Sybylla rejects subservient domestic employment, but also refuses to conform to novelistic, romantic ideals either, when she is displayed as marriageable material in more genteel surroundings. She survives humiliation as a household servant (where married women and mothers appear as her oppressors), and scorns the economic dependence of marriage, even when love is acknowledged.

The final realisation of Sybylla's personal and artistic ambition, the publication of her autobiography, is represented as a victory over the remoteness of the country. The publication of her book in Britain, while she remains alone in an isolated house not dissimilar to the one in which she was first seen, suggests she has overcome the obstruction of society and the landscape to achieve her goal. However, although the landscape may appear to represent and be a part of the social and patriarchal conspiracy against her, it also facilitates the solitary independence she enjoys at the film's close. As in the case of *The Getting of Wisdom*, the landscape in *My Brilliant Career* appears functionally, physically and symbolically as an obstacle to personal fulfilment, but in itself can also signify a proto-feminist resistance, allying the woman with the land which refuses to conform to male control: as in the case of Laura, Sybylla's 'gifts or assets are misrecognised ... as a "wildness of spirit" which must be tamed' (Collins, 1999: 19). In revealing, and in place of, the fabrication of national imagery associated with masculine control of the land, and in response to imported social constructions within the diegetic environments, the protagonists of female-oriented period films fabricate their own abstracted, literary, autobiographical and aestheticised creations of personal identity, in relation to or in defiance of the land itself. That these constructions can also embody a nascent, oppositional nationalism, in carrying Australian culture overseas (in parallel with the films in which they are depicted), appears the more subversive because it is incarnated by dis-empowered Australian versions of Victorian womanhood:

> The ambitious woman and the Australian writer are affirmed in Armstrong's 1979 landmark film, yet within the film's diegetic world of rural New South Wales in 1897 the Australian woman writer exists somewhere in the future, beyond the horizon of life in the bush. Visually there is no space in the film to accommodate Sybylla's ambi-

tions. Changes of scene, of landscape (from the most barren to the most fertile) and of social status (from the most privileged to the most illiterate) do nothing to open up a space for the woman artist in Australia. She is hemmed in, not by *nature* (the barren landscape bereft of cultural history) but by *culture*. (Collins, 1999: 23)

Landscape and recrimination

In the often hybridised generic territory referred to as the Australian Gothic, the landscape is a key element in the exploration of cultural anxieties arising from colonial experience. The questioning of the validity and durability of settler culture, in the face of a natural landscape antipathetic to colonisation, and overwhelming in scale and difference from European norms, lies behind the imagery and narratives of the Gothic.

Ironically, the film generally identified as the inspiration for the cycle of period dramas within the revival, *Picnic at Hanging Rock* (Peter Weir, 1975), offers a very clear articulation of the Gothic's basis of unease. A party of schoolgirls from a Victorian ladies' college visit the Hanging Rock on St Valentine's Day, and during the afternoon three girls and one teacher disappear without trace. More than a week later, one of the girls is found unhurt but stricken with amnesia. The stability of the college principal and the cohesion of wider society are threatened by the insoluble mystery, but subsequent searches reveal no more clues or survivors. The landscape, introduced via a series of dissolving impressionistic views of the rock, at once represents an irrational, irruptive challenge to establishment authority and a seductive, atavistic retreat for (female) adolescents escaping restrictive, patriarchal control. In the film's allusive, ambiguous and elliptical treatment, which mixes art-cinema style with the materials of horror cinema, the incongruity of (British Victorian) culture in the midst of an antagonistic Australian nature is again the crucial motif. *Picnic*'s suggestion of a sympathetic convergence between human sexuality and the landscape's primordial power can be related backwards to films such as *Walkabout* (Nicolas Roeg, 1971), which elegises the rape of the continent by white colonisation, and forwards to subsequent Gothic films, which probe an enduring guilt over the land's acquisition through allegory and abjection.

While the natural landscape is characterised as uncanny – with its remoteness, menace and fertility inspiring fear and loathing in (predominantly white) protagonists – the evocation of horror in the Gothic coalesces around two principal narrative and thematic areas: the danger embodied in the alien and unfathomable environment, and the moral and physical decline of representative human communities isolated within it. If the former epitomises settler responses to an unknown and inhospitable continent, the latter explores the land's influence and effect upon its colonisers.

In *Long Weekend*, the moral bankruptcy of a disintegrating middle-class marriage is brought to account for all the offences against the landscape committed throughout white settler history. The couple's trip, conceived as an attempt to run away from their recent crises (adultery leading to an abortion), develops into a heedless campaign of violence against the environment. The husband runs over a kangaroo during their journey at night. They ignore signs proclaiming the land to be private, and set up camp near the seashore. The wife decimates encroaching ants with insecticide, and the husband's reckless shooting with a newly acquired rifle orphans a group of ducklings. He also shoots and kills what he thinks is a shark, but the corpse of a harmless dugong washes up on the beach. Resisting the violent incursion, the flora and fauna fight back. The couple's pre-packaged food begins to rot within hours. A female eagle attacks them when her egg is stolen. Inexplicably, the decomposing dugong advances up the beach towards their camp. The husband discovers other camps apparently attacked and overrun by nature (an overgrown tent which contains only a frightened dog, and another car submerged off shore). In terror, the husband kills his wife by accident during the night, and gets lost in the bush when he tries to escape in daylight. Believing that he is safe when he reaches the main road, he is run over by a lorry carrying livestock to the slaughterhouse, completing the cycle begun by his killing of the kangaroo.

While its formulaic shocks are derived from the staples of horror film, *Long Weekend*'s representation of blatant exploitation and abuse of the land (and of an equally violent, symbolic and punitive reaction against invasion) needs to be read in terms of the 'self-loathing of liberal Australians for their material and spiritual sins against the continent' (Dermody and Jacka, 1988: 126). The images of destruction are more graphic and less stylised than those in *Walkabout*, and *Long Weekend* also lacks the earlier film's yearning for a pre-lapsarian paradise in the Australian landscape, to which non-Aboriginals may be granted access. Notably, the violence is perpetrated against (and returned by) emblematic Australian fauna: the kangaroo, a possum which bites the husband, the dugong which embodies a mute indictment, a cockatoo which makes the lorry driver swerve. More than simply being associated with destruction, the incongruous suburbanite couple are tainted specifically with the killing or harming of offspring: the smashing of the eagle's egg, and the killing of the mother duck and dugong (which is seeking its lost pup), all serve to re-invoke and magnify the pre-existent crime against nature, the adulterous wife's abortion. Within this pattern of escalatory violence, the couple's actions appear as a frenzied attack upon an accusing, Archaic Mother Earth, personified in the rampant processes of procreation, death and decomposition.

In *Long Weekend*, the rapacity of nature clearly functions as a mirror to the insatiable acquisition of territory and resources attributed to white colonisation, but the landscape registers a different accusation and judgement upon non-Aboriginal Australian culture in other examples of the Gothic. One of the most common images in Australian Gothic is of the idyllic rural town. Rather than being seen as the repository of old-fashioned values, outback towns are characterised by repressive forms of conservatism which, paradoxically, are expressed through bizarre, violent and anti-social behaviour.

This representation of the rural community is initiated in *Wake in Fright* (Ted Kotcheff, 1971), in which a school teacher on his way to the coast stops over in Bundunyabba, 'the best little town in Australia'. At first he remains aloof from the town's dissipation, but is soon subsumed within its culture of drinking and gambling. His chastening moral disintegration occurs with drunken sexual encounters, and involvement in a horrific kangaroo hunt. Any supposed superiority in education and class is wiped out, and when his efforts to escape from the town are thwarted, he attempts suicide. Although the relentless hospitality of the townsfolk is implicated in the teacher's downfall, the moral of this morality play is that circumstances merely reveal innate failings; the town's isolation may induce the behaviour of its inhabitants, or simply provide the setting and opportunity for its manifestation.

The association of the outback town with moral decline, perversity and barbarism is furthered by later Gothic examples. These vary in tone and emphasis between the fantastic (in *The Cars That Ate Paris* [Peter Weir, 1974] a secluded town with a waning economy turns to engineering car crashes in order to bring fresh goods and new blood into the community), the polemical (in *Shame* [Steve Jodrell, 1987] a female lawyer enters a town in which the female inhabitants have been subjected to recurrent and institutionalised sexual abuse), and the political (in *Deadly* [Esben Storm, 1990] a city detective comes to a rural backwater to investigate Aboriginal deaths in custody). In echoing the Western, in each case the presence of an objective outsider is necessary to uncover the scandalous secrets behind the community's façade of normalcy. This characterisation of the outback town even extends to later, more popular and comedic productions, such as *The Adventures of Priscilla, Queen of the Desert* (Stephan Elliott, 1994), in which the tolerance of the gay and transsexual travellers is tested in the towns of Broken Hill and Coober Pedy. The obsessive probing and revelation of guilty secrets (often based upon violent crime, questionable paternity or incest, in films such as *Summerfield* [Ken Hannam, 1977] and *Cassandra* [Colin Eggleston, 1986]) connote a problematic re-imagining of colonial history in the Gothic, in contradistinction from the reassuring certainties of period films and male adventures, which assert an unproblematic acquisition and mastery of the continent. The 'phobia-ridden relations with the land' (Dermody and Jacka, 1988: 82), which are epitomised by the beleaguered, degenerate outback town and its inhabitants, represent a denial of the validating national narratives of pioneering male endeavours, and an articulation of a pervasive cultural culpability: 'unlike the "problem identity" for other Australians, Aboriginal [sic] and Islanders are seen as having a secure identity and sense of belongingness … Their dispossession is becoming – like slavery and the US state – the settler culture's "original sin", its genocide, its holocaust' (O'Regan, 1996: 276).

Landscape and reconciliation

In traditional Aboriginal thought, there is no nature without culture, just as there is no contrast either of domesticated landscape with wilderness or of interior scene with an expansive 'outside' beyond four walls. In its focus on specific sites in the landscape, this type of art is centred on linked points marked by their social and religious significance in human affairs, not on their appearance alone. Site-based, mythic representations in Aboriginal art are landscapes of landscapes, or conceptual maps of designs already wrought, not views of nature. As one Cape York man once said, 'The land *is* a map' (Sutton, 1989: 18–19).

Representations and interpretations of the maintenance, and denial, of Aboriginal cultural links to the Australian land constitute an area of inevitable controversy in the national cinema. Arguably, as the above quotation suggests, the cinematic apparatus itself is simply inappropriate, in aesthetic or institutional terms, for the expression of the connections between the territories and the culture and history of the country's indigenous inhabitants. In film representations, Aborigines and Aboriginality have been synonymous with guilt and fears of an Other, preternaturally endowed with a spiritual, antecedent and inviolably authentic connection with the land which non-Aboriginal Australians cannot comprehend or replicate. Relatively few films attempt to illuminate the significance of the land to Aboriginal people in cultural terms which evade stereotyping, or in personal terms which explore individual experiences.

Radiance (Rachel Perkins, 1998), adapted from a play by Louis Nowra, depicts the unhappy family reunion of three sisters for their mother's funeral, at their former home in a coastal town. The middle sister Mae, who has tended the mother in her last illness, is joined by the younger sibling Nona, who returns from the city, and the eldest sister Cressy, who is an internationally famous opera singer. While the film operates along conventional, melodramatic lines, with sequential (and sexually based) revelations (Mae's hatred of the mother's promiscuity, Nona's unplanned pregnancy, Cressy's secret motherhood) punctuating and driving its narrative, the setting of the action within the home is expanded legitimately and relevantly beyond the confines of the play.

Although the house serves as their meeting point, it is not regarded with affection by the sisters. It has become devalued, not only by Mae's recent experience of caring for the demanding and erratic mother, but also by other long-standing, undisclosed associations. After the church service, Mae drives demonically to the house of her mother's white, married lover, who actually owns the mother's house. She calls for him to come out and speak to them, and when he fails to appear she fights with Nona over his wreath. The sisters' journey from the church and the town, through fields of regimented crops to the married lover's well-tended garden, underlines the superficial respectability which the scandalous history of the mother's life disrupts, for the sisters as much as for the white inhabitants. Mae's desire to burn down the house, initially thwarted by Nona, becomes a shared necessity for all the sisters when Cressy reveals that Nona is really her daughter, conceived when she was raped by one of her mother's lovers.

The absence of responsible, authoritative parental figures, which the death of the mother and the invisibility of her black and white lovers suggest, becomes a thematic consistency within the film, and in its treatment of land and ownership. Nona's wish to scatter her mother's ashes on an island close off shore is stymied by the discovery that it has been sold to Japanese property developers. The conspiratorial destruction of the house purposefully dispossesses its white owner, and also destroys the site of the mother's memory and influence. Removing the house breaks the ties between the mother and her lovers, but also frees the daughters from their distressing connection to its site and memories. Rather than standing as inviolate loci for familial and cultural meaning, in *Radiance* the land and the home are characterised as repositories for debilitating memories and associations, which must be purged for progress to be made. The anti-climactic reconstitution of a 'family' is therefore highly qualified: the sisters depart on a road trip back towards the city, with Nona declaring that she will never be able to call Cressy 'Mum'. The film's generic and cultural connotations remain mixed: the purposes of melodrama may be served by the house's destruction, and an updated 'walkabout' is provided by the road trip, but the cliched connections between Aborigines, rural environments and cultural and familial continuities have been heavily modified, or dismissed.

Rabbit-Proof Fence (Phillip Noyce, 2002) also modifies and politicises Aboriginal connections to land, in its discomforting depiction of the history of Australian race relations through the conventions of the period film and documentary drama. The 1,200-mile journey home made by three 'half caste' Aboriginal children, Molly, Gracie and Daisy, who were forcibly removed from their mothers at Jigalong and taken to the Moore River Native Settlement, becomes an allegorical passage in the history of reconciliation between

Australia's indigenous and white populations. This retrospective understanding is underwritten by the appearance of the surviving family members in the film's epilogue, and their collaboration with non-Aboriginal filmmakers in the production.

In narration Molly's voice-over states the origins of the conflict in terms of the marks left by white settlement on her family and territory. The erection of a station house in their region and the institution of a 'ration day' are followed by the establishment of the Aboriginal camp at Jigalong, and the ominous growth of the fence. The connection which Molly, the narrator and eldest child, feels with her home is conveyed in a compact series of introductory images and sounds of the natural landscape (including her mother's identification of the 'Spirit Bird' which will always look after her), which are linked to her point of view. At this point, and throughout the subsequent escape and pursuit, the experience and location of Molly, Daisy and Gracie are contrasted with the Perth offices of the Chief Protector of Aborigines, Mr Neville.

On their train journey to Moore River, the girls travel through a landscape marked by farming, and habitation hastened and facilitated by the railway. (Significantly, it is when the girls approach the railway again that Gracie is recaptured). After the girls' escape, the aerial landscape shots seen in the opening sequence reappear to differing effect. Following a rain storm which hides the girls' tracks, a shot of the forest from high altitude fades into a zoom into the hollow where they sleep intertwined. The three white-clad bodies hidden from the sight of their pursuers evoke an ironic comparison with the Pre-Raphaelite images of Victorian school-girls, lost in sublime reverie in the bush, in *Picnic at Hanging Rock*.

The apparently abstract patterns of contour and vegetation seen in the aerial shots of the opening sequence also return in the point-of-view shots ascribed to the Aborigine tracker Moodoo, when he scans the ground. Pans around the horizon, which sometimes function as Molly's point-of-view and at others observe the girls *en route* in extreme long shot, maintain this sense of the landscape's ambiguity: its distance and harshness are overwhelming, and efforts by the police to find the girls are hamstrung by reliance upon supplies of food and petrol, but for the girls the land is both an obstacle and an ally to their freedom. Similarly, during their journey the girls are assisted by whites as often as they are betrayed by Aborigines.

The same ambiguity is attached to the titular fence, which symbolises arbitrary attempts to control and compartmentalise the continent (and by implication its indigenous inhabitants, who are equated with the continent's fauna), but which is used by Molly as an aid to navigation home. The girls' joyful discovery of the fence is marked by a cut away to Molly's mother, still hundreds of miles to the north, laying her hands on the wire simultaneously, underlining the subversive use of the fence as a connection rather than a division. That the girls are finally saved by the fence's re-emergence from the desert (heralded by the reappearance of the 'Spirit Bird'), confirms its paradoxical endowment with oppositional meaning.

These depictions of the landscape and its value from Aboriginal perspectives incorporate significant departures from the stereotypical, spiritualised labelling of the environment and indigenous people encountered in other Australian films. In parallel with contemporary political impetuses towards the recognition of history and reconciliation between communities, the landscapes revisited and traversed in *Radiance* and *Rabbit-Proof Fence* are used for restitution and reconstitution, on familial and cultural grounds. Aboriginal experience, in individual and wider social terms, is mapped onto the land, with an appreciation of the history of connective, cultural ownership, and a frank acknowledgement of a problematic personal and national past.

Conclusion

The Australian natural environment has undergone a complex series of dynamic deployments within the film revival, and as a consequence has exemplified and elucidated a proportionate number of politicised, gendered and ethnically based positions within the national cinema. The significance of the landscape, as a signifier of national cultural difference and as a uniquely expressive national cinematic resource, has ensured its inclusion and relevance in films portraying the most abiding and recognisable Australian images for home and overseas audiences, and exploring the most enduring divisions and differences in Australian society (between men and women, between immigrants and indigenous peoples). The representation of the land provides an appropriate accent to the Australian cinema's idiom: the mountains, the desert, the bush and the coast may have acquired specific, but not necessarily one-dimensional, meanings in characterisation and *mise-en-scène*, and these environments appear as much as agents as atmospheres within the national film industry's products.

The landscape has also become an integral part of the genres which have come to define the output of the Australian film industry, in each decade since the revival. While the conventional valuation and evaluation of the land has persisted through the continuing production of literary adaptations and historically based films, the conceptualisation of the landscape in terms of the abject, the uncanny and the unacknowledged has also remained a consistent element in Gothic films (and in Gothic elements within mainstream films). However, the industrial and thematic development of the film industry has also influenced the textual and aesthetic properties of Australian film in more recent years. If it is 'not by chance … that a crop of extensively publicised and acclaimed films highlighting a unique Australian landscape' should appear 'during a decade of resurgent nationalism' (Gibson, 1983: 47–51), it is equally unsurprising that the Australian cinema of the 1990s, in essaying the representation of contemporary multicultural diversity, should concentrate upon abidingly urban settings, suiting the experience, concerns and environments of immigrant communities. Into the new century, the landscape cinema maintains its significance for the articulation, interrogation and contestation of national ideas, ideals and images, for the diverse audiences of the Australian cinema.

Notes

1   In relation to the depiction of Boer War, and the actions of Australian soldiers on the Veldt in *Breaker Morant* (Bruce Beresford, 1979), Susan Dermody and Elizabeth Jacka suggest that 'the similarity of the diegetic locale to Australian terrain is part of the film's meaning'. The Australians are not simply more at home in these lands than their British commanders, they are seen to be specifically 'at home' within the filmic event (Dermody and Jacka, 1988: 155–6).

References

Brabazon, T. (1999), 'A pig in space? *Babe* and the problem of landscape', *Australian Studies* 14(1&2): 149–58.

Collins, F. (1999), *The Films of Gillian Armstrong* (St Kilda, Victoria: AFC).

Dermody, S. and Jacka, E. (1988), *The Screening of Australia Vol. II: Anatomy of a National Cinema* (Sydney: Currency).

Gibson, R. (1983) 'Camera natura: landscape in Australian feature films', *Framework* 22–23 (autumn): 47–51.

O'Regan, T. (1985), '*The Man from Snowy River* and Australian Popular Culture', in Moran, A. and O'Regan, T. (eds), *An Australian Film Reader* (Sydney: Currency Press), pp. 242–51.

O'Regan, T. (1996), *Australian National Cinema* (London: Routledge).

Sutton, P. (ed.) (1989), *Dreamings: The Art of Aboriginal Australia* (London: Penguin).

3

Nation and nature in North Korean film

Carol Medlicott

Introduction

North Korea. The common name of the Democratic People's Republic of Korea (DPRK), that truculent little pariah state, conjures an Orwellian image of grim dystopia where the repressed population struggles under poverty as appalling as the dogma is rigid. Proclaimed by George W. Bush as part of an 'axis of evil', North Korea since the mid-1990s has garnered international attention for such paradoxical happenings as a devastating famine and alleged nuclear weapons development. A state that siphons the lion's share of its meagre resources to maintain its million-man armed forces, leaving infrastructure and economy in shambles, is surely among the last places on earth where one would expect a sophisticated approach to the visual arts or an advanced film industry. Yet, probably *because* North Korea relentlessly shields its population from exposure to ideas and images from the world beyond its borders, it has developed a system of cultural production that makes clever use of visual imagery for the inculcation of political ideology.

Since the division of Korea by the superpowers in 1948, North Korea has sought to project the notion that it – not its rival to the south – is the single authentic modern Korean state, the inheritor of long centuries of a rich social and cultural tradition. Just as its imposing military and showpiece capital city have been utilised to project this notion outwardly to the international community, the arts are utilised to project the same notion inwardly to the North Korean population itself. Over the fifty-five or more years of its existence, North Korea has poured a fortune into producing an array of representational texts and visual displays that underscore its cultural and political authenticity as the 'true' Korea. At the centre of this authentication enterprise is the personality cult of Kim Il Sung, who ruled North Korea for forty-eight years and continues, eerily, to rule it symbolically from his posthumous condition. North Korea's unrelenting hagiography elevates Kim as the author of the modern Korean nation and hero of Korea's twentieth-century struggle against imperialism and aggression. The veneration of Kim (and by extension his son Kim Jong Il and his parents) is the over-arching goal of all artistic, aesthetic and media production in North Korea, from song texts to billboards, urban design to school books, sports performances to theatre.

Indeed, the dominance of the Kim Il Sung personality cult in North Korean artistic production is a commonplace among scholars of North Korea and need hardly be commented upon. But examination of North Korean artistic production also reveals other visual themes much more subtle than simply the crass glorification of Kim Il Sung, and these evoke a North Korean regime influencing perceptions with even greater cunning. The manipulation of rural landscape images to reinforce both the personality cult and North Korea's particular variant of Korean nationalism is one feature both notable and subtle in North Korean artistic production. Although rural landscape images of various types persist throughout an array of propaganda media, this chapter will consider a specific set of northern Korean rural landscapes represented in visual arts, particularly film and stage productions. It proposes that the North Korean state selected a precise countryside image as the prototypical landscape of nationalism and that this landscape type serves as a canvas against which dramatised versions of nationalist myths unfold. Drawing from film and stage versions of several important North Korean 'revolutionary operas', this chapter explores how the North Korean regime has articulated the nation in a specific rural setting, namely that of the mountainous and thickly forested far-northern border area of the Korean peninsula. It pays particular attention to the construction of mountainous and isolated wilderness as both a metaphor for the nation and a cradle of revolutionary ideals, and also to the layered meanings of forest in revolutionary dramas.

North Korea's geography of nationalism

Korean nationalism coalesced as a consequence of Japan's growing influence in Korea from the late 1870s and its colonial occupation of Korea from 1910 to 1945 (Chandra, 1988; Robinson, 1988; Eckert *et al.*, 1990; Wells, 1990; Armstrong, 2002; Schmid, 2002; Cumings, 2004). The various oppositional events and movements that emerged in a colonised but undivided Korea later provided the bases for each rival Korean state's national 'founding myth' in a post-1945 Korea that was liberated but quickly divided. Nationalism employs founding myths centred upon feats performed in a particular temporal setting, regarded as a 'golden age' (Smith, 1997). Although scholars of Korean nationalism imply that each Korean state's idea of a 'golden age' of Korean national-ism involves different people and somewhat different temporal settings, it is less common to specifically consider the sharply different spatial settings of these competing nationalist narratives. The physical and aesthetic settings of the Korean founding myths in fact provide motifs for a range of nationalist texts and artistic productions. In a broader sense, the landscape images underpin-ning nationalist narratives are 'representative landscapes' that provide 'visual encapsulation of a group's occupation of a particu-lar territory and the memory of a shared past that this conveys' (Agnew, 1997).

Formally declared on 9 September 1948, the DPRK traces its political sovereignty and cultural legitimacy to the 1930s, when anti-Japanese resistance was fomented by Koreans and Chinese in Korea's far-northern cross-border region. Kim Il Sung had been active in the cross-border resistance movement, which partly explains North Korea's dogged insistence upon Korea's far north-ern area as the location of its founding myth. Born as 'Kim Song ju' near Pyongyang (North Korea's capital) in 1912, Kim Il Sung soon migrated with his family to Korea's far north. After a stint in a Japanese jail before 1930, he became involved with a Manchuria-based anti-Japanese resistance movement dominated by Chinese Communists. Kim remained involved with this resistance group (there were other decisive outbursts of anti-Japanese resistance elsewhere on the Korean peninsula, besides that in which Kim was active) in the rugged and mountainous cross-border region, punc-tuated by some time spent in the nearby Russian Far East, where his son was born in 1942, until he returned to Pyongyang under Soviet sponsorship and bearing the new pseudonym 'Kim Il Sung' after Korea's liberation. Both biographical accounts of Kim produced outside North Korea (Cumings, 1981: 35–8; Suh, 1988) as well as Kim's own state-produced 'autobiography' (Kim Il Sung, 1992) maintain that most of his life under Japanese occupation was spent along the remote China–Korea frontier. Kim himself maintains – along with myriad state-produced materials – that he specifically inhabited the slopes of Korea's highest mountain, Mt Paektu (hereinafter 'Paektusan', the commonly Romanised Korean equivalent), which straddles the Korea–China border (Figure 2.1). It was on the slopes of this mountain, according to North Korean state materials, that the institutions leading to the establishment of the post-liberation North Korean state were established. Specifically, North Korea claims that its primary military and revolutionary institution, the Korean People's Army (KPA), was established in April 1932 from Kim's first anti-Japanese guerrilla group, giving foundation to what would become the core state institution of North Korea.

In analysing the appearance in cultural production of natural motifs from the locale of North Korea's founding myth it is useful to consider geographers' descriptive work on that region. Examination of one acclaimed and comprehensive colonial period text of Korea (Lautensach, 1988 [1945]) reveals two key claims. First, despite the presence of rivers as definite geographical boundaries, the northern border between Korea and China is a political device only and represents neither a definite cultural boundary nor a morphological one. Referring to the rivers that mark the Korea–China boundary, German geographer Lautensach states:

> Geologically and morphologically the Yalu-Tumen line is not a definite boundary, except in a few places. From the standpoint of climate and vegetation it is even less of a boundary. The entire immense upland area extending from the northern end of the peninsula to the Manchurian plain is a decidedly transitional zone. (1988: 3–4)

Lautensach asserts that the Paektusan region, political boundary notwithstanding, should be treated as a unified whole both culturally and morphologically. Delineating 'the area around Paektusan and the surrounding basalt plateau', Lautensach states that of Korea's entire border with China, this Paektusan environment is

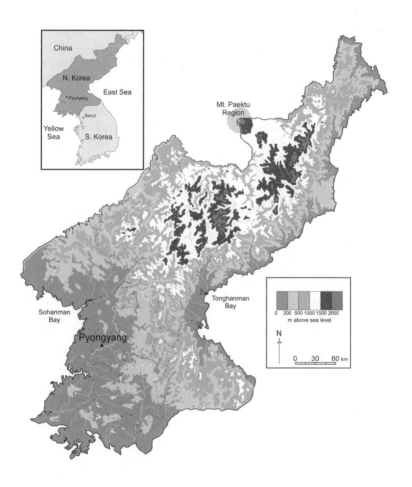

2.1 North Korea and the Mt Paektu Region

'the only part in which the political boundary dissects a landscape of profound individuality ... In this area the geographical boundary cannot coincide with the political boundary' (1988: 4).

Secondly, Lautensach contends that the Paektusan region, along with an adjacent volcanic upland area on the Korean side of the border, is so distinct morphologically that it should be regarded as decidedly atypical of the entirety of the Korean peninsula. Lautensach describes Paektusan and its adjacent upland area not only as unique relative to the rest of the border region and adjacent Manchuria, but also as uncharacteristic of the Korean landscape as a whole: 'it contrasts quite highly with the rest of Korea ... One no longer has the impression that he is in central East Asia ... [T]hese plant associations form an alien high altitude zone that is otherwise found only in much more restricted range on the highest peaks of the upland' (1988: 243).

In describing Paektusan's flora and human habitation patterns, Lautensach identified its mixed pine, fir, larch, birch, spruce and maple, giving way to pine, fir and larch only in the timberline zone. And Paektu's timberline forest pattern (occurring at the 1,950-metre level of the mountain's 2,700-metre reach) is replicated in the timberline forests of the highest peaks of the adjacent uplands. Lautensach wrote of the dominant pattern of 'fire field farmers' in both the Paektusan area and adjacent uplands. These he characterised as the lowest strata of landless peasants (peasants thrown out by landlords elsewhere), who 'burn a clearing, build a log cabin nearby, raise subsistence crops for a few years, and move on' (1988: 161). The least sedentary of Korea's agricultural lifestyles, this cultural pattern is characterised by Lautensach as largely confined to the Paektusan and upland area, with only a few pockets extant in the few thickly forested mountainous areas of the south.

For Lautensach the Paektusan area presented a fieldwork conundrum relative to Korea as a whole. But it was also an aesthetic highlight of his fieldwork. His vivid description of the forested landscape from the volcanic pumice cone summit, where one looks downslope to see nothing but conifer and birch forest, punctuated by lakes and marshes and huge patches of white lichen and looks inward to see the cobalt lake in the volcanic crater (Lake Chonji), is worthy of the most extravagant North Korean propaganda text: 'All observers agree that the contrasts that this twofold view unites makes the scene viewed from Paektusan one of the most enthralling sights on earth.'

It was to this geographically unique zone that Kim Il Sung allegedly retreated while a very young man to begin reorganising a coherent resistance movement that, according to North Korean history, would eventually oust the Japanese colonial aggressors from Korea. Of course, Kim's actual whereabouts have been historically established as further north (Cumings, 1981; Suh, 1988), with only occasional forays south of the Yalu-Tumen rivers to attempt the odd raid on a Japanese police outpost. North Korean materials steadfastly place him in the environs of Paektusan at all times; and they assert that his son, North Korea's current bizarre leader Kim Jong Il, was born at a 'secret camp' concealed within the forested slopes of this mountain.

But the actual setting of Kim's exploits matters, of course, far less to the construction of nationalist narrative than the alleged setting. Cumings offers a potent reminder of the power of these nationalist fables (and, by extension, of nationalist fables more generally) when he says, 'At the core of almost every grandiose, prideful, hyperventilated North Korean myth ... there is a kernel of truth ... One underestimates the hold of these stories at one's peril' (2004: 107). In this case, the myth involves Kim rallying thousands of demoralised local peasants, transforming them into a disciplined and uniform-clad army, and conducting full-scale assaults from their forest strongholds against the Japanese colonial infrastructure. The North Korean Constitution summarises this myth using a strikingly biblical cadence:

> And the General said, 'We must build secret bases in the form of semi-guerilla zones by creating a network of secret camps in the large forests on Mt. Paekto for the Korean People's Revolutionary Army to carry on its activities and organizing the people in the surrounding wide areas. Thus we will set up bastions of revolution invisible to the enemy.'[1]

For Cumings' posited 'kernel of truth', we return to Lautensach, from whose biased narrative we can plainly infer that there was more than enough anti-Japanese agitation (he terms it 'banditry') in the Paektusan area to later provide grist for the North Korean propaganda mill:

Banditry, which has become a severe political problem in all of Manchuria, has reached its prime in the forests of Paektusan and has encroached into the Korean sector. The hamlets inhabited by Chinese and Koreans are raided, the harvest robbed ... and the inhabitants killed. The bandits' log cabins ... are scattered throughout the forests ... Because of the danger from bandits the fire-field farmers have left the plateau and retreated to the larger settlements in the valleys. In the Korean sector, these are protected by Japanese police stations, which have been converted into small fortresses ... It will be possible to get rid of the bandits only when the plateau has been opened up to traffic. So far the natural forests are criss-crossed by hunting paths only. (Lautensach, 1988: 240)

Considering that Lautensach's own fieldwork in the region had taken place in the late 1930s, a time when Kim Il Sung was probably present there, it would not be far-fetched to speculate that Lautensach's 'bandits' might have included Kim Il Sung himself! Cumings' work reinforces the notion that the forest-dwelling peasants of the Paektusan area were being gradually transformed into Kim's guerrilla resistance force (Cumings, 1981: 35–8; 2004: 103–27). And Cumings quotes Japanese police records, which note that the guerrillas 'had to move like monkeys through the woodmen's paths in the dense forest' (2004: 116), using language curiously evocative of Lautensach's reference to hunting paths as the most viable mode of travel.

Nature motifs from Korea's far north also hold folklore significance, another factor that one must consider as affecting the inclusion of motifs in nationalist narratives. As the highest mountain on the Korean peninsula, Paektusan has long dominated the origin myths of Korean folklore. Fables tell of a supernatural union at the summit of Paektusan between animals infused with divine spirit, from which was born a boy who would become Korea's first king. Scholars of Korea commonly accept the notion that North Korean propaganda places both Kim Il Sung's fabled guerrilla exploits and Kim Jong Il's birth in the environs of Paektusan so as to fully exploit that mountain's complex and longstanding mythosymbolic cultural capital (Cumings, 1993; Armstrong, 1995; Cumings, 1997; Schmid, 2002; Cumings, 2004). By setting its most potent nationalist stories in one of Korea's 'thick places',[2] that is, a place already deeply implicated in a folk belief system, the North Korean state invested Paektusan with new meanings and reinvented it as the site of national and class struggle against Japanese imperialism, and in turn, as the site of the birth of modern North Korea.

Similarly, the pine tree has a long association in Confucian ideology with wisdom, filial loyalty and longevity. Pine trees are often singled out as a metaphor for Kim Il Sung in North Korean propaganda. For example, the pictorial magazine commemorating Kim's death bore a back cover image of a tall mature pine tree growing near Kim's birthplace. A poem titled 'Green Pine on Nam Hill' is attributed to Kim Il Sung's father, and appears in multiple contexts in North Korean art and propaganda,[3] and probably is intended to symbolise Kim's lineage and source of wisdom. A North Korean folk-music tape opens with a song whose lyrics tell of a baby boy born as the seeds of pine trees are scattered in all directions, covering the land with forest.[4] Because the high-altitude forest of the Paektusan region happens to be dominated by conifers, North Korean producers of a range of nationalist texts are availed of the opportunity for double entendre when employing the pine-tree motif.

Film and revolutionary opera as instructive texts

Early in its existence, the North Korean state recognised the power of film to convey political ideas across its population. Its first feature film, *My Hometown*, was released in 1949. Although it produced only a handful of films during the 1950s, by the mid-1960s its production averaged over a dozen films per year; this swelled to as many as thirty per year in the 1970s and 1980s (Lee 2000: 34–9).[5] From roughly the mid-1960s through to the end of the 1980s, the regime actively competed with its southern rival in urban construction, industrial development and cultural production. The resources it poured into its film industry should be seen in that light. The regime produced films that revealed the nation's heroic beginnings, followed its ongoing struggle against American imperialism, showcased the state's modernisation trajectory, revealed the country's majestic scenery, and portrayed people throughout the country leading productive and enjoyable lives – all the while making claims that South Korea was a correspondingly grim place gripped with poverty and violence. Taking no chances that its efforts to use film as a mass indoctrination tool would be wasted, viewing of all films produced – not only feature films, but also documentaries and children's films – became 100 per cent compulsory (Lee, 2000: 41).[6]

North Korea's film industry undoubtedly received a boost from the fact that Kim Jong Il evidently became a film enthusiast as a young man. The film industry is among only a few production sectors in North Korea in which the younger Kim – or 'the Dear Leader' – was known to be actively engaged.[7] As early as 1968, Kim Jong Il involved himself in film production by visiting filming locations and addressing directors and actors (Kim Jong Il, 1989a). By 1973 he had produced his own book-length work on filmmaking, *On the Art of the Cinema* (Kim Jong Il, 1989d). Short pamphlets purportedly authored by Kim Jong Il followed in the 1980s and 1990s, all oriented towards the performing arts: *The Character and the Actor* (1987), *Let Us Effect a New Upsurge in Producing Works of Revolutionary Art and Literature* (1989b), *On Consolidating and Developing the Successes Achieved in the Creation of Revolutionary Operas* (1989c), *Let Us Create More Good Music, Dances, and Films* ... (1990) and *For the Further Development of Our Juche Art* (1992). But the single factor that decisively demonstrated Kim Jong Il's obsession with film was undoubtedly his kidnapping in 1978 of a famous South Korean movie actress, Ch'oe Eun Hee, and her equally famous movie-director husband, Shin Sang Ok. The couple lived and worked in North Korea until 1986, making at least seven feature films and entering Kim Jong Il's private social circle, before they 'escaped' from a North Korean embassy in Eastern Europe and announced their intent to return to South Korea (Lee 2000: 32, 41).[8]

In addition to film, the North Korean artistic sector heavily invests in a closely related genre called 'revolutionary opera'. In revolutionary opera, the plot is moved along with liberal use of songs (both solo and chorus) and choreographed dances. A limited repertoire of five revolutionary operas exists in North Korea, and all share the distinction of being set in the far northern Korea–China cross-border region near Paektusan. The first revolutionary opera, *Sea of Blood*, was adapted from a lengthy novel that follows the plight of a Korean peasant family in 1930s Manchuria, and this novel was allegedly penned by none other than Kim Il Sung himself. Although the five revolutionary operas were first designed as stage productions, they were also adapted to film. One of the five, *Flower Girl* (1972), received accolades at an international film festival in 1973. In many ways these five serve as prototypes for other North Korean films. And although the film versions are all some thirty years old, they are regarded as among North Korea's 'classic' films, and they are continually reproduced in live theatre. Thus, the influence of the imagery they contain arguably remains strong. By exploring the alleged highlights of Kim Il Sung's anti-Japanese struggle, which purportedly not only freed Korea from foreign domination but also began a class revolution, the revolutionary operas offer an ideal array of dramatic elements, moral qualities and character types.[9] Although Kim Il Sung himself never appears as a character in any of the revolutionary operas, he is alluded to by name or by title in the plots, and he is a strong unseen force. Collectively, the revolutionary operas dramatise the national founding myth of North Korea, but instead of offering biographical accounts of Kim's own exploits they elaborate on various anti-Japanese themes against the distinct backdrop of the Paektusan region.

Nature motifs and nationalist meaning

Several nature motifs dominate North Korean revolutionary opera, including Paektusan mountain itself, the rugged and climatically harsh topography, and the characteristic timberline coniferous forest of that high-altitude zone. This section discusses three revolutionary operas in particular – *Sea of Blood*, *Flower Girl* and *Tell, O Forest*. It will identify the instrumental use of these rural images and note how the three dramas construct a national landscape more generally.

That film scenery offers important symbolic elements intended for audience interpretation is a key theme in the field of theatre studies. American Westerns are widely acknowledged as a genre in which the natural landscape itself often functions as character; the renowned director John Ford was particularly known for engineering scenery and landscape features for dramatic effect (Budd, 1976; Tuska, 1985). Scholars have noted the Western as a genre proffering distinct landscape types that serve as backdrops for particular morality tales, some of which function as American national myths (Coyne, 1998; Slotkin, 1998; Hausladen, 2003). In Westerns, landscape and the forces of nature can function as both friend and foe to the characters. Filmmakers utilise the physical settings to signal such features as characters' struggle against adversity, characters' insignificance relative to broader cosmic forces, or characters' moral triumph and spiritual harmony. Given the abundant testimony from North Korean defectors and former 'insiders' about Kim Jong Il's obsession with film and his vast personal collection of American films, it is not surprising that landscape's function in revolutionary opera bears some superficial similarities to American Westerns. Certainly nature as a whole is pressed into service in North Korean visual propaganda in rather uncomplicated ways to reinforce the beneficence of the state, the supremacy of Kim Il Sung, and the cities and countryside as a utopian paradise. State publications abound with gorgeous spring blossoms, fields of waving grain, and pastures crowded with healthy flocks. Moreover, magazine images of holidaymakers hiking amid the picturesque peaks of North Korea's mountainous regions often include views of some of the many political slogans that have been cut deeply into exposed rock faces, suggesting to the spectator that nature itself is a political actor in North Korea. The North Korean pictorial magazine commemorating the death of Kim Il Sung includes images of turbulent and unsettled nature – stormy seas and crashing waves – to indicate the grief of the nation.[10]

The three revolutionary operas highlighted here unfold in similar physical settings but have quite different plots. *Sea of Blood* (1969; 1977; 1990)[11] follows a widowed peasant woman and her three children who migrate across Korea's northern border to the Manchurian zone of the Paektusan region. From their humble forest log cabin home they are catapulted into the partisan movement led by the distant, unseen General Kim Il Sung. Japanese officials in a nearby town provide constant provocation, and the widow's youngest son is killed by a sadistic Japanese soldier. Finally, the widow leads a peasant uprising that successfully overruns the nearby Japanese garrison.

In *Tell, O Forest* (1974), a respected man in a small peasant enclave is chosen by nearby Japanese officials to serve as the village head and report on the peasants' activities. He agrees to cooperate, much to his fellow peasants' consternation: they believe he is a traitor and collaborator. Moreover, his daughter is deeply ashamed and believes her marriage prospects to be threatened by his actions. He must conceal from his community that his 'collaboration' is actually by direction from a distant partisan cell; his true purpose is to gain the trust of the Japanese, so as to eventually defeat them. He bears this heavy burden and is vindicated in the end when he leads the Japanese to a trap from which they cannot escape and the partisans decimate them.

Like *Sea of Blood*, *Flower Girl* (1972) follows the fortunes of a widow and her children – an older son and two daughters, of whom the younger is blind. But the children are the main characters in *Flower Girl*'s more complex plot, the older daughter – the 'flower girl' – in particular. Each day the flower girl and her mother go to town where the flower girl sells bouquets she has gathered in the forest and the mother labours as a maid in the household of a cruel aristocratic couple. An early flashback reveals that the younger girl was blinded years before when her mother's sadistic mistress 'accidentally' shoved the child into a kitchen fire. Angered by such cruelty to his little sister, the son soon is caught up in a scuffle with Japanese soldiers and is sent off to prison. The mother dies from overwork. The flower girl, who has continued gamely to peddle her flowers despite the townspeople's rebuffs, decides to set out alone in search of her brother, intending to return with him thereby reuniting the remainder of the family. After briefly landing in jail herself, she is taken in by some kindly peasants in the distant forest. Meanwhile, the mother's sadistic mistress lies ill and dying and is haunted by the memory of having caused the little girl to be blinded. Convinced that his wife will recover if the little girl is dead, her aristocratic but clueless husband decides to lure the little girl away into the snowy forest, whereupon he returns alone. A new scene reveals the missing brother, now older and wiser, making his way home through the wintry forest. He takes shelter overnight in a peasant's log cabin, only to discover the peasant is also sheltering a little blind girl whom he had found abandoned in the snow (believing she would soon die, the aristocrat had left her there). The brother joyfully recognises his little sister. Soon the flower girl also arrives and the siblings are reunited. Now a partisan, the brother gathers the other peasants and instructs them in how to resist the Japanese. In the end the peasants are dwelling happily in the town along with townspeople who had previously shunned them but have now mended their ways. Revolutionary ideas are on the rise, and a newspaper marked 'Bolshevik' is passed among the youth. The flower girl is still selling flowers, but now her bouquets are larger and brighter and townspeople flock to buy them.

Other than the commanding presence of the Paektusan summit itself, the region's natural features, as they are presented in these three revolutionary operas, seem to fall into three categories: generally rugged mountain terrain, coniferous forest vegetation, and harsh winter weather. Considering the terrain itself, the mountain terrain is a strong motif in all three dramas. All unfold in the same far-northern setting, where the peasants subsist in a rugged forested environment and mountain slopes are visible in the distance. In *Sea of Blood*, Paektusan's close proximity is clear – characters speak of it frequently and it appears in the distance. Paektusan is more ambiguous in *Tell, O Forest*, but the protagonist sees it in a dream; and the surrounding mountain zone, pathless and impenetrable, is indicated in song lyrics: 'The only way to get to Hongsan-gol is through the sky ... An axe and a sickle, Hearing the roars of tigers nearby ... Though I know the way, I won't go, Because there are guerrillas there' (Libretto, Act 4, Scene 2). In *Flower Girl*, no location is specified, but the snowy landscape, prevalent mountain scenery and the implied close proximity of the partisans all suggest that it unfolds near Paektusan.

In all three dramas, the forested mountain slopes are a wholly positive setting for the characters, in contrast to the American Western genre in which rugged wilderness often symbolises danger and evil. In revolutionary opera, good things happen to the characters when they are in the forest or on the rugged mountain slopes. They appear happy and fulfilled, as when the sisters in *Flower Girl* cheerfully cavort and gather flowers or the brother in *Sea of Blood* walks contentedly with a visiting partisan and listens to his wise words. Moreover, the peasant characters appear in control of their environment when they are in the forest or on the mountain slopes. In *Sea of Blood* the widow capably camps with her children in mountain woodlands as they journey to their new home at Paektusan; and later her older children pass happy and productive hours with other partisans in a cave on the slope of Paektusan, where they efficiently prepare supplies and organise themselves for the coming confrontation with the Japanese. Discouraged when no one will buy her flowers, the daughter in *Flower Girl* resourcefully gathers herbs in the forest, which she sells to a kindly peasant to buy medicine for her mother. Unlike the towns, where, until each drama's closure nothing but bad things happen to the characters (the little girl's blindness, confronting Japanese jailers, forced collaboration, suffering at the hands of aristocratic bosses), the deserted forests and mountains are sites of the characters' positive experiences and the revelation of important truths to the audience. Alone, deep in the forest, the protagonist in *Tell, O Forest* reveals to only the listening trees that he is not really betraying his village, but is in fact acting as a spy for the partisans. And while the audience initially thinks that tragedy has befallen the blind girl in *Flower Girl* when she is taken to the forest, it soon learns that the forest has actually been the site of her rescue and is the location of her reunion with her brother.

Audiences receive continuous reminders that these three dramas are set in or near pine forest. In all three stories, the protagonist families live in log cabins. As geographers such as Lautensach indicated, this dwelling type was unique to the 'fire field farmers' of the far-northern forests, seldom used elsewhere because of the relative scarcity of logs. Other positive characters, such as kindly peasants, also reside in log houses. In contrast, the buildings associated with negative characters – aristocrats or Japanese officials – are never log, but rather appear to be built of plaster and milled lumber. All three stories depict the characters happy and empowered when among pine trees. *Tell, O Forest* makes plainest use of the pine forest motif. Not only does nearly the entire story unfold in the midst of deep forest, but the forest is actually a character in the plot. The protagonist explicitly confides his secret to the pine trees, and the trees shake and respond to his emotions, according to stage directions in the libretto. And as in other instances of the pine motif in North Korean cultural expression, the pine in *Tell, O Forest* can be construed as a metaphor for Kim Il Sung. As the protagonist sings of his longing to 'be embraced by the General', he is embracing a large pine tree (Figure 2.2).

Flower Girl and *Tell, O Forest* both contain pivotal scenes in which the setting is not only forest, but snow-covered forest. In *Flower Girl*, the lost brother treks through the snowy forest as he finds his way back to his family and home. However, instead of struggling against wintry elements that actively oppose him, the character is shown wandering peacefully in stillness amid snow softly blanketing the rounded contours of hills and trees. Instead of a threatening barrier, the snowy landscape appears as a soothing

I cannot bear to see the misery of my villagers, though I can endure any personal insult

2.2 'When will I be embraced by the General?'

maternal setting of comforting quiet. And although the film ends in the spring amid blooming flowers, the plot resolution of the siblings' reunion occurs in the winter amid deep snows. A similar suggestion of wintry weather being friend, not foe, to the Korean people is found in Kim Jong Il's own 'directives' to North Korean filmmakers (Kim Jong Il, 1989a: 31–2). Kim urges special care in presenting wintertime scenes of revolutionary struggle. Evaluating a specific film scene and taking into account the elements' impact on *all* opponents, Kim points out 'Nevertheless, the regiment makes use of the cold and snow to make the enemy troops exhausted'. Therefore, Kim says, the images of the snowy landscape should be prolonged because of the 'greater sense of security it gives the audience that the headquarters of the revolution is safe, protected by the enveloping blanket of snow in which the enemy is bogged down'.

In all three films, the tension between the characters' difficult confrontations and powerlessness in the towns and their rejuvenation, empowerment and contentment in the rugged and wooded mountain environment is a palpable theme. In addition to conveying nature as a positive resource for the characters and the origin of their happiness and inspiration, this theme could also serve to remind the audience of the class conflict that is so critical to North Korean political identity. The forest peasants are alienated from the town-dwellers of 'civilised' Korea – Japanese officials and Korean aristocrats, alike. As Lautensach's field research confirmed, the forest peasants of Korea's Paektusan region occupied the lowest social strata. Seeing the peasants' empowerment in the forest accentuates nature itself as the nation and as the source of the peasants' strength and happiness. By contrast, the Japanese (who have come to Korea for no discernible reason, according to characters' remarks in *Tell, O Forest* and *Sea of Blood*[12]) are a straightforward menace to peasants' lives, but – tellingly – a town-based menace. The Japanese derive their power from towns, and they can't operate very effectively outside the towns, as the Japanese susceptibility to the protagonist's trap in *Tell, O Forest* indicates. The Japanese need infrastructure of towns and institutions, but the peasants don't. For the peasants in the far north, the Korean nation is not its town-based civilisation. Rather, the nation is unspoiled nature itself.

Conclusion

Territorial claims are central to nationalist discourse precisely because the crises from which the nation springs are spatial: they occur (or are remembered to occur) in particular places (Schmid, 2000). For North Korea, asserting the authenticity of its control over territory involves elevating and mythologising events and individuals associated with Korean nationalism that were spatially located within the landscapes of the northern part of the Peninsula. Thus, the North Korean regime can claim to be legitimate legatees of these nationalist icons. North Korea has constructed patently nationalist myths set in the distinctive landscapes of the far-northern cross-border region near the symbolic mountain, Paektusan. This distinctive spatial setting of the events of North Korea's founding myth has not gone unnoticed by Korean scholars. Noting that the liminal space between Japan's colonies in Korea and the adjacent provinces of China's Manchurian region were the spatial backdrop of Kim Il Sung's anti-Japanese guerrilla exploits, Armstrong (2003: 9) observes that a new Korean state 'had been imagined at the interstices of colonial control and unregulated frontier'.

However, scholars of Korea have been slow to systematically examine the consequences for artistic forms of the North Korean founding myths' spatiality. This chapter begins the process of analysing how the nationalist founding myths of North Korea have been aesthetically and symbolically articulated in the country's cultural production. The natural objects, patterns and motifs associated with the specific region in which Kim Il Sung's anti-Japanese campaigns allegedly occurred – namely, Paektusan and adjacent rugged mountain-strewn uplands, coniferous forests and harsh winter weather – are fundamentally important in representing and sustaining North Korea's idea of nation. And the North Korean variant of nationalism is deeply implicated in the person of Kim Il Sung, so that nature motifs, the nation and Kim are easily conflated symbolically.

Nature as a source of metaphors for nation is of course quite commonplace; and nature motifs underscore nation and national ideals in cases of cultural representation throughout the world. But the landscape type that is designated as significant in nationalist narrative is generally representative of the dominant landscape type within the nation's claimed territory as a whole. What makes the North Korean case so remarkable is the atypicality of the chosen national landscape relative to the Korean peninsula as whole. Indeed, the physical setting of the North Korean foundation myths is not clearly even in Korea itself. Rather, the myths transpire in a cross-border region identified by geographers as morphologically coherent but entirely distinct from the rest of Korea. In short, the *typical* landscape of North Korean nationalism is *atypical* of Korean landscape as a whole. Nature gives birth to nation in North Korean nationalist narrative, but it is a distant parent. North Korea employs as nationalist motifs the features of the remote Paektusan region so as to pay homage to its far-flung nativity.

Notes

1 *On the Socialist Constitution of the Democratic People's Republic of Korea*, 1975.
2 The term 'thick places' is used by Entrikin (1999) to refer to sites laden with multiple cultural meanings whose interpretation is continually contested.
3 For example, *DPRK Pictorial* (March 1993: 4); and *Korean Central Historical Museum*, 'edited by the Editorial Staff of Picture-Albums, the Bureau for Direction of Cultural Preservation, the DPRK' (1979: 118).
4 'I have been travelling various mountains everywhere, / Picking up seeds, spreading them all around the mountains, / And the pine trees are in full bloom. / North, south, east, and west – in all directions, / The pine trees grow to cover the mountains. / A baby is born that will be the joy of the nation.' *Choson Minyo Gok-jip* (*Korean Folk Songs*). Pyongyang. Cassette tape.
5 There is little literature outside of North Korea that documents its film industry. See Hyangjin Lee (2000) for a comparative survey of North Korean filmmaking. Even working with rare North Korean sources it is possible to deduce much about the North Korean film industry. A 1993 North Korean songbook compilation, *Yeong-Hwa No-Rae: 1100 Gok Chip* (*Movie Music: 1100 Melodies*) indicates that some individual years in the 1980s saw the production of over two dozen films.
6 Erik Cornell, a Swedish diplomat to North Korea in the 1970s, suggests that film viewing in North Korea is compulsory (Cornell, 2002).

7 Nuclear energy and terrorism are other sectors in which the Dear Leader is believed to exercise direct authority. See, for instance, the documentary film *Kim's Nuclear Gamble* (Public Broadcasting Service, 2000).

8 Shin and his wife now live in Southern California. They tend to avoid the English-speaking press, and the authenticity of their abduction and subsequent escape from North Korea has been called into question.

9 Character types include the strong mature peasant mother, the faithful and unspoiled young virgin, the evil Japanese official, the devious collaborator, and the brave and loyal elder brother.

10 *Korea* (English Language Edition) (1994).

11 *Sea of Blood* (1969) (film version, VHS tape); *Sea of Blood: Revolutionary Opera Based on the Immortal Classic Sea of Blood – Libretto* (1977) Pyongyang: Foreign Languages Publishing House; *Sea of Blood* (1990) (stage production, VHS tape).

12 In the revolutionary operas, Japanese invasion is tantamount to a natural disaster that challenges but does not defeat the peasants. Moreover, offering no formal explanation for the imperial aggression further dehumanises the aggressor.

References

Agnew, J. (1997), 'Geographies of nationalism and ethnic conflict', in Agnew, John (ed.), *Political Geography: A Reader* (New York: John Wiley), pp. 317–24.

Armstrong, C. (1995), 'Centering the periphery: Manchurian exile(s) and the North Korean State', *Korean Studies* 19: 1–19.

Armstrong, C.K. (ed.) (2002), *Korean Society: Civil Society, Democracy and the State* (London and New York: Routledge).

Armstrong, C.K. (2003), *The North Korean Revolution, 1945–1950* (Ithaca, NY: Cornell University Press).

Budd, M. (1976), 'A home in the wilderness: visual imagery in John Ford's westerns', *Cinema Journal* 16(1); 62–75.

Chandra, V. (1988), *Imperialism, Resistance, and Reform in Late Nineteenth-Century Korea: Enlightenment and the Independence Club* (Berkeley, CA: Institute for East Asian Studies).

Choson Minyo Gok-jip (Korean Folk Songs). Pyongyang, cassette tape, personal collection of author.

Cornell, E. (2002), North Korea under Communism: Report of an Envoy to Paradise (London and New York: Routledge; Curzon).

Coyne, M. (1998), *The Crowded Prairie: American National*

Identity in the Hollywood Western (New York: Tauris).

Cumings, B. (1981), *The Origins of the Korean War, Volume I: Liberation and the Emergence of Separate Regimes, 1945–1947* (Princeton, NJ: Princeton University Press).

Cumings, B. (1993), 'The corporate state in North Korea', in Koo, H. (ed.), *State and Society in Contemporary Korea* (Ithaca, NY: Cornell University Press), pp. 197–230.

Cumings, B. (1997), *Korea's Place in the Sun: A Modern History* (New York: Norton).

Cumings, B. (2004), *North Korea: Another Country* (New York and London: The New Press).

Eckert, C.J., Lee, K., Young, L., Robinson, M. and Wagner, E. (1990), *Korea Old and New: A History* (Seoul: Ilchokak Publishers).

Entrikin, N.J. (1999), 'Political community, identity and cosmopolitan place', *International Sociology* 14(3): 269–82.

Hausladen, G.J. (2003), 'Where the cowboy rides away: mythic places for Western film', in Hausladen, G.J. (ed.), *Western Places, American Myths: How We Think About the West* (Reno and Las Vegas: University of Nevada Press), pp. 296–318.

Kim Il Sung (1992), *Reminiscences with the Century, Volume I* (Pyongyang: Foreign Languages Publishing House).

Kim Jong Il (1987), *The Character and the Actor* (Pyongyang: Foreign Languages Publishing House).

Kim Jong Il (1989a), *Some Problems Arising in the Creation of Masterpieces: Talk to Creators of the Film* Five Guerilla Brothers, *April 6, 1968* (Pyongyang: Foreign Languages Publishing House).

Kim Jong Il (1989b), *Let Us Effect a New Upsurge in Producing Works of Revolutionary Art and Literature* (Pyongyang: Foreign Languages Publishing House).

Kim Jong Il (1989c), *On Consolidating and Developing the Successes Achieved in the Creation of Revolutionary Operas* (Pyongyang: Foreign Languages Publishing House).

Kim Jong Il (1989d), *On the Art of the Cinema* (Pyongyang: Foreign Languages Publishing House).

Kim Jong Il (1990), *Let Us Create More Good Music, Dances, and Films Congenial to the National Sentiments of Our People and the Aesthetic Sense of the Times* (Pyongyang: Foreign Languages Publishing House).

Kim Jong Il (1992), *For the Further Development of Our Juche Art* (Pyongyang: Foreign Languages Publishing House).

Korea (English Language Edition), August 1994, No. 460 (Pyongyang: Foreign Languages Publishing House).

Lautensach, H. (1988), *Korea: A Geography Based On the Author's Travels and Literature* (original publication 1945), translated and edited by Dege, E. and Dege, K. (Berlin: Springer-Verlag).

Lee, H. (2000), *Contemporary Korean Cinema: Identity, Culture, Politics* (Manchester and New York: Manchester University Press).

On the Socialist Constitution of the Democratic People's Republic of Korea (1975) (Pyongyang: Foreign Languages Publishing House).

Public Broadcasting Service (2000), *Kim's Nuclear Gamble*. 'Frontline' Series.

Robinson, M.E. (1988), *Cultural Nationalism in Colonial Korea, 1920–1925* (Seattle and London: University of Washington Press).

Schmid, A. (2000), 'Looking North toward Manchuria', *The South Atlantic Quarterly* 99(1): 219–40.

Schmid, A. (2002), *Korea between Empires, 1985–1919* (New York: Columbia University Press).

Sea of Blood: Revolutionary Opera Based on the Immortal Classic Sea of Blood – Libretto (1977), Pyongyang: Foreign Languages Publishing House.

Slotkin, R. (1998), *Gunfighter Nation: The Myth of the Frontier in Twentieth Century America* (Norman: University of Oklahoma Press).

Smith, A. (1997), 'The "golden age" and national renewal', in Hosking, G. and Schopflin, G. (eds), *Myths and Nationhood* (New York: Routledge), pp. 36–59.

Suh, D. (1988), *Kim Il Sung: The North Korea Leader* (New York: Columbia University Press).

Tell O Forest! A Revolutionary Opera (1974), libretto booklet with production photos (Pyongyang: Foreign Languages Publishing House).

Tuska, J. (1985), *The American West in Film: Critical Approaches to the Western* (Westport, CT: Greenwood Press).

Wells, K. (1990), *New God, New Nation: Protestants and Self-*

Reconstruction Nationalism in Korea, 1896–1937 (Honolulu: University of Hawaii Press).

Yeong-Hwa No-Rae 1100 Guk-Chip (Movie Music: 1100 Songs) (1993) Mun Hak Ye-sul Chong-hap Ch'ul P'an Sa [Literature and Art Collection Publishing Company].

4

Mapping the nation and the countryside in European 'films of voyage'

Maria Rovisco

Introduction

As cultural artefacts, films create and express meaning about the individual and collective identities people make for themselves, yet cinematic representations of countryside rarely animate debates about the socio-cultural context in which these identities take shape. The way in which specific films or cinematic traditions reflect upon the countryside can, this chapter argues, prove crucial for the construction of identities, particularly those with a territorial dimension. It does so by exploring European 'films of voyage', a cinematic tradition that articulates, both narratively and visually, representations of the countryside with questions of boundaries and cultural diversity.

European 'films of voyage' show how ethnic or cultural cleavages challenge both internally and externally the political boundaries of the nation-state. In deploying a particular physical and 'mental' landscape such films refuse to express an idealised or uniform image of the nation. In European 'films of voyage', the iconography of the countryside plays an important part in mapping the nation as a diverse rather than a homogenous cultural space. Two case studies based upon a close analysis of two films will be presented: *Voyage to the Beginning of the World* (Oliveira, 1997) and *Ulysses' Gaze* (Angelopoulos, 1995). In each case study, an analysis embracing stylistic, narrative and thematic aspects will elucidate how a specific imagery of the countryside expresses the sociological and historical contingencies of a given spatiality. The two films concern two distinct spaces which can be comprehended across cultural, geographic and political boundaries. On the one hand, *Ulysses' Gaze* relates to the ill-defined and transient Balkan space whose cartography has changed widely in an area where different ethnic groups and religions have mingled for many centuries. On the other, *Voyage to the Beginning of the World* relates to the Portuguese national space, where political borders have remained substantially unchanged since the late Middle Ages, and where the attainment of early statehood, and the absence of conflicts with neighbouring countries and of ethno-linguistic minorities favoured the model of the homogenous nation (Martins, 1971).

Mapping the countryside in European 'films of voyage'

The tradition of European 'films of voyage' generally encompasses those fiction films in which the journey shapes, both thematically and narratively, a tale of self-discovery and social learning about 'us' and 'them', self and other.[1] The general criteria for distinguishing the European 'film of voyage' from other fiction films which also present a narrative journey are: a sense of a route as perceived by the voyager; a quest motif, in other words the existence of at least an implied drive to be on the move; a process of inner change and learning by the voyager which is enabled by the journey; a depiction of an experience of otherness as enacted by the voyage itself; and an episodic and open-ended narrative that aims at exploring the relation between the characters and the space travelled. We are dealing with stories which are commonly structured as a succession of episodes, marked by a slow-paced narrative and a relative lack of narrative closure. Such narrative devices befit the reflection upon complex characters and a more reflexive stance regarding the socio-historical context being depicted.

European 'films of voyage' generally fit the thematic and narrative concerns of modern European cinema that flourished in the aftermath of the Second World War. This cinematic trend spans across a period of more than fifty years and includes films cutting across diverse film traditions and movements in film history. *Voyage to Italy* (Rossellini, 1953) and *La Strada* (Fellini, 1954), two iconic films of Italian neo-realism, find their place within the tradition of European 'films of voyage'. In a similar vein, the acclaimed *L'Avventura* (Antonioni, 1959) and *Pierrot le Fou* (Godard, 1965) are also representative. Wim Wenders' *Alice in the*

Cities (1974) and *Kings of the Road* (1976) deploy two fictional journeys whilst reflecting upon the post-war historical amnesia and legacies of Fascism in 1970s Germany. In the 1990s, the films by the Greek director Theo Angelopoulos (such as *Landscape in the Mist* (1988), *The Suspended Step of the Stork* (1991) and *Ulysses' Gaze* (1995)) and the 'nomadic cinema' of Tony Gatlif (for example *The Crazy Stranger* (1997)) forcefully embody the thematic, narrative and stylistic features of the European 'film of voyage'.

In European 'films of voyage', the journey involves ultimately an 'encounter with otherness' in which the 'foreign' is being rendered 'familiar' (see Chard, 1999). The narrative evolves around the forceful relation between the voyager and the space travelled. In fact, the act of being in transit shapes the journey as a movement through a recognisable geographical and social space. Not surprisingly, the iconography of the countryside plays an important role in depicting the national space as being culturally and geographically diverse. Rural environments or particular geographic details (for example mountain, river) get visually enhanced as the countryside springs up as a remarkable marginal space. This is also to say that the countryside, in representing socially and geographically marginal areas, is not usually associated with dominant images, symbols or narratives of the nation. In this context, it is not only the cultural complexity of the national space that becomes apparent, but also the smothered artificiality of the political boundaries of the nation-state. The voyager is confronted with local and regional aspects of a space that is either manifestly alien, or seemingly familiar but which has been found strange through the experience of the journey. There is a sense that the voyager is confronted with a spatiality that he or she cannot avoid contemplating (Augé, 1995: 87), whilst often engaging in active observation and interaction with others.

Both visually and narratively, European 'films of voyage' draw attention to the textures and subtleties of locally bounded forms of social belonging in their connection, and often conflict, with a perceived national community. The relation between place and identity is therefore of the foremost significance when looking at such films. As observed by Entrikin (1999: 269), the 'moral significance of place becomes evident when place is conceived not as location in space, but instead as related to an individual subject'.

The countryside is cinematically crafted as a desolate space peopled by those who are objectively (that is, in terms of their material conditions of existence) or subjectively (that is in terms of their psychological or existential needs) at the margins of society. What we usually find, then, is an iconography of the countryside that comes with characters who, whilst eventually embodying the figure of the voyager, present themselves in some marginal condition. Individuals suffering an identity crisis (for example Robert, the child psychologist, in *Kings of the Road*, or Catherine, the upper class English lady, in *Voyage to Italy*), minority groups (such as the gypsy community in *The Crazy Stranger*), itinerant artists (for example Zampano and Gelsomina in *La Strada*) and petty thieves (such as Ferdinand in *Pierrot Le Fou*) constitute some classic examples. In this respect, the countryside turns out to be a space which is, both literally and metaphorically, connected to the physical (in other words geographic), psychological or social marginality of people living in a specific socio-historical context. Of course, urban locales are not simply erased, either visually or narratively, from films where the countryside is a prevailing spatiality. Instead, the narrative deploys the textures of a physical and mental landscape which might embrace disparate urban elements whilst blurring the contrast intrinsic to classical configurations of both 'the city' and 'the countryside'.

The countryside is depicted not as mere background, but as an important source of visual and affective cues to comprehend the space travelled and its inhabitants. This is achieved by means of a narrative that carefully draws attention to the interaction between the voyager and the surrounding space, and stylistically through camera work, settings and lighting. The films are usually shot in location, which helps to render the countryside into a visually dominant spatiality. In some films, this cinematic feature facilitates a naturalistic approach to landscape.

An important characteristic is the way settings do not work as background to frame character action and interaction. The viewer is thus often pushed away from the storyline to centre attention on the space where the voyager and other protagonists move. In many films, this is enabled by framing characters moving in the distant background of a multi-layered space shot in deep focus. This means, for instance, that the portion of space available in the screen to explore *mise-en-scène* is rarely limited. The use of long shots to frame characters also helps the viewer to more easily relate the characters to the space in which they exist. Long travelling shots of landscape revealed from the perspective of the moving vehicle are also pervasive. This stylistic device plays an important part in bringing the countryside to the centre of the story being told. The travelling shot facilitates, in fact, the emphasis on the contrast between diverse instances of the passing landscape. It enhances, for example, the imbalances of a surrounding country-side landscape while also highlighting the contrasts between rural and urban visual details.

The voyager is also rarely depicted in traditionally homely environments, such as home or the work place. One of the predicaments of the journey is that the voyager is continuously moving from one place to another, which necessarily implies a wide exposure to outdoor environments away from the bounded-ness of place. Furthermore, the iconography of the countryside does not comply with the idea of an idyllic rural region which celebrates closeness with Nature whilst admonishing against the dangers of life in the 'Big City', as it is recognisably the case in the American road movie. In respect of cinematography, European 'films of voyage' often avoid the use of bright and sharp colours[2] which are commonly equated with warm and summery environments. Stylistically, this feature helps to express a sense of desolation associated with winter and misty environments (such as the misty landscapes in *Ulysses' Gaze* or *The Suspended Step of the Stork*). In other instances, the cinematography relies strongly on a naturalistic use of lighting which lays emphasis on specific visual details, such as the exterior lighting conditions in a particu-lar social context (for example the images of the destitute gypsy community living over the severe winter in *The Crazy Stranger*).

In European 'films of voyage', the narrative is beset, after all, by a powerful imagery of the countryside concerning the relationship between the characters and the space in which the characters move around. *Voyage to the Beginning of the World* and *Ulysses' Gaze* are worthy of this complex and rich cinematic tradition.

Nation, boundaries and cultural diversity in *Voyage to the Beginning of the World*

Voyage to the Beginning of the World follows the journey of Afonso, a French actor of Portuguese descent, who is coming to the North of Portugal to act in a film. On the way, he wants to visit Lugar do Teso, the village his deceased father was forced to abandon many years before to escape a poverty-stricken life. Manoel, the elderly director (a role played by the late Marcello Mastroianni), and two fellow actors, Judite and Duarte, come along to help him. Manoel recalls the memories of his privileged childhood and youth as they pass by and often stop at places he knew well as a child. He recounts the stories of his past in long expository sequences that encourage in Afonso an even stronger desire to visit the village of his ancestors.

As they get closer to their intended destination, Afonso tells his journey companions about his father's hardships. Having left his village at the age of fourteen, he crossed Spain during the Spanish Civil War, got arrested by the Republicans, entered France illegally, worked in a garage until he became his own boss, and died at the age of forty. When they reach Lugar do Teso, Afonso visits his father's sister, Maria, who is at first reticent, unable to accept the identity of a nephew she knew nothing about and who she realises cannot even speak her language.

Voyage to the Beginning of the World deals with questions of homogenous representations of 'us' in unfolding the tension between regional and national dimensions of space. We are presented with a story which concerns a certain discourse of Portuguese national identity in relation to questions of boundary-definition. On the one hand, the film concerns the depiction of Portugal as a territory where political boundaries have remained substantially unchanged through almost eight centuries of unbroken statehood. Such historical factors have favoured claims, mostly amongst historians and intellectuals, about the homogeneity and stability of Portuguese society (see, for instance, Almeida, 1994). These discourses were mostly forged by the enclosed circles of the cultural elites (Santos, 1994: 49–50) and only very recently, in particular from the late nineteenth century onwards, gained wide popular support (Sobral, 2003). On the other hand, *Voyage to the Beginning of the World* also contests this apparent cultural homogeneity.

The film deliberately explores the social, geographic and economic asymmetries of a society that emerges, after all, as remarkably disparate. Most oral stories told in the film's long and expository dialogue scenes embrace detailed descriptions of historical events and social upheavals of Portuguese official history. Issues such as the traditional domineering influence of the Catholic Church on Portuguese social and cultural life emerge in Manoel's recollections of severe discipline at the Jesuit boarding school where he was educated. The perils of a historical mass migration are raised in Maria's accounts of life in a village where so many young men were forced to emigrate to escape poverty-stricken lives.

Crossing boundaries, in other words the physical act of crossing or of being faced with a political boundary inscribed in the landscape, is a process that is both symbolically and affectively linked to the topics of ongoing conversations and to specific visual details of the passing landscape. A good example of this is the conversation about the medieval origins of the fortress city of Valença, a historical border-town in the northwest. The conversation takes place as we are offered images of the group passing through the gates built in the extremely thick city walls. The tracking shot has a powerful effect in symbolically linking the extraordinary depth of the city walls to the idea of the historical Portuguese separateness from its neighbouring Spain. Here there is a strong reference to an important historical border that is being symbolically emphasised by the physical crossing of a boundary marker (that is, the town's walls). The fortress-town of Valença signals, both literally and symbolically, the distinctiveness of Portugal in relation to the 'Spanish other'. Attempts to ensure the political independence and cultural distinctiveness of the Portuguese nation are even today visible, for instance, in events such as the public holiday celebration of the restoration of the independency in 1640 after a period of six decades under Spanish rule (see Monteiro and Pinto, 1998).

Another example of how questions of boundary-crossing are linked to issues about the specificity of the Portuguese national territory and identity can be found in the scenes set at Lugar do Teso. Here, the inaccessible mountain range rising in the background acquires a more symbolic meaning as we learn through Afonso's elderly aunt of how so many young men were forced to cross such mountains to find a better life elsewhere. The tales of emigration that follow when the group finally reaches the house where Afonso's father was born help to illustrate and 'authenticate' the relevance of an enduring historical border.

Voyage to the Beginning of the World is a film in which the countryside is both visually and narratively a dominant spatiality. Urban settings are visibly absent as the journey evolves through a typically rural terrain. But, more importantly, this is a story *about* 'the interior' in which the rural is equated with underdevelopment. An important question being raised in the group's conversations is the issue of Portuguese emigration and the negative consequences of this for rural populations faced with a mass departure of young men. This pattern was particularly noticeable in emigration to central European countries (especially France and Germany) during the second half of the twentieth century (Baganha, 1998; Garcia, 2000).

During the 1960s, the opposition between a highly populated and 'modern' littoral, and a rural 'underdeveloped' interior replaced the historical dichotomy of North/South (Ferrão, 2002). When in 1986 Portugal joined the EU the economic and social asymmetry between different regions of the country soon became less prominent. This was achieved especially through an improvement in the networks of transportation and communication, as well as the expansion of common patterns of consumption (Villaverde Cabral, 1992). Although we have to acknowledge the homogenisation of the Portuguese social space in recent years, we still have to accept the continuing costs of the 'deserting of the interior' for the many rural populations of such insular regions. It comes as no surprise that Maria speaks of Lugar do Teso as a place forgotten by the world, since the village has for so many years faced geographic and economic isolation. Ultimately, she hopelessly asks 'who cares about us?' She wonders aloud who is going to cultivate the land after the elderly who stayed in the village die, and remarks bitterly that these are stories that nobody tells.

Visually, it is also significant that *Voyage to the Beginning of the World* refuses to display a picturesque image of the Portuguese countryside. The film draws particular attention to economic, social and geographic dimensions of space whilst portraying a rich and diverse landscape. Entering the country from northern Spain, the group travels by van along the most northerly province of Portugal. This area is part of the Minho region known for its green vineyards and fertile soil. As the journey proceeds, we become aware of differences in the landscape that are powerfully conveyed by the consistent use of the travelling shot, which allows us to make sense of the layered landscape of northern Portugal. A landscape encompassing green and fertile areas composed mainly of large vineyards and small vegetable plots soon changes to sharply contrasted rough mountain ranges, punctuated by rapid brooks of cold water, and rocky areas scattered with old Roman remains. An imagery at first pervaded by rich vineyards and large houses with the distinctive stone granaries typical of the 'green Minho' disappears when the group enters a harsh area of high and irregular slopes. It soon becomes clear that this is a terrain of limited desirability for agriculture due to the rocky properties of the land.

As they approach Lugar do Teso, the growing sense of the remoteness of rural communities is clearly connected to a perceived rough landscape. At Maria's house, a table displaying local food illustrates the warm welcome visitors get in these villages, a traditional custom already anticipated by Duarte's comments on their way to Lugar do Teso. Moreover, the vision of Maria and her daughter-in-law, Christine, dressed in black mourning costume and with their heads covered with black kerchiefs turns out to be the expression of another local custom. Christine explains that such a costume marks the respect for the absent husband, who has most certainly emigrated abroad. These traditional customs, which only endure within small communities that escaped 'modernisation', are also indicative of the enclosure of Lugar do Teso.

Instead of 'enchanting villages' spread across an 'unspoilt countryside' we are faced with the dramas of ageing local communities confined to villages that still live on the basis of old communitarian habits. It is also the case that the places and spaces depicted are meant to represent genuine locations; that is to say, that the fictional Lugar do Teso coincides indeed with the genuine Lugar do Teso. Here, characters' mood is sombre, the landscape depicted is rough, interiors are gloomy and destitute, and a sense of the felt remoteness of those still inhabiting the village is convincingly conveyed in both the conversations taking place and a naturalistic approach to landscape. What is also being suggested is the topographic and cultural diversity of the Portuguese national space, which is apparent in strong narrative and visual references to the interior/littoral dichotomy. This is because the boundary separating the 'interior' and the 'littoral' translates the subjective delimitation between the 'included' and the 'excluded' in modern Portugal (Ferrão, 2002: 156–7).

In the end, this voyage to the 'beginning of the world' functions as a metaphor for Portugal as a country crisscrossed by sharp social and economic asymmetries whose complexity is often dismissed in both the political and the media agendas. The unwavering 'reality' of geographically and culturally isolated small rural communities that remain at the margins of the new enterprises of valuation of a local rural patrimony (see Peixoto, 2002; see also Fortuna, 1997) constitutes a threat for the advertised image of 'modern' and 'European' Portugal.

Nation, boundaries and cultural diversity in *Ulysses' Gaze*

Ulysses' Gaze covers the journey of a Greek-American filmmaker (who is only known as 'A') across the Balkans in search of three missing film-reels by the Manakis brothers, two pioneer filmmakers. The film-reels contain aspects of daily life in several Balkan locations as recorded in the early twentieth century. A's personal obsession with this 'lost gaze' leads him to travel across the complex Balkan space, from Florina, in Northern Greece, to war-torn Sarajevo, in Bosnia. Whilst searching for information about the possible whereabouts of the lost film-reels in different Balkan film archives (first in Monastir and then in Belgrade), he also makes a brief incursion into Constanza, in Romania, where he has a recollection of his childhood in the late 1940s. This diversion can be seen as a result of A's all-encompassing drive to come to terms with his past and roots in the Balkans. In the end, we are dealing here not with a single storyline but with several sub-stories all interwoven with each other by means of a main storyline: the story of A's ongoing journey across the Balkans in search of the missing film-reels. There are two other sub-stories told in a non-linear manner and only symbolically inter-related; there is a story about the real-life figures of the Manakis brothers that is being set against the backdrop of important political and social stirrings of modern Balkan history, and a story about A's past life in the region.

The film's highly self-conscious and unorthodox stylistics constantly blurs the boundary between fiction and reality. This involves, for instance, playing with intertextuality (such as a direct quotation from Homer's *Odyssey* or the use of lines from Angelopoulos' *The Suspended Step of the Stork* coming from loudspeakers in the square in Florina) and the use of clips of old documentary footage (for example shots by the real-life figures of the Manakis brothers) which alternate with the sequences covering A's ongoing journey. An important aspect of Angelopoulos' style is the use of highly stylised and non-chronological tableaux pointing clearly to the 'unreal' but embedded with important historical references (for example the scene of A 'revisiting' his childhood, though with his adult appearance, when his family was exiled in Constanza at the time of the Greek Civil War). These unorthodox scenes are interlocked with the more conventional and temporally arranged scenes that cover A's current voyage.

Ulysses' Gaze unfolds the textures of a rich and diverse rural landscape where imposed political boundaries cut across lasting ethno-cultural divides. The journey evolves across a countryside terrain, mostly constituted of remote borderland areas, and punctuated by ruined cities barely resembling the urban as a site of prosperity. Moreover, A's trajectory leads him across several Balkan countries (Albania, Former Yugoslav Republic of Macedonia, Bulgaria, Romania, Serbia and Bosnia), and their contested political borders, at the troubled time of the Bosnian war. In this sense, the film appears to be laying the ground for us to understand how the politics of nation-building in the region evolved through an ethnic conception of the nation.[3] In consequence, the discourse of 'ancient hatreds' (well illustrated in Huntington's 'clash of civilisations' thesis) was legitimated as the primary source of conflicts in the Balkans. The tragic, and perhaps unwilled, outcome of such a process was a stiffening of political borders and the concomitant wars disputing imposed national borders at the expense of the displacement of many ethnic minorities.

Ulysses' Gaze strongly concerns the controversial question of political borders as hardly permeable divides across the ethnic patchwork of the Balkans. To start with, every political border A crosses is narratively signalled. In fact, our voyager travels (sometimes illegally) along carefully patrolled rivers which, as effective 'natural' divides where a political boundary can easily lie, play an ambivalent role in the film. By travelling along the Danube, A gets from Constanza to Belgrade, and from here again along the

Danube, and then along the Sava and its tributaries, to Sarajevo. In travelling along the Danube, A is, in fact, travelling *along* the border, in other words the political divide, and not *across* the border. It is noteworthy that in the cartography of the Balkans the Danube offers a political boundary for countries like Bulgaria, Romania and Serbia. Thus the underlying idea here that the Danube has a hardly permeable political border at the time of A's ongoing journey is, paradoxically, also offering an alternative route to travel across the Balkans.

The scene of A travelling in a barge along the Danube is strikingly illustrative of the elusive role and meaning of political borders in the Balkans. The barge travels from Odessa to Germany to deliver a broken giant statue of Lenin to a collector. The landscape unfolded in long, slow travelling shots is one populated by faceless people, including many children, who gather by the riverbank to observe the huge statue of Lenin passing by. Meanwhile, A's minuscule figure standing on the bow of the barge is framed in the distant background facing the landscape. Several watchtowers and shabby thatched houses aligned along the river leave no doubt that this is an area of strict surveillance and a border zone. If, on the one hand, *Ulysses' Gaze* shows how political borders can work more as a divide, that is as a barrier to the mobility of people, than as a gateway in the complex and ill-defined Balkan space; on the other, and at a metaphorical level, the film it is also raising the question of the possibility, however improbable, of a trans-Balkan identity by transforming the political divide, the fissure, into a path. If there is something which has been central to all modern borders, it has been the efforts of people to use, manipulate or avoid the resulting border restrictions (Baud and Schendel, 1997: 214–15).

The film also provides important narrative and visual cues that draw attention to the role of geographic formations such as rivers and mountains in offering suitable barriers to the mobility of people. Images of highly patrolled border-stations are recurrent and visually emphasised in *Ulysses' Gaze*. At the same time, the *de facto* lack of porosity of the political border is also narratively and visually unfolded. This is visible in all the scenes in which A manages to pursue his quest by overcoming political borders that are meant to constitute an obstacle to the movement of people.

The film's visual imagery plays a very significant part in depicting a strange and alienating scenery which hardly finds room within the limits of the rural/urban dichotomy. Representations of bleak countryside landscapes alternate with images of ruined and deserted urban settings. The remote countryside lands that A travels play an important role in foregrounding the forgotten 'reality' of people living in war-torn environments over different times of modern Balkan history. The landscapes represented, accompanied by the post-romantic and melancholic music of composer Karaindrou, evoke an overall sense of desolation and nostalgia. The cities that our lonely voyager visits all share the same ghostly aura amidst rundown buildings and empty streets. Although space is represented realistically, which helps us to situate scenes and the 'unreal' tableaux in their precise temporality, A and the people he meets along the journey are never depicted in homely environments. Instead, most scenes of interiors correspond to conventional public settings (for example cinemas, border-stations, train compartments) but all being depicted as derelict.

Though courageously shot in location (with the impossibility of shooting in Sarajevo at the time of the Bosnian war, Angelopoulos sets his fictional Sarajevo in the equally war-torn town of Mostar), *Ulysses' Gaze* never displays a visual imagery rich in those iconic landmarks or striking countryside landscapes which are commonly associated with a specific locality. It becomes difficult to distinguish between different places despite the precise narrative references that enable us to identity each specific location. In this sense, there is not a sharp division between the rural and the urban, or between one Balkan state and another, or even between one locality and another; we are faced with a space that hardly fits those classic dualities (such as rural versus urban, regional versus national) through which people comprehend territorial forms of collective belonging. The space depicted is one where everyone appears as displaced; everyone is paradoxically both at home and living the condition of exile. The cultural boundaries through which people subjectively construct their sense of social belonging do not necessarily coincide with the political divides which are the outcome of more than two centuries of fabricated traditions of nationhood.

In short, there is, in *Ulysses' Gaze*, an overall suggestion that the cause of conflicts and displacement in the region is, fundamentally, a consequence of the modern politics of nation-building

(Mazower, 2001; Roudometof, 1999). Arguably, then, the perceived sense of threat and fear most people endure in different Balkan locations determines the possibility for every individual to be constituted as an 'other'. There is a sensibility suggesting that enforced political borders separate and alienate people whilst undermining the possibility of any sense of community or collective life amidst different Balkan peoples. In the last instance, it becomes difficult for those personally affected by the social and political upheavals to distinguish between 'friend' and 'foe', 'us' and 'them'. In its reflexive and open-ended stance, the narrative does not aim to offer a 'solution' for the current conflicts in the Balkan space.

Yet, no one can remain indifferent to the fact that every character in *Ulysses' Gaze* is personally affected by past or ongoing conflicts and wars in the Balkans. The film ends by leaving a note of hope for those who attempt to live humanly and restore their lives in spite of the horror and absurdity of conflicts in the region: the Bulgarian peasant, grieving for her missing husband in a World War One setting, is prompt to offer A/Yannakis (A's persona often gets blurred with that of the filmmaker Yannakis Manakis, whose figure he appears to embody in some scenes) her vanished husband's clothes whilst helping him to escape from exile; Ivo Levy, the Jewish curator, and his family go for a walk amidst the deep fog in destroyed Sarajevo as a regular family would do in peaceful circumstances; A is compelled to pursue his quest whilst leaving behind his loves in the hope that the discovery of the 'first gaze' would bring him a new understanding of life in the region; the elderly Greek woman who has been separated from her sister for more than forty years is determined to cross the Greek/Albanian border despite being refused a taxi to go to 'the other side'; Nikos, A's long-term friend and war correspondent, is resolute to stay in Belgrade to put a stop to the Bosnian war.

In view of these people's efforts to defy imposed and rigidified political boundaries, *Ulysses' Gaze* dares to raise the question of whether it would be possible, in the Balkans, for an ideal of citizenship that could relinquish the political body of the nation. Finally, the film also mirrors Angelopoulos' predilection for that 'other Greece' of rural spaces and historically contested territories (Horton, 1997: 11–13).

Conclusion

European 'films of voyage' are imbued with a reflexive stance about fundamental aspects of human relatedness within the territories in which people exist. Our sense of belonging to a certain locality or territory is achieved by means of those symbolic boundaries, or 'mental maps', through which we define 'us' and 'them' (Lamont, 1995). In investigating how, in European 'films of voyage', the iconography of the countryside forcefully helps to contest the idea of the homogenous nation, I have attempted to shed some light on the significance of less inclusive forms of collective identity. The insurmountable cultural diversity of the national space goes along with the tension and the fractures enforced on the national unit by locally and transnationally rooted forms of collective belonging. In *Voyage to the Beginning of the World*, the geographic and economic marginality of the village of Lugar do Teso lays the ground for the inhabitants' sense of inadequacy and social isolation within the national community. In *Ulysses' Gaze*, everyone is compelled to defy, in one way or another, the crystallised political borders that cut across lasting cultural boundaries. Those remote rural borderland areas that A travels deploy a remarkable 'mental' landscape for the comprehension of collective identity formation in a region where different religions and ethnic groups have mixed and collaborated for many centuries. In conclusion, the countryside, as a visually and narratively dominant spatiality, offers a suitable terrain to comprehend the national space in its sheer diversity and inconsistency.

Notes

1 The European 'film of voyage' is distinct from the American road movie genre in both style and narrative structure. The latter typically presents a more linear narrative structure and a set of conventional devices to implement dramatic action (such as close association between driver and motorized vehicle that stresses the thrills of high speed driving, fast editing, a strong outsider motif, exciting encounters with strangers, and goals of various kinds). In terms of narrative closure, American road movies traditionally end with the death of the rebellious protagonists (for example Hopper's *Easy Rider* [1969], Penn's *Bonnie and Clyde* [1967]).

2 Some films were deliberately shot in black-and-white when colour

was available. This is the case with Petit's *Radio On* (1980) and Wenders' *Kings of the Road* (1976).

3 Gellner (1983) and Smith (1991) distinguish between a civic and 'Western' model of the nation based on the existence of a historical territory encompassing a political and legal community, and an ethnic and 'oriental' conception of the nation based in ancestry.

References

Almeida, O.T. (1994), 'Portugal and the concern with national identity', *Bulletin of Hispanic Studies* 71: 155–63.

Augé, M. (1995), *Non-Places – Introduction to an Anthropology of Supermodernity* (London, New York: Verso).

Baganha, M.I. (1998), 'Portuguese emigration after World War II', in Pinto, A.C. (ed.), *Modern Portugal* (Palo Alto: The Society for the Promotion of Science and Scholarship), pp. 189–205.

Baud, M. and Schendel, W.V. (1997), 'Toward a comparative history of borderlands', *Journal of World History* 8(2): 211–42.

Chard, C. (1999), *Pleasure and Guilt on the Grand Tour – Travel Writing and Imaginative Geography 1600–1830* (Manchester: Manchester University Press).

Entrikin, J.N. (1999), 'Political community, identity and cosmopolitan place', *International Sociology* 14(3): 269–82.

Ferrão, J. (2002), 'Portugal, três geografias em recombinação: espacialidades, mapas cognitivos e identidades territoriais', *Lusotopie* 2: 151–8.

Fortuna, C. (1997), 'Destradicionalização e imagem da cidade – o caso de Évora', in Fortuna, C. (ed.), *Cidade, Cultura e Globalização* (Oeiras: Celta), pp. 231–57

Garcia, J.L. (ed.) (2000), *Portugal Migrante – Emigrantes e Imigrados, Dois Estudos Introdutórios* (Oeiras: Celta).

Gellner, E. (1983), *Nations and Nationalism* (Oxford: Blackwell).

Horton, A. (1997), *The Films of Theo Angelopoulos – A Cinema of Contemplation* (Princeton, NJ: Princeton University Press).

Lamont, M. (1995), 'National identity and national boundary patterns in France and the United States', *French Historical Studies* 19(2): 349–65.

Martins, H. (1971), 'Portugal', in Archer, M. and Giner, S. (eds), *Contemporary Europe: Class, Status and Power* (London: Weidenfeld and Nicolson).

Mazower, M. (2001), *The Balkans* (London: Phoenix Press).

Monteiro, N.G. and Pinto, A.C. (1998), 'Cultural myths and Portuguese national identity', in Pinto, A.C. (ed.), *Modern Portugal* (Palo Alto: The Society for the Promotion of Science and Scholarship), pp. 47–62.

Peixoto, P. (2002), *Os Meios Rurais e a Descoberta do 'Património'* (Coimbra: Oficina do CES).

Roudometof, V. (1999), 'Nationalism, globalization, Eastern orthodoxy – "unthinking" the "clash of civilizations" in Southeastern Europe', *European Journal of Social Theory* 2(2): 233–47.

Santos, B.S. (1994), *Pela Mão de Alice – O Social e o Político na Pós-Modernidade* (Porto: Edições Afrontamento).

Smith, A.D. (1991), *National Identity* (Harmondsworth: Penguin).

Sobral, J.M. (2003), 'A formação das nações e o nacionalismo: os paradigmas explicativos e o caso português', *Análise Social* 37(165): 103–26.

Villaverde Cabral, M. (1992), 'Portugal e a Europa: diferenças e semelhanças', *Análise Social* 27(118/19): 943–54.

5

Lurking beneath the skin: British pagan landscapes in popular cinema

Tanya Krzywinska

Jagged monoliths, eroded earthworks, stone circles, hillside chalk figures: the enigmatic remnants of pre-historical landscapes in the British countryside have fired the imagination of artists, writers, historians, archaeologists and filmmakers. From folklore to feature films, the 'pagan' landscape has inspired mystery, horror and romance. Escaping the confines of contemporary written documentary sources, diverse fictions are easily projected into the historical void. However, the retrospective and apparently fanciful fictions that circulate around the existing features of ancient landscapes are frequently grounded in real cultural conflicts and tensions. Many of these contentions coalesce around competing narratives and accounts of what 'Britain' means. The argument of this chapter is that the existing features of ancient landscapes and their presentation in film and other popular media are often used to explore and create histories and identities that extend beyond, or challenge, those offered by conventional 'national' and historically grounded narratives. I explore the ways that pagan monuments that are strewn across the British countryside have acquired certain conventionalised and often subversive meanings. An 'archaeology' of such meanings reveals that these are not entirely grounded in contemporary culture, but stretch back to the rhetorical modes used by Roman writers, rhetoric that has come to serve the generic forms of horror and fantasy as well as the predilection for sensationalist spectacle inherent within audio-visual media. As such I cite representations of the British pagan countryside in popular culture within a matrix of cultural, formal and historical contexts.

'The Devil's Own': monumental pagan troubles

During the Summer Solstice of 1985, the area around Stonehenge became a ravaged battlefield: a standoff ensued between the 'keepers of culture' and what were considered officially to be anarchic violators of British heritage. Makeshift raggletaggle encampments, barbed wire, news cameras and police in riot gear are not perhaps the accoutrements that might be associated with the bucolic idyll promised by English Heritage marketeers. Assorted interested people clashed with the police in a standoff between very different notions of the meaning and use of an ancient 'pagan' monument. The Battle of the Beanfield, as it has become known, demonstrates the way in which the meaning of Stonehenge, as an icon of the British pagan landscape, has often been situated at the confluence of a variety of cultural contestations. What the Battle of the Beanfield exemplifies is that the remnants of an ancient British landscape offer themselves as emblems through which people have challenged dominant narratives of British history and identity. The fact that the terms 'British' and 'Britain' have no meaning in a pre-historical context plays a significant role in its post-1960s attraction. This enigmatic ancient past appeals to neo-pagans and some counter-cultures as a means of rejecting and challenging the implications of what is often considered to be the repressive nature of Christian-based authority.

Part of the subversive appeal, which also operates in a more populist sense, is derived from the way that monuments of British pre-history have been presented within horror and fantasy genres. However, many of these are informed directly or indirectly by older fictions. The miscellaneous ancient monuments that stand in mute testimony to an occulted past are laced with mythic explanations of their origin and use. Medieval mytho-historian Geoffrey of Monmouth suggests that Stonehenge was built by giants and that it was transported from Ireland to Britain by the magician Merlin (1982: 196). The notion that stone circles are the petrified remains of people punished by god for dancing on the Sabbath seems to have originated during the English Civil War (Hutton, 1997: 74; Ashe 2002: 40). Many seventeenth- and eighteenth-century interpretations compete between supernatural, folkloric, explanations of stone circles – witches or fairy circles, for example (Hutton, 1997: 74) – and more scientifically grounded ones, provided by proto-archaeologists such as John Aubrey and William Stukeley. Meanings assigned to inscrutable features of the British landscape have also been strongly informed by the sensationalist accounts of so-called 'Celtic' religion, outlined by Roman writers such as Caesar and Tacitus, in particular the alleged druidic practice of human sacrifice. In the eighteenth century Stukeley consolidated this link by publishing his engravings of stone circles as druidic temples (although later he changed his view to a more Christian orientation). (See Hutton, 2001, for an extended account of the treatment of pagan landscapes in British letters and literature.)

Poets John Keats, William Blake, William Wordsworth and Robert Graves and proto-anthropologist J.G. Frazer (1994), author of *The Golden Bough*,[1] also romanced with the alleged bardic-philosophical tradition of the Druids, which, Caesar had written, originated in Britain. Even Byron asked of Stonehenge what the 'devil is it' in his poem *Don Juan* (1821). In the main, poetic imagery of the Romantics is used to evoke the sublime majesty of the stone circles and often represents a lost Arcadian age when the poetry had religious status. Even here conflicts between the material presence of ancient monuments, which were taken as representing an apparently sophisticated pre-historical culture, and classical Roman accounts of their barbarous use are apparent. Matthew Schneider (1997) mounts a convincing argument that Wordsworth and Keats struggled in their poetry to square the druidic practice of sacrifice reported in Caesar with what they viewed as the noble aspects of druidism. The romance with druidism, and the landscape that speaks ostensibly of them, continues (even if archaeological evidence places most monuments as preceding the late Iron Age by millennia in some cases). But it is the sinister spectre of human sacrifice that lends such monuments their particular bloodcurdling resonance and it is this that has fuelled the sensationalism of many subsequent occult-based fictions. The Rev. J. Ogilvie commented in 1787 in *The Fane of the Druids* that with regards to druidic human sacrifice 'some ancient writers seem to dwell on this subject with a satisfaction' (cited in Schneider, 1997: 5). Many modern texts follow in similar vein, including some that do not fall within the category of generic horror fiction.

Within the context of the horror genre, prehistoric 'pagan' monuments are connected often with the presence of primal, supernatural evil. The use of Stonehenge in the opening credits of *Night of the Demon* (also known as *Curse of the Demon*, 1957, UK) provides an indicative example. A montage of canted shots of the stones, backlit and windswept in brooding black and white, appears, accompanied by a sonorous voice-over that intones 'It has been written since the beginning of time, even unto these ancient stones, that evil, supernatural creatures exist in a world of darkness. And, it is also said, that using the magic power of ancient runic symbols man can call forth these powers of darkness, the demons of hell.' Accompanied by dramatic music, and schlocky B movie graphics for the titles, the scene utilises all the lurid generic accoutrements of the horror film to jar the spectator's equilibrium. The film's story hinges on a common trope in the horror film: a sceptical hero comes to understand the full force of the occult, when he investigates the mysterious death of an academic. The chief suspect in the case is the leader of a cult, Karswell (Niall MacGinnis), whose manuscript was turned down for publication by the dead man. Hot on the trail of Karswell, our hero is given surreptitiously a note inscribed with runes that will invoke an ancient demon to kill him. Moral balance is restored when the note is returned to Karswell resulting in his death. The story arc has little to do with Stonehenge, however, but the powerful image of Stonehenge is used metaphorically to encapsulate the film's theme of vengeful desire and demonic magic that lurks beneath the civilised skin of middle England.

Iconic monuments of prehistory in horror-based cinema are also often linked to human sacrifice within the context of a barbarous paganism. *Blood on Satan's Claw* (also known as *Satan's Skin*, 1970), *The Witches* (1966) and *The Wicker Man* (1970) are British-made horror films that place 'pagan' sacrifice centrally as the source of horror: each are set in the British countryside and emphasise in different ways the links between the landscape and pagan practice. These films follow on from the commercial success of Dennis Wheatley's sensationalist and tendentious occult novels written between 1933 and 1974, which linked pagan practice with black magic. *The Devil Rides Out* ([1934] 1971) and *To the Devil a Daughter* ([1953] 1972) are structured morally and formally on Manichean lines, where Christian forces representing light and good do battle with evil in the form of black magic and 'lustful' pagan-derived practice. In one section of the former novel, a woodland glade, reproduced in the Hammer film of the same name, provides the stage for a bacchanalian orgy complete with a composite image of Pan, the devil and Baphomet, the alleged god of the Knights Templar, appearing at the height of the ceremony (see Krzywinska [2000] for an analysis of the figure). Later in the novel a child is to be sacrificed in a deconsecrated chapel in a manor house.[2] Here, however, Stonehenge escapes the brooding menace of its representation in *Night of the Demon*. One character asks why Stonehenge is a good place to find sanctuary against evil, given that it is associated with druidic sacrifice; the response from the occult-moral authority, De Richleau, is that even though druids practised human sacrifice at the site it is nonetheless 'one of most hallowed spots in all Europe because countless thousands of long-dead men and women have worshipped here – calling on the power of light to protect them from evil things that go in darkness' (Wheatley, 1971: 141). Like Wordsworth and Stukeley, Wheatley seeks to square the apparent contradiction between sacrifice and spirituality, thereby rescuing the monument for British moral heritage. Within this novel, as with other occult fictions, the landscape itself is a source of power, imbued with a moral-metaphysical dimension that accords neatly with the common horror Manichean-based convention of a universal battle between good and evil, which, in this case, precedes Christianity. Tom Holland's horror novel *Deliver Us from Evil* (2000) is partly set in Wiltshire and continues the tradition of associating remnants of a pagan landscape with the intrusion of hitherto repressed dark forces that are both supernatural and articulations of the collective unconscious. The novel blends together seductive villains with a Wheatley-esque take on black magic, weaving a tale around historical figures such as John Dee, John Milton and the British antiquarian John Aubrey, who surveyed Stonehenge and Avebury in the seventeenth century.

Deliver Us From Evil, alongside each of the films and novels mentioned above, invokes the British countryside as a place where pagan practices continue to abide in the Christian era. This trope provides the rationale for sensationalist stories of human sacrifice and orgiastic sexuality freed from repressive civilising agents. Most of these texts regard pagan sacrifice as inherently evil, and, particularly in Wheatley and some of the horror films, the return to the 'old religion'[3] and antique magical practice represents moral decay, a factor indicated by the presence of abandoned Christian churches in *The Witches* and *The Wicker Man*. In *Cry of the Banshee* (1970), a ruined church that lies deep in secluded woods provides a place for pagan-based nature worship, but here is the stage for the brutal massacre of the hippie-esque celebrants by those alleging to do their brutal work in the names of God and the King, resulting in a plot-driving curse on the house of their leader. Many British occult films made in the late 1960s and early 1970s, including *Eye of the Devil* (1967), *Cry of the Banshee*, *The Witches* and *The Wicker Man*, make use of the *League of Gentlemen*[4] model. The locals may look ordinary, but they are in fact members of barbaric pagan cults that practise human sacrifice. In *Blood on Satan's Claw*, the locals are god-fearing and their daily life is disrupted when a sub-human skull, complete with a set of rudimentary horns, is found in a field near their village. Through some strange magic this drives the local youth to a frenzy of murder and self-mutilation. While the muted tones of an autumn rural landscape lend a bucolic tone, the flesh-rending Bacchae-like events that take place are very far from being quietly picturesque. Such generically grounded othering of rural communities sits in sharp and delicious contrast to the saccharine 'Miss Marple' view of the English country village in which murder has no magical or supernatural cast. The type of myth-making found in occult-horror fictions draws some of its power from tacit references to antique religious practices outlined in the Roman 'colonialist' texts mentioned above. But their particular horrors are also rooted in the cultural context in which they were produced.

Counter/cultural issues

As Leon Hunt has noted, 'the conflict between "old" and "new" faiths was a way of talking about the relationship between the upheavals of the late 1960s – the emergence of youth and "counter" cultures, permissiveness, the possibility of revolution – and the backlash of the 1970s represented, in particular, by the "law and order" agenda of the new Heath government' (2002: 93). *Blood on Satan's Claw* and *Cry of the Banshee* are set respectively in the early seventeenth century and interregnum period, times that are associated with Puritanism and its goal to place piety and religious observance at the heart of the culture and government (*Witchfinder General* [1968] is also located in this period). The particular historical setting of these films, made during the early 1970s, is well suited to articulating modern cultural conflicts around the increasing 'permissiveness' of British culture. Manifestations of supernatural entities that destroy the order of things can be regarded as symptomatic of perceived repression (as well as having dramatic and sensationalist potential), the landscape serving as a metaphor for the stratified layers of the collective unconscious. While it is easy and attractive to glean a message about the danger of stultifying the free expression of sexuality in such films, the portrayal of pagan practice is often ambiguous, serving, as it were, with two hands. As with Wheatley's conservative Christian bias, these films yoke the return of the repressed with ritual sacrifice and black magic. The return of occulted atavistic supernatural forces expresses a warning about the effects of repression, yet they are frequently regarded as evil and overcome by the forces of 'Right' and 'Light' – terms of no liberal/relativist compromise that are closely associated with Mary Whitehouse's anti-permissive organisation, The Festival of Light. *Blood on Satan's Claw* is by far from a simple celebration of 'pagan' sex and magic; its sensation-driven narrative carries a health warning about the dangers that cults represent to youth (especially when considered in the light of the high-profile ritual murder of the heavily pregnant Sharon Tate by Manson's 'Children of God' in 1969). Yet the anarchic outbreak of barbarous behaviour in the film has a transgressive appeal that would not be lost on the well-developed counter-culture, which found many of the values and attitudes of conservative middle-England abhorrent, particularly as these tended to demonise aspects of youth culture as well as unfettered expressions of sexuality. However, not all horror-based fictions that use the British pagan landscape for their setting speak so directly of unregulated sexuality. The children's TV series *Children of the Stones* (1977, Harlech Television), set within the partially stone-encircled village of Avebury, is one such case, yet nonetheless the stones harbour dark forces of an extra-terrestrial nature that possess the local inhabitants and prevent them from leaving.

In terms of an 'archaeology' of the meanings assigned to the pagan landscapes in each of these horror-based texts, each draws quite strongly on the image of 'Celtic' paganism outlined in the writings of Caesar, Tacitus and Pliny. These Roman writers viewed

North European paganism as deeply barbaric, using human sacrifice as a means of demonstrating their claim. Yet, it should be noted that they had reasons to construct and maintain a difference between their own culture and that of the 'othered' barbarians. As with more recent fictions, they too projected lurid fantasies onto the strange landscape of 'Celtic' paganism. The conflation of 'barbarianism' and 'primitivism' inscribed in such work functioned as a means of justifying the colonial management of North European people, deployed according to various political and moral agendas. When their 'histories' are adopted in later fictions, it is the colonist gaze that prevails and it is the studied sensationalism of this viewing position that lends itself so well to the horror genre. This becomes extremely apparent when we examine the aforementioned horror fictions in relation to these 'classical' works. Tacitus, for example, comments that the Germans 'count it as no sin, on certain feast days, to include human victims in the sacrifice' (Tacitus, 1970: 108), and Caesar writes that the Gauls are much given to human sacrifice and employ druids to do it; he goes on to say 'Some of them use huge images of the gods, and fill their limbs, which are woven from wicker, with living people [...] They believe that the gods are more pleased by such punishment when it is inflicted upon those who are caught engaged in theft or robbery or other crime' (Caesar, 1996: 127–8/6.17). There is a clear, if tacit, superior self-promotion in the deployment of the binary opposition civilisation/barbarism here. This binary is also played out obsessively in the horror genre and is frequently allied to the psychoanalytic notion of the return of the repressed. British occult-based films and novels that look back to the 'old religion' consistently mobilise human sacrifice as the indicator of barbarity and moral bankruptcy, as was also the case in Tacitus and Caesar. This model also threads its way through Christian discourse, and many clerics used such rhetoric as a means of outlawing and demonising paganism: old gods become new devils. The legacy of such demonising plays a crucial role in the meanings that popular culture, and particularly the horror genre, assigns to the British pagan landscape. In a neat redeployment, the othering of 'Celtic' paganism within Roman and Christian discourse, has provided recent popular culture with a powerful counter-discourse with which to 'other' Britain, as well as deploying sensationalist images to attract horrified fascination.

Caesar's powerful evocation of the wicker man as a tool for human sacrifice in Celtic culture is resurrected directly in *The Wicker Man*, a film that is often hailed as the most significant British horror film. The local inhabitants of a fictitious Scottish island, Summerisle, practise a version of paganism that they believe ensures the fruitfulness of their harvests, which has been re-introduced to them by their Laird in the nineteenth century. For the first time their crops have failed and they entice a carefully chosen 'virgin' policeman, Sergeant Howie (Edward Woodward), to the island to investigate the death of a child. He witnesses pagan practices that affront his fundamentalist Christian sensibilities, and ends up being a substitute sacrifice for the current Laird, Lord Summerisle (Christopher Lee), the aim of which is to restore fertility to the land. As a policeman and as a hard-line Christian who believes strongly in sex only within the sanctity of marriage, and who lets everyone know that they are sinners, Howie is multiply determined as a representative of outmoded puritanism and authoritarianism. This character coding is pointedly directed to the libertarian counter-culture as a figure of ridicule and contempt, however. Nothing could be more timely and fitting than the sacrifice of an agent of 'repression'; a man who is horrified by the sight of young woman jumping naked over a fire placed at the centre of a circle of standing stones, and who does not yield to his sexual urges (despite the best efforts of a witchy-seductress played by Britt Ekland). Like *Blood on Satan's Claw*, the film is riven by contradictory meanings. These can be viewed within the context of contemporary counter-cultural investments, and exhibit themselves in disagreements about the meaning of the film between the screenwriter and the director, as well as in the film's ambiguous dealing with sacrifice as both horrific and thrilling, rational and irrational. Are we meant to commend the pagans for killing the policeman? If so, then the death of an arrogant and self-righteous cop wasn't working to gain my sympathy. Robin Hardy, the director, claims his aim was to communicate the dangers of paganism (see Krzywinska [2000] for an extended analysis), whereas Anthony Shaeffer, the film's screenwriter, claims that the impetus for the film lay in the need for 'someone to go right back to the beginning and explore ... what lay behind religion as we know it' (cited in Brown, 2000: 24). For many fans of the horror genre and those with contemporary pagan leanings, it is Summerisle's paganism that offers up an alternative to repressive laws and puritan-style moral frameworks. Throughout most of the film paganism is presented as vital and generally life-affirming, and appeals to the senses through the connections it makes between sexuality and seasonal cycles. Thereby the film addresses itself most directly to those viewers inclined to baulk against the repressions of conservative, authoritarian, parent culture (even if Summerisle has its own brand of authority).

Paganism in British films of the 1960s and 1970s is frequently coupled with the full expression of 'natural' sexuality, a factor that has informed various interpretations of standing stones as fertility, phallic or vaginal symbols. The link between stone circles and fertility rites is evoked in the image from *The Wicker Man*, yet other rites are rather less benign. In *Deliver Us From Evil* the central male character is impregnated by the Devil within the inner circle of Stonehenge. Rather than a site associated with the invocation of forces of light as in *The Devil Rides Out*, here it is presented as a dark and blood-soaked monument, the 'natural' home of a corrupting evil that makes a mockery of the gendered order. The paganism paraded in the British horror genre articulates in its cultish way, for some at least, an anarchic atavistic spark that re-invokes a rhythm that has been lost under urban tarmac and clock (on) time. Yet within the context of horror and sexploitation, witch-power and magic are rendered perverse, amoral and connected to violent death (which in itself provided for some viewers a welcome transgressive fantasy thrill that put two vicarious fingers up to the moral order). By deploying familiar pre-historical monuments as settings for such narratives, and drawing on pseudo-historical sources, the British pagan countryside becomes infused with subversive resonance.

These few examples show how the sacred landscapes of ancient Britain have become entrenched in the popular imagination under the seductive sign of 'transgression'. Prehistory, with its connection to the primitive, acts as literal and metaphoric terrain for conjuring up buried histories, identities and narratives that have been, or are imagined to be, suppressed by 'civilisation' and the dominant order.

Recent departures

In the more benign context of recent fantasy fiction, the pagan past becomes a place for evoking a time when the land and people worked in harmony, to which magic was instrumental. Here a rather different register operates to that which colours the 'demonic' vision of paganism in the horror film. Boorman's *Excalibur* (1981) carries a strong authorial signature, and is perhaps best described as having an art cinema aesthetic. With mainstream cinema embracing strongly the notion of the 'auteur' at that time, as a means of branding products that evaded generic affiliation, the context was right for Boorman to explore the Arthurian myth from a personal perspective, one that dovetailed with the considerable counter-cultural interest in myth and magic. As he is quoted as saying, 'When you recount a legend you find yourself speaking more about your own period than you think [. . .] What is essential, then, is not to refute the myth but to refresh it' (cited in Frayling, 1995: 23). What is *new* in Boorman's rendering of the myth is its insistence on *old* paganism (at least old paganism filtered through nineteenth- and twentieth-century mediations). Merlin and Morgana (both practitioners of ancient magics) belong to the old pagan world and act outside the newly established Christian/democratic/patriarchal order. The film presents the pagan countryside through iconic representations such as stone circles, but paganism also plays a structural role. Despite Arthur's Christianity, the seasonal rhythms of nature are also at some deep level tied into the trajectory of Arthur's life. When Arthur is young, perpetual spring reigns, when he marries it is full summer and when he grows ill a hard winter sets in; on his drinking from the grail the land becomes bright and lush again and cherry blossom petals fill the air. This romantic synergy is derived in part from J.G. Frazer's contention in *The Golden Bough* that many pre-Christian myths coalesce around the notion that the king and the land are one. This takes on a symbolic and allegorical resonance in the film that is informed by Jung's work on archetypes. Frazer also presents this king/land synergy as the basis for human sacrifice: if the land falls sick the king, or his substitute, must be ritually sacrificed. This myth-based trope provides both structure and horror-based spectacle in *The Wicker Man*, *Eye of the Devil* (a horror film set in Northern France) and, in an art movie context, Pasolini's *Medea* (see Krzywinska, 2000).

For Boorman's purposes, Arthur is of less interest than Merlin.

Merlin crops up in various guises in many of Boorman's films, representing in archetypal terms a lost world of magic. Not wholly absorbed by the traditional chivalric focus of the myth, Boorman makes use of novelist Mary Stewart's strategy of locating the Arthurian myth within the context of the transition between paganism and Christianity; and it could be said that the shift itself is 'mythologized' by the film. Boorman states, '[Merlin] says to Morgana "The days of our kind our numbered". There are also echoes of the coming of Christianity and I couldn't resist putting my own feelings into this. I feel that the imposition of Christianity – a desert religion – on northern Celtic people, was a very alien thing . . . They destroyed the magic of those people and we are still suffering from that today' (cited *Film Directions*, 1981). This sense of spiritual loss distilled a more general trend at work in the mystically inclined hippie counter-culture. The ascendance of Arthur does not herald a golden age, as traditionally couched, but a fall that entails the loss of a rich and meaningful relationship with the landscape and nature. Boorman uses Merlin and powerful images of the living, changing landscape as means of evoking that missing connection, thereby providing an implicit criticism of some of key tenets of traditional British culture and identity. In so doing the film mediates a burgeoning dissatisfaction with the more traditional celebration of British culture and identity that is embedded in many versions of the Arthurian golden age. Whether the film's nostalgia is considered conservative, with a small c, or subversive depends on the interpretive framework that viewers bring to the film. For those aligning themselves with the hippie-oriented counter-culture the film expresses through the appropriate rhetoric of myth-based fantasy the latter.

There is also a notable gender dimension to the film's representation of paganism that warrants consideration because it has a bearing on the burgeoning counter-cultural investments in the 'old religion' at the time the film was made. The 1970s saw a growing interest in the development (or rediscovery as it was sometimes couched) in feminist/feminine modes of spirituality and expressions of power. This has a bearing on the representation of the figure of Morgana in *Excalibur*. As a witch of the old religion Morgana is intent on overthrowing Arthur's glorious age of men, which makes her available to be read as a threat to both patriarchal and Christian values. Her representation resonates within the feminist appropriation of witchcraft as a discourse of gender dissidence, as is evident in Cixous and Clement's (re)appropriation of witchcraft as an anarchic discourse of female empowerment with capacity to subvert patriarchal power (1986). Within this context pagan witchcraft, and its related myths of powerful female deities, constitutes a challenge to the status quo, speaking, at least to some receptive viewers, of a lost and othered 'herstory' that melds together imagination and historical fact. With a recent re-witching of popular culture – evidenced across various media with the *Harry Potter* franchise, *Buffy the Vampire Slayer*, *Sabrina the Teenage Witch*, *Charmed*, and the presence of playable shamanic magic casters in role-playing games such as *EverQuest* and *SpellForce* – the links between paganism and witchcraft are often consolidated through quite wide-spread cultural investments in 'girl power'. The figure of Queen Mab (Miranda Richardson) in made-for-TV film *Merlin* (1998, Hallmark/NBC) utilises this resonant link. Dressed in gothic black and purples, with powerful magics at her fingertips, she has the requisite bad-girl kudos through her attempts to destroy Arthur, lure Merlin to the 'dark side' and rescue the old gods, of which she is one, from oblivion. She first appears as a standing stone made flesh, stepping out of the stone which establishes her connection with the pre-historical landscape. Open to a variety of interpretations, this association might be read by those with an interest in witchcraft, and perhaps seeking new ways of figuring a female-based spirituality, as a way of aligning the female body to the rhythms of the earth, rhythms masked by industrial clock-time. For some feminists, however, this association might be construed as supporting essentialist ideas about the definition of femininity. In either case Queen Mab is a very contemporary figure, who is made entirely in the light of recent popular interest in paganism and witchcraft (or Wicca).

Both *Excalibur*'s Merlin and *Merlin*'s Queen Mab are intrinsically linked to the pagan landscape: Arthur can only speak to the imprisoned Merlin through the conduit of Stonehenge. Unlike *Excalibur*, *Merlin* is far more in keeping with the more traditional Arthurian narrative (Queen Mab excepted). The figuration of Merlin (Sam Neill) is clearly built around his being an active and morally upright agent of change, rather than a darkly ambiguous and playfully arch representation of the old order of shamans, as he is in *Excalibur* ('I have walked my way since the beginning of time.

Sometimes I give, sometimes I take. It is mine to know which, and when'). In *Merlin*, Queen Mab is defeated by Merlin and Arthur's court, composed predominantly of men, by a simple act of forgetting. They turn their backs on her and the old world that she presents. Given that she is presented in such deliciously mischievous ways, presenting an affront to the patriarchal and Christian order, I for one did not want to forget her so easily. The film may evoke the attraction of the pagan-witch but her disruptive purpose is overcome with no diegetic sense of loss. It then takes a recuperative interpretational act to remember the magical counter-world that she stands for. By contrast, in *Excalibur*, the audience is actively invited to reconnect with an imagined pagan past that has been lost in the smog of industrial time. As such, the landscape itself is re-enchanted and anthropomorphised, rescued from being more than simply a dumb, exploitable commodity. This is set to speak to those with an interest in ecology, magic and pantheistic religions. While both films are clothed in the special effects of the type typical of the fantasy genre, they seem to look in different directions. *Merlin* looks to the bright, rational, future, celebrating the loss of the old magic and its wickedness. *Excalibur* looks back with melancholy to an unrecoverable, mythic, past to show the hubristic folly of the 'time of men'. As Merlin says from his tomb of crystal: 'the earth is being torn apart, its metals stolen, and the balance is broken and the lines of power no longer converge'.

A conclusion

All the narratives addressed in this article deploy elements of transgression in their depictions of the pagan countryside, although the type of transgression differs from text to text, interpretation to interpretation. The screen of pre-history provides a context through which to evoke an imagined lost world that resonates in accord with the socio-geographic fault-lines of contemporary culture, whether this is a lost spiritual vitalism or something repressed by the machinations of civilisation/industrialisation/patriarchal institutions. Pagan prehistory as rendered by these popular texts is often set against the loaded authority of traditional history, as well as helping to diversify the very concept of 'Britain'. The competing narratives that invoke British pre-history demonstrate that what constitutes Britishness is far from fixed or settled. As Barbara Bender has suggested, the pagan landscape provides contemporary British culture with a means of what she calls 'differential empowerment' (1999: 5). The presence of pagan landscapes in popular fiction is, at least in part, based on the spectacular attraction of magic, myth, sex and sacrifice, which are well suited to audio-visual media. The rhetorical alignment of transgression to the pagan landscape provides for some a vehicle by which to challenge and reconfigure the meaning of Britain and identity. And perhaps the recent enthusiasm for British *pre-history* reflects a desire to re-invest the landscape with a sacred dimension, as well as distaste for a very dirty and repressive British *history*.

Acknowledgements

I am grateful to Professor Julian Petley and Leon Hunt for reading versions of this paper.

Notes

1   *The Golden Bough* was first published in twelve volumes between 1906 and 1915 and abridged in 1922. It is a study in comparative myth, magic and folklore, often described as a work of classical anthropology.
2   Large old houses are often used in British horror films of the 1960s and 1970s as the fitting domicile of decadent aristocrats; an articulation of what Carol Clover (1992) terms the 'terrible place', a staple location used in various guises in many horror films.
3   Pagan-witchcraft is in fact a new religion, which, according to Hutton (2001), is the only religion to have developed in the historical era in Britain. Many writers, including anthropologists such as Margaret Murray (1970) have claimed erroneously that there is a continuity of practice between pre-history and contemporary 'Wicca'. This notion has informed many occult fictions including *Eye of the Devil*, however.
4   The BBC Television series comedy *The League of Gentlemen* (1999–2002) has made explicit references to *The Wicker Man* as well as parodying horror-movie conventions and plot formulas.

References

Ashe, G. (2002), *Mythology of the British Isles* (London: Methuen).

Bender, B. (1999), *Stonehenge: Making Space* (Oxford: Berg).

Brown, A. (2000), *Inside the Wicker Man* (Basingstoke and Oxford: Sidgwick and Jackson).

Caesar, J. (1996), *The Gallic Wars [De Bello Gallico]*, Hammond, C. (trans.) (Oxford: Oxford University Press).

Cixous H. and Clement, C. (1986), *The Newly Born Woman*, Gilbert, S.M. (trans.) (Minneapolis: Minnesota University Press).

Clover, C. (1992), *Men, Women and Chainsaws: Gender in the Modern Horror Film* (London, BFI).

Film Directions (1981), 'John Boorman talks about *Excalibur*' 4(15): 16–19.

Frayling, C. (1995), *Strange Landscapes: Journey Through the Middle Ages* (Harmondsworth: BBC Books/Penguin).

Frazer, J.G. (1994), *The Golden Bough: Abridged* (abridgement by Fraser, R.) (Oxford: Oxford University Press).

Geoffrey of Monmouth (1982), *The History of the Kings of Britain*, Thorpe L. (trans.) (Harmondsworth: Penguin Books).

Hetherington, K. (2000), *New Age Travellers* (London: Cassell).

Holland, T. (2000), *Deliver Us from Evil* (London: Abacus).

Hunt, L. (2002), 'Necromancy in the UK: witchcraft and the occult in British Horror', in Chibnall, S. and Petley, J. (eds), *British Horror Cinema* (London, Routledge), pp. 82–98.

Hutton, R. (1997), *The Pagan Religions of the Ancient British Isles: Their Nature and Legacy* (Oxford: Blackwell Books).

Hutton, R. (2001), *The Triumph of the Moon: A History of Modern Pagan Witchcraft* (Oxford: Oxford University Press).

Krzywinska, T. (2000), *A Skin for Dancing In: Possession, Witchcraft and Voodoo in Film* (Trowbridge: Flicks Books).

Murray, M. (1970), *The God of the Witches* (Oxford: Oxford University Press).

Schneider, M. (1997), '"Wrung by sweet enforcements": druid stones and the problem of sacrifice in British romanticism', *Anthropoetics*, II(2): 1–11.

Tacitus (1970), *The Agricola and The Germania*, Mattingley, H. (trans.) (Harmondsworth: Penguin Books).

Wheatley, D. (1971), *The Devil Rides Out* (London: Arrow Books [1934]).

Wheatley, D. (1972), *To the Devil – A Daughter* (London: Arrow Books [1953]).

6

Militarised countrysides: representations of war and rurality in British and American film

Rachel Woodward and Patricia Winter

Representations of war, representations of rurality

Platoon, and the men of Bravo Company, 25th Infantry Division US Army, set out on patrol 'somewhere near the Cambodian border' in Vietnam. It is September 1967. We fly over an endless canopy of trees, then cut to the forest floor, looking up as shafts of sunlight filter down upon us through the leaves. The light fades, tingeing the world blue, and the platoon patrols upslope, following the line of a rocky stream. This could be paradise, but it isn't. The climb is arduous. A man tumbles down the slope. A snake slithers through the undergrowth. Our protagonist, Chris Taylor, a new arrival to the jungles of Vietnam, hacks through the undergrowth; the leaves are razor-sharp and cut his hands. All the men sweat profusely. Flies buzz, and we see in the blue gloom what looks like a tree-trunk. But it is not a tree-trunk. We, and Taylor, can just about see that it is the corpse of a Viet Cong soldier rotting gradually into the base of the tree – hence the flies. Ants crawl over Taylor's skin, along his neck and down his shirt. He vomits, collapses. His initiation as a soldier has begun, here in the strange, dangerous, deadly rural of Vietnam.

What do representations of rurality, representations such as *Platoon*'s, bring to war films? How do they function? In this chapter, limiting our discussion to British and American cinema, we look at the use of representations of the rural to explore how the cinematic countryside functions in war films. War films in British and US cinema are riddled with rural representations, used as scenic devices for narrative and plot purposes and as metaphors for broader arguments and anxieties about national identity and the morality of armed conflict. We explore a small selection of these representations from a vast array of possibilities, our choice of films for discussion determined by three criteria – the significance of particular films for the topic, the availability of films to us for viewing, and our own preferences and prejudices. As a result, we are not claiming that our choice is representative of the whole possible array of ruralities displayed and used in war films, but we hope to indicate some dominant themes. Before we do so, we shall start with some observations about the genre of war films.

War films as a genre – a surprisingly small genre given the ubiquity of violent armed conflict (Hayward, 2000) – are as old as cinema itself. Some of the earliest moving images captured and reproduced as film for entertainment were taken of British troops in the South African War (1899–1902). The development of war films as fictionalised accounts of real engagements emerged during the First World War (1914–18) as a strategy for illustrating for domestic audiences some of the 'realities' of ongoing military campaigns. *The Battle of the Somme* (1916), famously, combined documentary footage with reconstructions of specific events for the purposes of cinematic entertainment. Small though the genre might be, given the long history of violent conflict as a subject for feature films the diversity of the genre is unsurprising. Indeed, war films struggle against their classification as a unified category. We have epic stories from all the main theatres of combat of the First World War (from *All Quiet on the Western Front* to *Charlotte Grey*) and the Second (*The Dam Busters, A Bridge Too Far, In Which We Serve*), from Korea (think *M*A*S*H*) to Vietnam (from *The Green Berets* and *Rambo* to *Born on the Fourth of July* and *Apocalypse Now*), and through to the armed conflicts in the Middle East (*Three Kings, Courage Under Fire, Rules of Engagement*) and Bosnia (*Behind Enemy Lines, Saviour*). Military metaphors and images also militarise the future (see, for example, *Starship Troopers, Aliens*). We have war films made whilst armed conflicts have been raging and their outcomes uncertain, and films made after ceasefire reinterpreting conflicts for subsequent generations. Although our focus here in this chapter is not chronology and reinterpretation *per se*, this is always an issue; war films are inherently political.[1] We have stories from home fronts and stories of foreign fronts, stories of prisoners of war and stories of escape, stories of lone spies and stories of mass military campaigns, stories of heroes and stories of traitors, stories of villains and stories of victims. War films constitute an extremely diverse genre.

Resistant as war films are to categorisation, some key themes are almost always present. The first is a set of plot conventions, usually revolving around a mission. This is not in itself surprising – the narrative structured around a protagonist's task is a dominant theme in feature films. In war films, however, the mission is usually a deadly one. A second key theme is the articulation of beliefs and anxieties about the utility and morality of armed conflict and military violence; indeed, the cultural significance of war films rests with their primacy as one of the few popular cultural forms which engages explicitly with questions about militarism and its consequences. The third key theme, given the role of war films as morality tales, is the legitimation offered to the use of military violence through references to nationhood and national identity. All national cinemas have produced war films (Hall, 1989; Williams, 2002). War films engage directly with issues of national identity, and articulate ideas about nationhood.

Given the significance to the genre of ideas about national identity, it is unsurprising that war films reflect so consistently on the meanings of the spaces of home and the spaces of foreign engagement. Furthermore, given the significance to both British and US cultural traditions of 'the rural' (or even, the non-urban) as key spaces in the national imaginary, it is unsurprising that war films in the British and US cinematic traditions speak so frequently and vocally about the rural.[2] The ruralities represented in British and US war films draw heavily on these cinematic traditions, but our intention here is not to plot war film ruralities onto these. Rather, we are interested in what the rural offers in the way of narrative devices and broader metaphors to films about armed conflict. As we've already noted, war films are riddled with rurality (and we consider why this might be in our conclusions). Given this ubiquity, we limit our discussion to three types of representation; the rural as hostile territory; the rural as a legitimate space for national defence; and the rural as a space in which anxieties about armed conflict can be played out.

Things that leap out of the bushes: the rural as hostile territory

Let us return to *Platoon*, and to Chris Taylor. After stopping to rest and re-supply, the squad is sent out on an ambush. They leave camp at sunset and head into thick jungle. Lighting flashes through the sky and a voice sings a lament from the Deep South: 'Oh I came from Alabama/my banjo on my knee/and I'm going to Louisiana/my true love for to see'. Thunder rolls through the valley drowning out the voice, and as it fades and the squad depart from our sight, it concludes the song. '...don't you cry for me...'. It rains. The squad lay an ambush, and Taylor and another soldier, Junior, are put on watch to detonate claymore mines should the Viet Cong come down the trail. Their ambush site is watched over by a huge stone Buddha. They fall asleep. The rain stops. A lizard scuttles across the Buddha. Insects buzz around Taylor. He wakes with a start. The jungle is quiet, smoky, moonlit, mysterious. But there's a rustling. He doesn't yet know what, but there's definitely something lurking out there. This is Vietnamese jungle, after all. He huddles, a blanket pulled tight around his head, peers out up the trail to a gap between two trees. He sees nothing. We share his point-of-view and we see nothing either. He looks again. We look again. Tension mounts, suspense builds, we hear his heart beating fast. This is a Vietnam war film, after all. But what's there? Gradually, subliminally, we see the silhouette of a human figure, emerging by degrees from what we thought was an empty space between two trees, in dense jungle. It is an enemy soldier, his outline blurred by camouflage, his gun pointing directly at Taylor. Three more enemy figures emerge, seemingly out of nowhere, and move towards him ...

This figure, of an unseen enemy emerging from (it seems) nowhere to confound the offensive strategies of the US Armed Forces, is a common one in American films about Vietnam. In *We Were Soldiers Once*, a unit is stranded for two nights in a remote part of the central highlands of southern Vietnam and forced to hold out in a clearing in a forest which they know is held by the People's Army of Vietnam. The men wake to sense and then (terrifyingly) to see, emerging from trenches a matter of a few metres before their frightened eyes, armed soldiers stealthy and silent in the morning mist. The point is clear; this is their country, they know how to use it, tactically for military gains. An early scene in *Hamburger Hill* makes the same point. The film tells the story of the virtual annihilation of a group from the 101st Airborne Division on Hill 937 in the Ashau Valley. Early on, the platoon sergeant instructs recruits on the lethal jungle-fighting skills and tenacity of the North Vietnamese Army; behind him, a loin-cloth-clad, RPG-toting NVA soldier slithers through mud and beneath barbed wire to demonstrate the point; he knows this place, he is born to the place, and knows how to fight in it. The US Armed Forces are doomed to fail before they even start; deadly things leap out of the bushes here. Inevitably, Captain Willard's journey up the Mekong River, the narrative which drives *Apocalypse Now*, is interspersed with sudden, unexpected assaults by an unseen enemy. To underscore the point that this is hostile, foreign, dangerous and alien territory, even Nature itself turns against them; *Platoon*'s razor-sharp leaves and *Hamburger Hill*'s quagmire mud are as nothing to the sheer fright of a roaring tiger leaping out of the undergrowth at Willard and Chef as they stroll through the forest in search of mangoes. 'Never get out of the boat. Absolutely goddam right.'

These films use a strange, threatening, unknowable rural to emphasise that the US Army is out of place in Vietnam, as an inca-pable fighting force, and as a foreign occupying power (and we return to this issue below). The same device is easily inverted when the politics of a film require it. *Rambo, First Blood: Part II*, set in an early 1980s Vietnam swarming with Soviet troops fighting their corner of the Cold War ('Do we get to win this time?' asks John Rambo/Sylvester Stallone) underscores US global military power (or aspirations to global military hegemony) through Rambo's heroic and absolute soldierly capacity. Through his qualities and skills, we see him utterly at home in the jungle. A mere twenty-four seconds after he is parachuted into hostile territory, he proves this to us by strangling a snake bare-handed. He's so at home here that he runs (runs!) through the jungle – no silent, stealthy tactical advance to battle here. Later, escaping pursuit, he merges into a low cliff, caked in mud, becoming one with the sticky yellow clay of the cliff-face; thus concealed, he ambushes an unsuspecting pursuer. His weapon of choice – a cross-bow armed with explo-sives-tipped arrows – and his uniform of choice (long damp hair, headband, necklace with lucky charm, scanty clothing) identifies him as a rightful inhabitant of the jungle, in contrast to the conventionally uniformed Vietnamese and Soviet assailants, encumbered by their short hair and starched trousers.

The devices used to denote a specific rural and to portray John Rambo, Ultra-Soldier, as master of this rural are not confined to this one film. Consider another patrol, and another war; Captain Miller leads a (reluctant) US Army squad through the French countryside, a few days after the Normandy landings in June 1944. Their mission? *Saving Private Ryan*. Yet despite journeying through (we presume) hostile enemy territory, this feels like a country ramble. They walk in file along June-green hedgerows, past grazing sheep and lush pastures. The sky is overcast, there are a few flies, but nothing threatens them; this rurality is a place of safety. We sense that they feel at home, relaxed enough to complain about their mission, to joke with the reserved Captain Miller, to make fun of the interpreter bought into the squad at the last minute. (According to the logic of the film, at this point nothing can happen; the primary purpose of the scene is to introduce the characters and their view of their mission.) Nothing leaps out of the bushes here. Rather, they are the ones doing the leaping from hedgerows, to attack, for example, a less skilled enemy guarding a radar with a machine-gun nest, or to ambush a small convoy in the middle of a cornfield (which is when they find Ryan). The rural is hostile territory only when directors choose it to be. This is not so much hostile enemy territory as temporarily enemy-occupied friendly territory. The squad's sense of fitting in, their relaxation in this space, naturalises the rightness of their presence there as a liberating force and underscores that their function is 'defence', rather than 'offence'. Whereas Rambo has to transform, bodily, to merge with the other, in order to be at home in the foreign rural, these men are already (to an extent) at home there.

Defending the country: the rural as space for national defence

The ruralities represented in war films are, like any other cultural construction, temporally and spatially specific. In 1942, Britain faced very real fears of invasion from Germany. The country was mobilised for the war effort; children and women evacuated from urban areas, the Home Guard ('Dad's Army') was mobilised;

young, unmarried women were conscripted into the Women's Land Army, mass male conscription was enforced. Military morale had been badly dented by the evacuation of the British Expeditionary Force from the north French beaches around Dunkirk. Civilian morale sagged under the weight of family separations, rationing and the nightly bombing of all major urban and industrial centres. And Ealing Studios went into production of *Went the Day Well?* (1942) (Houston, 1992).

If cinema is a medium through which ideas and anxieties about nationhood and national identity are played out, and war films constitute a prime site for such debates, *Went the Day Well?*, as a number of commentators suggest, is an archetypal example (Richards and Aldgate, 1983; Houston, 1992; Aldgate and Richards, 1994; Richards, 1997; Chapman, 1998; Murphy, 2000). The film revolves, in its entirety, around a specific representation of a southern, rural, English ideal, which in turn is held up as representative of the values, culture and social structure of a wider Britain in answer to questions as to 'why we fight'.

The opening credits roll, and we see a signpost pointing to Bramley End, two miles distant. We are taken down a broad, cornfield-lined country lane into an archetypal southern English village, stopping in its heart, by the green, the pub and the church. This idyllic rural scene, as we know, connotes the 'real' England. A short poem accompanies us on the drive:

> Went the day well?
> We died and never knew
> But, well or ill
> Freedom, we died for you

The link between this landscape and the war's project, liberty, is made explicit from the very start. A man greets us in the churchyard, and a celestial choir provides a musical soundtrack:

Good day to you! Come to have a look at Bramley End, have you? Pretty little place. And a nice old church too. Thirteenth century, parts of it. Still, it won't be that that's brought you, I don't suppose. It'll be these names on this grave here, and the story of them that's buried along with them. Look funny, don't they? German names in an English churchyard. They wanted England, these Jerries did. And this was the only bit they got. The Battle of Bramley End, that's what the papers called it. Nothing was said about it after the war was over, and old Hitler got what was coming to him. Whitsun weekend it was, 1942. As peaceful and quiet here then as it is now, even though there was a war on. It was Saturday morning when those army lorries came rolling along the road from Upton ...

The camera cuts back to the road along which we as viewers have just been taken, and to the sight of army lorries trundling along it. These are not, however, German lorries. They are British, and therein lies the hook on which the plot suspends. The film tells, in flashback, the story of how this fictional English village deals with the threat when it is chosen by an advance guard of German soldiers as the bridge-head for an invading German force. Rural England, or rather, a specific representation of rural England, is established for us as the context in which this invading force lands. The postmistress and the shop girl chatter, milk is delivered to a cottage door framed with flowers, birds sing, the sun shines, and the vicar and his daughter have breakfast in the Vicarage. The social structure and hierarchy of the village is stable and traditional. The centres of authority are the manor house and the vicarage, and there is easy deference to the upper-class figures of authority – the lady of the Manor, Mrs Frazer, and a local gentleman, Oliver Wilsford, leading member of the Home Guard. This is a place of harmonious social relations, the war a distant but necessary activity fought in their defence.

But now the war has come to Bramley End, disguised as British engineers, the German soldiers ask to be billeted in the village. It is soon revealed to the spectator that Wilsford is in fact a traitor, a German agent in the heart of the community and in league with the invaders. Some of the villagers begin to piece together clues that these 'British' soldiers are not what they seem (a bar of 'Chokolade', a number seven written in the continental style). Their cover blown, the Germans put their 'Plan B' into operation and round up the villagers in the church. There are murders – all the more shocking for their idyllic rural context (Richards, 1997). The vicar is shot dead in his own church as he tries to ring the alarm on the church bells. The four men of the Home Guard are mown down by German fire as they come whistling down the lane on their bicycles. The Germans, however, had reckoned without the courage and determination of the villagers, some of whom die heroically for their cause. Mrs Collins the postmistress kills a German soldier in her parlour with an axe, before being felled by a German bayonet. Mrs Frazer, grenade in hand, sacrifices herself for the evacuee children. The vicar's daughter Norah shoots Wilsford in the Manor House, which has become the site of the villagers' last stand against the German invaders and a metaphor for England under attack (Barr, 1977). Ironically it is an urban incomer – the evacuee boy George – who succeeds where others failed in raising the alarm. He does so, however, using the skills of the countryman, having been trained by the village poacher in the ways of escape and evasion in the countryside. And having repelled the invaders, the village of Bramley End, we know from the opening scene of the film, buries them in its churchyard and returns to its timeless existence, as peaceful and quiet now as it was then.

The Silent Village (1943), made by the documentary filmmaker Humphrey Jennings, offers an alternative representation of the invaded British rural. Unlike the invasion fantasy of *Went The Day Well?*, the story told here is based on a true one. In 1942, following the assassination of the Nazi Reinhardt Heydrich, German security police took their revenge on a small Czech mining village, Lidice. The men and boys were lined up and shot, women and children sent to concentration camps, and the village razed to the ground. In *The Silent Village*, the story is transposed to the Welsh mining village of Cwmgiedd, the parts taken not by actors but by real people of the village. The film shows the occupation of the village by faceless Nazis, the resistance of the villagers, chilling scenes of the lining up and shooting of the men (while singing 'Land of My Fathers'), and the burning of the village. The rural imagery at the opening of the film resonates with that of *Went the Day Well?*, showing timeless nature (shots of the babbling stream that runs through the village, birdsong), and images of spirituality (the chapel) communality (choral singing), and everyday life (people working, washing, gardening). But where the image of rural Britain in *Went the Day Well?* was a Southern, agricultural, English one, this is different – working class, industrial and, of course, Welsh. It is most different in that the villagers are Welsh speaking – one of the oppressions perpetrated by the Nazi invaders is to force them to speak English, underlining their loss of identity. The representation of the rural here has some similarities with that of *Went the Day Well?* but serves also to connect Britain to a wider world, and to a wider internationalist struggle.

Went the Day Well? is an extreme. A propaganda film in all but name (Chapman, 1998), it projects a specific rurality for specific purposes. It is not the only film of the era to do this by any means. Powell and Pressburger's *A Canterbury Tale* (1944) (Richards and Aldgate, 1983), fleshes out a flimsy plot about a mysterious 'glue man' threatening young women in a wartime Kentish village, with scenes valorising the aesthetic, social and moral orders of the countryside. *Tawny Pipit* (1944), another wartime feature, naturalises the military presence in the countryside through the conservation antics of a recuperating airman; the rural is equated with the nation, to be loved, cherished and defended. The equation of a locationally specific, idealised rural is a powerful idea; the children's film, *Bedknobs and Broomsticks* (1971) draws on precisely these ideas, with a climax involving a would-be (and rather ineffectual) witch, a magician/con-artist and a trio of evacuee children summoning Arthurian knights, medieval swordsmen, Cavaliers and Roundheads to defeat a party of invading Germans.

Where such direct references to a specific ideal/idyll are impossible, for reasons of plot credibility, British cinema in the post-war period still manages to sneak rural suggestions under the wire, to help consolidate the links between Britishness, 'character', wartime endurance and (ultimately) military victory. For example, in *A Town like Alice*, a group of British expatriates in colonial Malaya are rounded up by the Japanese following the invasion, and deal with flight and the threat of internment by holding fast to their rurally inflected markers of cultural identity. A fleeing family at the centre of the story cower in a roadside ditch at the sound of an approaching vehicle, fearing for the Japanese. 'Stopped for a picnic?' chuckles the driver in an upper-class accent, on finding them. Later in the film, the Malayan jungle rural becomes dangerous – two children in the charge of the central character (Jean Paget) die as direct result of the strange foreign rural – one from a tropical disease, the other from snakebite – and many others in the group die from the rigours of the strange land in which they are forced to walk endlessly in search of a suitable internment camp. But Paget soldiers on, carrying an orphaned baby on her hip, transcending through 'character' the trials and tribulations of the beastly rural. She also survives the ordeal through adopting Malay dress (conical hat, shirt, sarong) and learning the language, secure enough to relinquish some of the key markers of her British identity to survive this hostile rural. Other ladies in the party limp on and struggle in their garden-party skirts and high heels.

'Character' enables endurance, often of appalling privations; in building *The Bridge Over the River Kwai*, Colonel Nicholson (eventually) is 'persuaded' to contribute to the Japanese war effort by helping in the construction of the Burma railway. His determination to assert the superiority of British values entails not only constructing a physically sound bridge, but also in conquering the dangerous, disease-ridden, hostile rural in which they are imprisoned. The same 'character' is a dominant theme in *Ice Cold in Alex*; flawed as it is in the shape of Captain Anson, it helps a quartet of retreating Brits (well, one is foreign, who turns out to be German) prevail in the North African desert as they flee Rommel's Afrika Corps and Tobruk for the sanctuary of Alexandria. The desert is a hostile, sandy, wind-swept, burning hell, but the green fields of home are never far away; moral support when the going gets tough. One of the nurses dies on the journey. Her companions build a cairn above her grave, like those on upland British hilltops, thereby establishing their morality (and thus superiority and 'character') as Christians. They stand above the bare arid landscape, drawing succour from the rural imagery of Psalm twenty-three (The Lord is my shepherd/I shall not want/He maketh me to lay down in green pastures') as enemy tanks bear down upon them from out across the hot sandy wasteland.

If foreign rurals are dangerous, deadly, beastly places, ripe for intervention and subjugation from a dose of British 'character' and will, domestic rurals provide space for tests of other, less assertive qualities. Barnes Wallis's moments of greatest despair, as he tries to perfect the bouncing bomb for use by *The Dam Busters* on the dams of the industrial Ruhr, come on the beach used as a testing range. But the beach, a liminal space (Shields, 1991) is also a place for new starts, renewed resolve; he takes off his socks and shoes, rolls up his trouser legs, and in a caricature of British seaside manhood, wades out through the receding tide to collect the fragments of his bomb. Later, the tests are successful. All the while, the nerve of the men of 617 squadron RAF, to fly low and fast in heavy Lancaster bombers over hostile enemy territory, is forged over the dark hills and glinting silver waters of the Derwent and Ladybower Reservoirs. The low flying is practised to the disgust of a local poultry farmer, from whose rattling cottage a letter is despatched to the Air Ministry, complaining about the effects of noise disturbance on his hens' egg production; his war efforts are superseded by a greater need.

Symbolic rural landscapes: anxieties about armed conflict

Above all, in war films the rural is a symbolic space in which rural metaphors and allegories are used to explore anxieties about the morality of armed conflict and military intervention. Vietnam films invariably establish the jungle as a place of horror, drawing on the conventions of 'the terrible place' used so effectively in horror films (Clover, 1992). The impenetrability of the jungle, the clogging of mud, is a common theme; the logistics of fighting and the morale of troops becomes cloudy, clogged, muddied, a metaphor for the quagmire that the Vietnam War had become. As Klein (1997) notes, the *Platoon* patrol in Vietnamese countryside may be part of a regional pacification programme involving the destruction and resettling of villages, but if so we're not provided with the information. Given the discourse of the film we simply share the soldier's perspective, that somewhere out in the jungle we, like the soldiers, are being hunted by an alien and evil antagonist, and we, like America, are surrounded by Third World, Communist aliens. This is such a well-worn metaphorical use of jungle space that Kubrick deliberately avoided it in *Full Metal Jacket* (LoBrutto, 1998); the film has an entirely different feel from other 1980s Vietnam films in its use of settled, urban-industrial and urbanised agricultural landscapes.

The symbolism of landscape is overwhelming in *Southern Comfort*, an allegorical film which transposes the American military experience in Vietnam to the Louisiana swamps. A patrol of Louisiana National Guard get lost in the swampy bayous, and after a misunderstanding over the use of some small boats, resulting in the death of their commanding NCO, the Guardsmen are pursued through the bayous by vengeful Cajun locals as they struggle to reach the Interstate and 'civilisation'. Even though this is American soil, and thus home territory, these soldiers are foreign to it, strangers, out of place in this scary rural. Only two soldiers of the original nine survive, the rest killed by pursuing locals; an experienced patrol sergeant (denoting the Cajuns as 'the enemy', treating the exercise in tactical terms) is shot, a young African-American guardsman is spiked on a man-trap, a gung-ho Latino guardsman drowns in mud, the all-American football coach goes mad and ends up hanging from a railway bridge. The two survivors are a self-confessed city boy (identified from the start as urbane and sophisticated by his arrangements to have a group of prostitutes meet the patrol at the end of the exercise for a little R and R) and an incomer and stranger to the group (a college graduate in chemical engineering and teacher from Texas). The message of the film, about belonging and rightful presence, violence and retribution, is clear.

Anxieties about US military engagement in the 1991 Gulf War are played out in the desert landscape, where bleak expanses of nothing (to North American eyes) represent the anti-climatic nature of that war for the huge number of ground troops deployed (Swofford, 2003). *Three Kings*, a tale of an errant squad in search of hidden gold, opens in the flat, grey-buff sand and grit. We hear a voice, asking about what can be seen. One soldier inspects another's eye for a particle of sand as they stand surrounded by a featureless, flat, un-vegetated landscape where nothingness is readily apparent. The desert hides things, obscures things, enemy soldiers (one is shot in the opening scene – is he surrendering? It is hard to see in the desert) and underground bunker complexes. An American journalist, in the course of the film, is distracted from the story of gold by being purposefully lost in the desert. In *Courage Under Fire*, a film revolving around the investigation of an act of heroism by a helicopter pilot, the act itself is obscured by the landscape where it takes place. The contours of the wadi and the bare rocky slopes hide a contested story, the facts of which are so hard to verify for the investigating officer precisely because so little could be seen by the obscuring desert. The ability of the desert to obscure visibility is a central narrative in the film – the investigating officer is himself responsible for a friendly fire incident in the dusty black of a desert night, when he and his tank crew were unable to see.

Some war film landscapes are represented as ultimately unknowable, a metaphor for conflict itself. A navy pilot lost *Behind Enemy Lines* lies hiding from his renegade Serb pursuers beneath a pile of rotting corpses, ethnically 'cleansed' victims of mass executions. From a control room deep in the bowels of an American aircraft carrier, the pilot's commanding officers use high-tech gadgetry (infra-red devices, satellite imagery, global positioning systems) to locate the man. They see his prone body, they see his advancing pursuers, but they cannot understand what is going on. The Serbian forests are as unseen and thus unknown on their computer screens as the intricate contours of the Balkan conflict itself. The

watching commanders are as powerless to help the man as the UN
peacekeepers were themselves.

War in the city

We have argued in this chapter that war films speak to narratives
about mission, national identity, and the morality of violent armed
conflict, and that they do so frequently, though not exclusively,
through their engagement with rural imagery and rural metaphors.
Not all war films are rural in character, metaphor or context.
However, a great many are, explicitly or incidentally, because of
the significance of rural (that is, non-urban) space as a traditional,
even 'natural' location for military engagement.[3] Pre-modern and
modern warfare was warfare conducted in the open, in non-popu-
lated, non-urban space, for strategic and practical reasons. Cities
were to be avoided, warned Sun Tzu in the fifth century BC. War
films reflect this.

We conclude with the observation that this connection between
warfare and the rural is being destabilised, in the age of 'postmodern' war and the Revolution in Military Affairs (Gray, 1997), as
new military technologies, new strategic doctrines and new geopolitical imperatives urbanise political violence by making urban
warfare either more possible or, more correctly, inescapable
(Graham, 2004). *Black Hawk Down* re-enacts the loss of US
soldiers in the Somalian capital Mogadishu in 1993, with attempts
at urban engagement having calamitous and terrible consequences
for both the soldiers and the much larger number of civilians. The
incident on which the film was based has been heralded as a marker
for a new mode of military engagement, urbanised warfare. This
new way of war, we can confidently predict, will be replayed and
repackaged cinematically; war films are perhaps *the* key contemporary cultural space in which we engage directly with militarism and
its consequences.

Acknowledgements

Rachel Woodward would like to acknowledge the support of the
Defence Studies Forum of the Australian Defence Force Academy
for providing a Visiting Fellowship during writing of this chapter,
and the Academy Library for access to their comprehensive stock

of war films. Trish Winter acknowledges the support of the Centre for Research in Media and Cultural Studies, University of Sunderland, for research leave in support of this project. The opinions expressed in this chapter are our own.

Notes

1 See, for example, Murphy (2000) on British cinematic reinterpretations of the Second World War, and Dittmar and Michaud (1997) on American reinterpretations of Vietnam.
2 See introductory chapter to this volume for a fuller discussion of the use of rural imagery in different cinematic traditions.
3 See Woodward (2004) for a broader discussion of the connections between rurality, militarism and environmentalism.

References

Aldgate, A. and Richards, J. (1994), *Britain Can Take It: The British Cinema in the Second World War* (Edinburgh: Edinburgh University Press).

Barr, C. (1977), *Ealing Studios* (London: Cameron and Tayleur/David and Charles).

Chapman, J. (1998), *The British at War: Cinema, State and Propaganda, 1939–1945* (London: IBTauris).

Clover, C. (1992), *Men, Women and Chainsaws: Gender in the Modern Horror Film* (London: BFI).

Dittmar, L. and Michaud, G. (eds) (1997), *From Hanoi to Hollywood: The Vietnam War in American Film* (New Brunswick, NJ: Rutgers University Press).

Graham, S. (ed.) (2004), *Cities, War and Terrorism* (Oxford: Blackwell).

Gray, C.H. (1997), *Postmodern War: The New Politics of Conflict* (New York: Guilford Press).

Hall, S. (1989), 'Cultural identity and cinematic representation', *Framework* 36: 68–81.

Hayward, S. (2000), *Cinema Studies: The Key Concepts* (London: Routledge).

Houston, P. (1992), *Went the Day Well?* (London: British Film Institute).

Klein, M. (1997), 'Historical memory, film and the Vietnam era', in Dittmar, L. and Michaud, G. (eds) (1997), *From Hanoi to Hollywood: The Vietnam War in American Film* (New Brunswick, NJ: Rutgers University Press), pp. 19–40.

LoBrutto, V. (1998), *Stanley Kubrick: A Biography* (London: Faber and Faber).

Murphy, R. (2000), *British Cinema and the Second World War* (London: Continuum).

Richards, J. (1997), *Films and British National Identity: From Dickens to 'Dad's Army'* (Manchester: Manchester University Press).

Richards, J. and Aldgate, A. (1983), *British Cinema and Society 1930–1970* (Oxford: Blackwell).

Shields, R. (1991), *Places on the Margin: Alternative Geographies of Modernity* (London: Routledge).

Swofford, A. (2003), *Jarhead: A Marine's Chronicle of the Gulf War and Other Battles* (New York: Scriber).

Williams, A. (ed.) (2002), *Film and Nationalism* (New Brunswick, NJ: Rutgers University Press).

Woodward, R. (2004), *Military Geographies* (Oxford: Blackwell).

Part II

Mobile productions and contested representations

7

Mediating the rural: *Local Hero* and the location of Scottish cinema

Ian Goode

The landscape of Scotland – whether it is in the shape of the Highlands and Islands of the north, or the Lowlands of the south – represents a key economic and cultural resource to the nation. In economic terms the land and sea contain natural resources and support fishing, agriculture and tourist industries, and in cultural terms they are key to literature, music, theatre, film and television produced in Scotland.

The importance of the Scottish landscape to Scottish cinema is underlined by the role given to locations by Scottish Screen, the body set up in 1997 to 'develop, encourage and promote every aspect of film, television and new media in Scotland' (www. scottishscreen.com). Scottish Screen was formed in order to bring together the previously separate agencies of the Scottish Film Council, Scottish Screen Locations, Scottish Film Archive, and the Scottish Film Production Fund. The locations office of Scottish Screen co-ordinates a growing network of Film Commissions and Film Liaison Offices, dedicated to facilitating production in Scotland. Regional film commissions such as the Scottish Highlands and Islands Film Commission now offer a service to film and television producers that includes information and advice on locations and permissions and contacts for cast, crew and facilities.

The choice of the Scottish landscape as a location for feature-filmmaking is confirmed by both recent Hollywood productions such as *Braveheart* (Mel Gibson, 1995) and *Rob Roy* (Michael Caton-Jones, 1995) and the earlier and more indigenous productions of Alexander Mackendrick's Ealing comedy *Whisky Galore!* (1949) or more recently the adaptation of Christopher Rush's autobiographical novel *Venus Peter* (1989) and Lars von Trier's

Breaking the Waves (1996). It is the polarity between representations of Scotland produced by agencies located outside Scotland and those that emanate from inside Scotland that has informed much of the critical debate concerning Scottish cinema (McArthur, 1982, 1994, 1996; Cairns, 1983; Petrie, 2000). The opposition between external constructions produced by the Hollywood film industry, and the viability of local filmmaking, is one of the underlying tenets of the idea of national cinema (Higson, 1995). *Local Hero* (Bill Forsyth, 1983) represents an example of a film that resists this opposition by virtue of being written and directed by the Glaswegian director Bill Forsyth, and produced and financed by David Puttnam and his production company Goldcrest Films with the backing of Warner Brothers in the United States. The films of Bill Forsyth in general and *Local Hero* in particular formed a significant contribution to the meaning of Scottish cinema during the early 1980s. The central theme of *Local Hero* is the encounter between an outsider and the Scottish landscape, which results from the journey of an oil executive based in Houston, Texas to the rural location of the fictionally named coastal village of Furness in the northeast of Scotland. It is this meeting between urban and rural that I wish to examine at the levels of production, text and critical reception in order to reassess how the rural in *Local Hero* has been claimed by and for critics of Scottish cinema.

Negotiating rural resources: the production of *Local Hero*

During the 1980s the Scottish Film Council was the solitary agency responsible for film in Scotland and its primary role was concerned with education rather than promoting Scottish locations to the decision-makers involved with a film production.

According to the Associate Producer, Iain Smith, the decisions regarding the location for the film were a result of a compromise between the characteristics of the beach and village imagined by Forsyth during the writing of the script and the practicalities of film-production; in other words, was it possible to transport and accommodate a cast and crew to the preferred location, once it was found?[1] Originally, Forsyth had the village of Valtos on the Isle of Lewis in mind for the film. The Hebridean island of Barra, which was the location for *Whisky Galore!*, was also considered before

Smith and Forsyth decided to confine the search for a location to the Scottish mainland. After a thorough survey of the Scottish mainland the locations chosen and rendered continuous in the final film were Camusdarroch beach near Arisaig on the west coast, and the village of Pennan near Banff on the east coast. The process of securing permission to use these locations was uncannily prescient of the apparently oppositional encounter between urban America and rural Scotland that structures the film.

The village of Pennan in Aberdeenshire has become a haven for *Local Hero* tourism since the film was released 1983, but prior to the production of the film the village was as anonymous as other rural coastal villages in the north of Scotland. At the time of the decision to locate the film in Pennan, the village was suffering from unemployment, a declining population and a lack of the economic resources urgently required to reinforce the ailing sea wall and protect the village from the encroaching sea. The initial encounter between the film producers and the village was reported by the local press in Aberdeen as an encounter between the local and the national: 'It seems ironic to villagers that there is national interest in Pennan through the film industry but they have problems in finding cash to preserve their village – steeped in the heritage of the north-east' (*Evening Express*, 15 May 1982). As Smith states, 'rather like the story of the film, the villagers of Pennan thought their dreams were about to come true when we rolled in'.[2] What happened was not so much an agreement regarding the cultural importance of making a feature film that fictionally represented rural Scotland, than an argument concerning ownership of, and access to, the locations in and around the village that were required by the film.

The situation that developed involved negotiations between the film's producers – *Enigma*, who were represented by Smith – and the villagers en masse, whose principal spokesman came to be the village pub landlord Les Rose, and the feudal superior David Watt.[3] Rose went to the lengths of hiring a lawyer and accountant to assist in the negotiations and for his efforts he was dubbed an unofficial *Local Hero* by the local press (*Evening Express*, 19 March, 1983). The encounter seemed to echo the themes of the film in that the locals confounded any shared cultural expectations that outsiders might have assumed them to have. Smith observes that 'we were the idealistic film makers encountering the locals who were much more interested in reality than we could ever have imagined'.[4] For the villagers of Pennan in the early 1980s 'reality' was economically determined and the negotiations between the film producers and the population of the village were protracted. The budget for the film meant that the amount of money available for negotiating access to the locations was restricted rather than limitless. According to Smith the villagers did not accept this: 'they just misunderstood what we were. They thought we had an open chequebook and their interest in money was brought on by the desperate plight of their village.' At the end of the negotiations the location agreement decreed that from the location budget – 'a total of £10,400 was paid to a general village fund, various local committees, and certain individuals by way of disturbance money, and some of this money would be used for village improvements' (*Evening Express*, 19 March, 1983).

The negotiations between the villagers and the film producers demonstrate how the villagers' relationship with their natural environment (the coastal village) exists in tension with the producer's relationship with the natural environment, which is ostensibly national. Forsyth and Smith scoured Scotland in search of a location that corresponded to the way that they imagined the landscape should appear in their film. The discrepancy between the image of the Scottish village and landscape required by the fiction of the film and the material relationship of the villagers with this lived environment was revealed in the course of the negotiations. Indeed, this struggle between the material/economic and symbolic/cultural is not only pertinent to the production of *Local Hero* but also pertinent to the text of *Local Hero*, the critical response to *Local Hero*, and the ongoing debates about the contested formation of both Scottish cinema in particular and national cinema(s) in general.

The claim by Scottish cinema of *Local Hero* because it is predominantly set in rural Scotland and directed by Bill Forsyth is mitigated by the contribution and influence of David Puttnam, a figure who is crucial to the history of British cinema in the 1980s. The success of Puttnam's prior production *Chariots of Fire* (Hugh Hudson, 1981) and the fanfare that followed its Oscar-winning success allied with the critical approbation that gathered around Forsyth's *Gregory's Girl* (Bill Forsyth, 1982) meant that, as Nick Roddick suggests, 'in some respects the future of British cinema depends on its ability to merge the Puttnam tradition with the

Forsyth one' (Roddick, 1983: 138). For Puttnam the motivation for *Local Hero* was the tradition of the Ealing comedy, and the theme for the script was prompted by his reading of press stories involving oil companies and local communities (Roddick, 1983). Importantly, Puttnam also believed that such localised subject matter could find an audience outside of its country of origin:

> What we're trying to make is a modest-budget film that looks like a big film with universal implications ... I believe passionately that only by being specific do you become global ... Cinema is about the transference of personality to that of someone on the screen and you can only do that if they have a fixed, clearly rooted identity. (Yule, 1988)

After the success of *Chariots of Fire* Puttnam signed an agreement with Warner Brothers which meant that he had to offer them the opportunity to invest in, and acquire the distribution rights to, any film in which he was involved in return for a commitment by them to spend $1.5 million on the promotion of *Local Hero* (Eberts and Ilott, 1990: 115–16). Puttnam's production company Goldcrest retained control of *Local Hero* by committing a budget of £2.6 million (Eberts and Ilott, 1990: 115–16). The film went on to become a critical and commercial success recording a profit of £338,000 (Eberts and Ilott, 1990: 293).

Analysis: the text of *Local Hero*

The opening of the film shows the oil company executive MacIntyre driving his Porsche along the busy freeway into the city of Houston. The combination of a busy freeway and the vertical tower blocks of the city in the background of the image confirm an urban milieu. However, the soundtrack is formed by the rapid banjo rhythms of southern country music associated with the Hillbilly, and the voice of a local radio disc jockey speaking with a folksy, southern drawl, and declares that 'you're with KOS, the radio sound of Texas sound'. This use of music and voice confounds the signalling of the Texan city as a place that is exclusively formed by the sources of modernity. The effect of this signification of the rural in the urban is to form an ironic counterpoint to MacIntyre's apparent security in the world of business and the mechanised trappings that accompany this role. In addition, the infusion of southern country music into Houston, Texas, a city and a state whose wealth is predicated upon the economic exploitation of the resources of the earth in the shape of oil, adds further irony to the inter-relation of the country and the city. This is underlined by the subsequent scene, which is revealed to be a film being screened for the management of Knox Oil and Gas. The voice-over on the film declares that 'nature guards her treasures jealously. Just over a decade ago these fields were beyond our reach – we didn't have the technology. Today a Knox engineer will tell you that he might need a little time but he'll get the oil.' The film goes on to reveal the geographical reach of the company through shots of pipelines being laid, and a young man wearing the Arab headdress of Agal and Ghutra whilst working on an oil installation. The final shot of the screen that is now in view bears the words 'A Knox Industries Film For The World'. The decision to include a screened film within the diegetic world of *Local Hero* underlines how significant the encounter between the expansive Texan oil company and Scotland will be, but also how Forsyth and Puttnam's film represents thematically – and also at the level of production – a meeting between America and Scotland, as well as Hollywood, Scottish and British cinemas.

Forsyth confirms how he imagined *Local Hero* as an encounter not simply between urban and imperialistic America and rural Scotland but also between the combination of these apparently oppositional terms: 'I saw it along the lines of a Scottish *Beverly Hillbillies* – what would happen to a small community when it suddenly became immensely rich – that was the germ of the idea.'[5] The implications of the Hillbilly figure acquiring wealth and taking the rural into the city formed the basis of the US television series *The Beverly Hillbillies* (1962–71), and it is this symbiosis thematically underlying the question of whether Knox Oil and Gas will manage to acquire part of the Scottish coast that lies at the centre of the film's narrative.

MacIntyre is to represent the company in their intended acquisition of a specified area of coastal Scotland where they wish to install an oil refinery. This is based on the assumption that MacIntyre is Scottish, but MacIntyre's apparent lack of a clear identity is indicated when he confesses to his colleague Hal that he is not Scottish and that his folks 'changed their name when they got off the boat from Hungary. They thought that MacIntyre was

American.' Hal's reply in front of the vending machine that 'you're not a Scotsman, you're not a Texan' indicates how MacIntyre represents the interests of the American oil company but in himself does not feel rooted to any particular nation.

The nature of the relation between Scotland and America is stated when the head of the company Felix Happer comments to MacIntyre that 'it will be like going home, like we're going home', and he points out that the founder of Knox Oil and Gas was a Scot, before he was bought out by Happer's father. The implication that MacIntyre and the company will be returning home to a place of origins that he cannot truly lay claim to suggests that the encounter between Knox Oil and rural Scotland is not only an economic one but also a cultural one. Both of these routes back to Scottishness are followed by references to Happer's eccentric interest in astrology, underlined by the instruments that furnish his elevated office in the sky. The combination of astrology with economics allied to Happer's odd behaviour serve to deflect attention from the economic muscle that he wields as head of a multinational oil and gas company.

MacIntyre's encounter with rural Scotland is initiated as the negotiation of a business venture that becomes an exchange between rural nature and urban culture that Duncan Petrie argues is based upon 'the romantic and elemental appeal of the beauty and remoteness of the landscape' (Petrie, 2000). MacIntyre and his Scottish assistant Oldsen arrive in Furness bearing all the signs of businessmen adjusting to a rural setting. They take a walk on the beach and MacIntyre suggests that 'we should come here when we want to discuss business; the hotel is too public'. As they walk along the beach that the refinery is intended to occupy MacIntyre replies to Oldsen's wonder at the plan with the words 'it's the only business' and he continues 'could you imagine a world without oil?' The exchange continues with a list of the manufactured products of industry: 'No automobiles, no paint, no ink, no nylon'. These words occur after a cut to a significantly longer shot emphasising the beauty of the gloaming, the natural features of the coastline and the size and scale of the characters in the frame.[6] As MacIntyre enquires about Oldsen's knowledge of the stars the scene is interrupted by the musical tune of MacIntyre's digital watch. This scene underlines not only the opposition between, and combination of, nature and culture, but also initiates what the

Glasgow Women's Film Collective describe as 'man's (certainly not woman's) search for a lost innocence' (1983).

The initial incongruity of the executives walking and discussing business on the beach lessens with each scene showing them on the beach. MacIntyre also witnesses a meteor shower and he steps up on to a rock in order to wonder at the spectacle of moving light in the sky over the sea. The use of electronic sources to produce a sonic and otherworldly sound heightens MacIntyre's reverie at the cosmic prospect that he is shown looking up to. MacIntyre is next shown having shed his jacket, tie and briefcase, and barefooted he collects shells from the rock pools on the beach. A symbolic image shows his technologically advanced digital watch left lying, isolated on the rocks, and submerged by the incoming tide of the ocean, emitting sounds that do not trigger a human response. MacIntyre's return to nature and Oldsen's attraction to the biological essence of the web-footed scientist Marina suggest that the two businessmen are not unaffected by the rural environment of Furness.

The representation of the rural in *Local Hero* reveals a place that outsiders are drawn to, and provides the possibilities for a loosening of the identity they arrived with. This possibility of exchange is confirmed at the ceilidh, where the traditional Celtic folk culture is given an international dimension by the dancing partnerships that are highlighted. The visitors to the village such as the black African Reverend MacPherson, the Russian seaman Victor, plus Oldsen and MacIntyre, are all shown dancing with local people. This is also the point of the film where the negotiations over the beach required for the oil terminal come to a halt when it is discovered that the beachcomber Ben Knox is the legal owner of the beach. Ben reveals that 'the beach has been in the family for four hundred years; the Lord of the Isles gave it to an ancestor of mine'. He continues to resist the offers of money and invites MacIntyre to use not monetary figures but to estimate the number of grains of sand that Ben holds in his hand. The contrast between the familiar quantitative scale of money and the less familiar but symbolic grains of sand functions as a means of drawing attention to the criteria used to determine the value of land. Ben's refusal to sell prompts the compromise that arrives from the skies through the arrival in Scotland of Felix Happer. After Happer descends from a light in the sky, he meets Ben and they, along with the prompts of Oldsen, arrive at the decision to build the marine laboratory originally suggested by Marina. The film closes with MacIntyre leaving Furness and returning to his apartment in Houston. The final image of an unanswered call to the telephone box in Furness under- lines the separation of MacIntyre from the coastal location he had become so attached to and changed by and echoes the opening sequence of the film where rural and urban meet as MacIntyre drives into Houston. The ambivalence of the close of the film given the prior scenes raises questions as to the possible meanings of the words *Local Hero*.

The caption from the promotional poster that accompanied the release of the film is instructive here, for it is illustrative of the geographical dispersal of those who seek to influence the fate of the land and which also create the conditions for the heroism implied by its title:

> A beautiful coast line ...
> A rich oilman wants to develop it.
> A poor beach bum wants to live on it.
> An entire town wants to profit by it.
> And a real life mermaid wants to save it ...
> Only one of them will get their way.

The distribution of vested interests from international business to marine biologists, pragmatic locals and eternal nature also under- lines how the narrative appears to offer positions, albeit unequal positions, to differently located characters who meet and interact in a rural setting. The ending suggests that there is no conclusive and singular hero, just as the localness of *Local Hero* is also lent a global dimension by the theme of the economics of land use. The apparent dispersal of the location of heroism and the degree to which *Local Hero* can be read as an open text is lent weight by the critical the reception of the film within and without Scotland.

The local, national and international reception of *Local Hero*

The reception of the film in the north of Scotland is clearly influ- enced by the locality of the subject matter and its potential economic dividends for the area. Coverage in Aberdeen's *Evening Express* highlights firstly the negotiations behind the production of *Local Hero* and also how the film played to full houses at the 800-

seat Odeon cinema in Aberdeen (*Evening Express*, 11 May 1983). The attention and potential economic gains brought to the northern area of Scotland by the production of the film clearly takes priority over the critical assessment of the film that is carried out in other parts of predominantly urban Scotland.

With the exception of the Glasgow Women's Film Collective, for Scottish critics the key criterion for evaluating *Local Hero* has been through its representation of Scotland. In *Scottish Field*, a publication dedicated to reflecting the interests of the rural population in its content, Mark Astaire and Allan Hunter argue that *Local Hero* 'deals with Scotland today and is able to transcend the frequently caricatured view of Scottish people and life which is often portrayed on the screen' (Astaire and Hunter, 1982). The urban critic from The *Glasgow Herald* concurs: '*Local Hero* is a triumph, It does to be sure, paint a romantic picture, which may cause a frown among those who hate that kind of portrayal of Scotland but there's nothing exploitative about it' (*Glasgow Herald*, 17 March, 1983).

Tom Milne, writing for a British film journal, detects in Ben Knox the presence of Scottishness as a brand image: 'the dread cliche of the pawky Scot hangs over *Local Hero* in the person of beachcomber Ben Knox, a man so content with his whisky, his wisdom and his wee plot of land that he is secure from the blandishments of the consumer society' (Milne, 1983). It is clear that certain Scottish critics are alert to, as well as critical and forgiving of, cultural stereotypes and a romantic view of the landscape. The national audience for the film, whether this audience is rural or urban, is taken for granted, and the film is situated in a context of previous representations of Scotland.

Scott Malcolmson and Brian Pendreigh are more generous towards Forsyth's attempts to simultaneously invoke and undermine some of the clichés that have come to be reproduced in representations of Scotland:

> [T]he real problems posed by the oil company's designs on the village are resolved by the fantastical plot device of the natural preserve – which, as it happens, is a pretty good metaphor for the timeless and sylvan marginality in which both Tartan and Kailyard seek to leave the Scottish countryside ... *Local Hero* dismantles many of the Kailyard clichés, yet ultimately serves some of the main purposes of that 'frozen discourse'. (Malcolmson, 1985)

Pendreigh counters:

> [A]ccusations that Forsyth had abandoned sparky contemporary comedy in favour of couthy stereotypes, sentiment, nice scenery and a big-name Hollywood star ... Forsyth builds stereotypes only to undermine them – the Highland idyll shattered by a low flying jet, the remote wee village whose minister is black, the Scottish American MacIntyre who turns out to have no Scottish connections at all. (Pendreigh, 2002)

Colin McArthur is less forgiving: 'A glance at the history of modern (particularly Highland) Scotland will indicate the gulf between what Scots are imagined to do, the autonomy over their own country they are posited to wield, in films such as *Whisky Galore!*, *The Maggie* and *Local Hero*, and what actually happens in the "real" world of politics and economics' (McArthur, 2003). Scottish critics clearly impose a framework of national responsibility on to a film written and directed by an eminent figure such as Bill Forsyth, despite the influence of Puttnam and Forsyth's expressed intention to draw upon the theme of the *Beverly Hillbillies*. The level of expectation that critics place upon the film in relation to Scotland's position in the world differs according to the degree of realism expected and the concessions that can be made for the pleasures of comedy and fantasy, as the last three responses demonstrate. It is clear that the film offers different positions of influence from different locations but the determining source of power lies with the character of Happer, as Nick Roddick confirms: 'Happer, the tycoon behind the deal in *Local Hero*, represents power – almost boundless power, the power to destroy the community of Furness. His conversion to ecological camaraderie at the end leaves untouched the threat ... posed to Scotland by Knox Oil and Gas' (Roddick, 1983).

The reception of *Local Hero* in Scotland positions the film, despite its content, in an exclusively national context. As John Caughie points out 'it is probably the first film ever in history which is identifiably (if arguably) Scottish in subject matter, location, origination, and with a substantially Scottish crew and cast to have achieved a real international success' (Caughie, 1983). The fact that the film is predicated upon the encounter between rural Scotland and America at the level of subject matter and production does render *Local Hero* an axiomatically national film, even though, paradoxically, it could be argued that its narrative concerns attempt to address international themes. If Caughie concedes that *Local Hero* is *arguably* Scottish in subject matter, in what ways is it not exclusively Scottish?

In an interview with a local newspaper in northeast Scotland Puttnam suggests that 'although *Local Hero* is filmed and based in Scotland it is an entirely international concept which could have been filmed equally well anywhere in the world with similar appeal' (*Banffshire Journal*, 23 June 1982). The international concept that Puttnam is keen to highlight, and Scottish critics are less willing to concede as universal, is the issue of ownership of land and land use. The success of the film with critics and audiences outside of Scotland suggests that Puttnam's assertion should be given further consideration.

The reception of *Local Hero* outside Scotland appears to acknowledge the role of comedy, albeit whimsical, and the visual appeal of the landscape. The British critic Philip French states that 'in the delightful *Local Hero* Forsyth has taken the potentially gritty subject of hard-nosed Texans set on ousting a remote Highland fishing community to make way for an oil terminal, and treated it as a pawky fairy tale' (*The Observer*, 13 March 1983). Critics in the USA similarly praised the film: 'one complacently envisions an ecological morality tale in which the quaint old-fashioned Scots fight off the rape of their beautiful beach. Not so: Forsyth is savvy enough to know that it's only outsiders who get sentimental over Scottish landscapes' (*Newsweek*, 28 February 1983); and, '*Local Hero* speaks obliquely in a comic mode of preserving things of value, the environment, a community, against decisions based strictly on profit. A film of sensibility, its humour is gentle, subtle, slyly subversive, rather than strident and righteous' (*Newsday*, 17 February 1983). And further afield in Australia and South Africa: 'a landscape captured in oil – the movie is a powerful plea for conservation' (*Daily Telegraph Australia*, 29 April 1983); and, 'the incongruous sharing and swapping of values between America's rat race and Scotland's rurality' (*Natal Mercury*, 3 August 1983).

In the reception of *Local Hero* there is a sharp distinction between the universal appeal that Puttnam claims for the film, which is supported by international critics and evident in the text of the film, and the exclusively national frame of Scottish critics.

The different responses place different degrees of priority upon character and the representation of rurality. The local reception of the film is bound up with the publicity and economic benefit that the production of the film brings to the area. The urban and national reception situates the film in a critical context where the material imperatives of rural life, borne out by the production negotiations and to an extent by the text of the film, are displaced by the cultural frame of the nation and the ongoing concern of how Scotland has been represented and should be represented. The relation between the cultural politics of the national and the environmental politics of conservation evident in the international reception of *Local Hero* appear to be mutually exclusive at the time of the release of the film in 1983. There are real issues of power underlying the themes that are introduced but ultimately not resolved by the film in a manner that equates with the necessities of national cultural politics.

However, the setting of rural Scotland in *Local Hero* does, I would suggest, create the conditions for a connected rather than separative view of the local, the national and the global. The introduction of MacIntyre at the opening of the film confirms how Forsyth exploits the Hillbilly theme, which is predicated on the overlap between urban and rural rather than their separation. This is continued by repeated suggestions that characters in the film such as Happer, Reverend MacPherson and MacIntyre feel a connection with and a desire to return to an imagined, rural Scotland. MacPherson says to MacIntyre 'you are not Scottish are you?' MacIntyre replies 'no', and the Reverend then says 'I am not Scottish either; I'm an African'. This exchange takes place on the land outside the church and it invites the spectator to consider the names people inherit, and the connections between the places they come from and arrive at. These affiliations are articulated through the rural location and the symbolic and narrative emphasis placed on the sea and the sky. As Marina points out, 'the North Atlantic drift comes in here, that's warmish water from the Caribbean. That's why it's special here, there's stuff fetching up here all the way from the Bahamas.' The colonial histories that lie beneath these routes are not explored but what is emphasised are the transcendental qualities of the environment. Forsyth stated his ambition to use the medium of film 'to present a cosmic viewpoint to people, but through the most ordinary things' (quoted in Hardy,

1990: 178).[7] He achieves this through the comic eccentricity of Happer and the reveries of MacIntyre. These connections across space are described by Avtar Brah as 'genealogies of dispersal' (Brah, 1996: 242) that he associates with diasporic spaces. *Local Hero* suggests, but does not work through, a diasporic reading position via the characters that arrive at and are affected by Furness. Euan Hague has observed of the Scottish diaspora in the USA that 'Americanness is not quite enough' (Hague, 2002: 145). Both MacIntyre and Happer are shown in their urban, domestic lives to be isolated bachelors. Their departures from urban Houston to encounters with rural Scotland offer a relationship with a natural environment that is not available to them in the city. The disjunction between urban and rural confirms the shifting and inverting of the Hillbilly theme from the USA to the Scottish coastal landscape of Furness. Viewing *Local Hero* less as an articulation of Scottishness only, than as a film formed by and produced from a desire to address an international audience, is to suggest that, following Trinh Ti Minh-ha, the film can be assessed productively, from a location that looks from the outside in, as well as the inside out (Minh-ha, 1989).

The subject matter and setting of *Local Hero* demands that it should be claimed for Scottish cinema, but it is undeniably a story about the encounter between the two sides of the Atlantic that attracted a favourable reception from an international audience. As Geoffrey Nowell-Smith points out, 'even *Local Hero* domestic and provincial though it is, stretches across the Atlantic to Texas' (Nowell-Smith, 1985: 154). One of the consequences of the international success of *Local Hero* was the influx of tourists from other countries to Scotland and the village of Pennan (www.geo.ed.ac.uk/home/scotland/tales/heros.html).

John Caughie demonstrates the reaction of Scottish critics located in urban contexts to the cultural implications of the economic exploitation of tourism by rural Scotland in the wake of the success of *Local Hero*. Caughie observed how the press in Scotland claimed the heroism of the film for Bill Forsyth and for Scotland: 'The local press is exceeded by the local tourist board: living in a land beyond self-parody The Scottish Tourist Board and John Menzies: "invite you to experience the rich delights of Scotland in a *Local Hero* competition, with a prize of two weeks in a Banff Springs Hotel, where the *Local Hero* production team stayed"' (Caughie, 1983: 45). Caughie argues that 'Local heroics depend on domination from elsewhere: they support and confirm each other' (1983: 45). Once more the terms of assessing national cinema are set from a defensive and urban inside, in response to the domination of the American film market from the outside. The economic necessities of tourism to rural Scotland are inimical to the cultural imperatives of representing Scotland to the satisfaction of the urban centre. As David McCrone points out, there is amongst Scottish intellectuals 'a deep aversion to everything native and local' (Beveridge and Turnbull, 1989: 58). The representation of the relation between rural Scotland and the United States, and the self-conscious attempt to unfix and merge identities in *Local Hero*, also functions to expose the relationship between not only Scottish intellectuals and rural Scotland, but Scottish intellectuals, rural Scotland and the Scottish diaspora. Deirdrie MacMahon also questions the consequences of cultural disdain: 'if Americans want to wear tartan and be whisky connoisseurs, why on earth should we discourage them? ... Scotland seems to sneer at its Diaspora while Ireland embraces it' (MacMahon, 2004).

The general suspicion of the use that the tourism industry made of *Local Hero* and the summary of the film as simply another romantic encounter with the landscape can be questioned by placing the film in a critical framework that is not restricted to the politics of the national. Writing nearly ten years after the release of the film in a historical context, Christopher Harvie and Stephen Maxwell describe *Local Hero* as a 'a green classic'[8] and a testament to conservation. Re-viewing the film some twenty years after its release and taking into account the stated aims of Forsyth and Puttnam, the international reading of the film as a testament to the use and conservation of the environment seems prescient in the light of current debates on renewable energy sources. In the light of this re-view, it is also helpful to interrogate a little more deeply just what kind of romantic encounter with the rural landscape is suggested in *Local Hero* and how it might connect with romanticism.

Placing the film in a contemporary frame of environmental politics does offer a means of connecting rather than separating the local, the national and the international that is supported by reviewing the encounter between America and rural Scotland in diasporic and transnational terms, rather than simply as a function of romanticisation and, by extension, tourism. Petrie points out that there is an established tradition of films about journeys to rural Scotland that construct a romantic vision (Petrie, 2000). However, to assume that this vision is completely deficient for the cultural politics of rural Scotland is challenged by the historian T.C. Smout, who carried out research on behalf of Scottish Natural Heritage, a national environmental body formed in 1992 by the Scottish Office (www.snh.org.uk). Smout makes a case for rethinking the assumption that the conservationist and romantic disposition to the Scottish landscape is solely the preserve of the outsider, through a re-reading of the history of romanticism. Smout traces the emergence of different types of attitude to the landscape and its use that he argues inform the roots of Green consciousness in environmental politics (Smout, 1991). These attitudes encompass the romantic, where the unspoiled landscape affects the contemplative spirit of those that gaze upon it, and the political and cultural attitudes towards its use (Smout, 1991). All of these attitudes are reflected in the narrative agents of *Local Hero* and suggest a more historicised and expansive understanding of a romantic disposition towards rural Scotland.

The developments in the culture and politics of rural Scotland offer an example of how encounters between outsiders and the landscape might be reconsidered in rural films as significant as *Local Hero*. The different, connected and unequal localities that *Local Hero* represents – and which gained a wide local, national and international audience – do suggest how the critical frame of Scottish cinema might be expanded to take account of the routes taken from the outside into rural Scotland, by fictional visitors, real visitors and cinema spectators.

Notes

1 Iain Smith, e-mail correspondence.
2 Iain Smith, e-mail correspondence.
3 In Scottish law every owner or tenant of a property that falls within the boundaries of a landed estate is subject to the demands of the feudal superior (www.scotland.gov.uk).
4 Iain Smith, e-mail correspondence.
5 Production notes. David Puttnam Collection. British Film Institute Library.
6 The Scottish word 'gloaming' refers to the part of the day in Highland

Scotland after the sun has gone down and before the sky is completely dark.

7 John Hill makes a similar argument about the unfixing of Scottish identity in Forsyth's previous film *Gregory's Girl* (Hill, 1999: 243).

8 Harvie and Maxwell point out that 'one platform construction firm settled on a site at Drumbuie in Wester Ross which had been covenanted to the National Trust for Scotland (an episode which provided the germ of that 'green' classic *Local Hero*)' (Harvie and Maxwell, 1992: 218).

References

Astaire, M. and Hunter, A. (1982), 'Hollywood hits the west', *Scottish Field* (November).

Beveridge, C. and Turnbull, R. (1989), *The Eclipse of Scottish Culture: Inferiorism and the Intellectuals* (Edinburgh: Polygon).

Brah, A. (1996), *Cartographies of Diaspora: Contesting Identities* (London: Routledge).

Cairns, C. (1983), 'Visitors from the stars: Scottish film culture', *Cencrastus*, 11 (January): 6–11.

Caughie, J. (1983), 'Support whose Local Hero?', *Cencrastus*, 14 (autumn): 44–5.

Eberts, J. and Ilott, T. (1990), *My Indecision Is Final: The Rise and Fall of Goldcrest Films* (London: Faber and Faber).

Glasgow Women and Film Collective (1983), 'Bill and Ben The Innocent Men?', *Cencrastus*, 14 (autumn): 42–4.

Hague, E. (2002), 'Tartan Day and the appropriation of Scottish identities in the United States', in Harvey, D.C., Jones, R., McInroy, N. and Milligan, C. (eds), *Celtic Geographies: Old Culture, New Times* (London: Routledge), pp. 139–56.

Hardy, F. (1990), *Scotland in Film* (Edinburgh: Edinburgh University Press).

Harvie, C. and Maxwell, S. (1992), 'Scottish nationalism and North Sea oil', in Smout T.C. (ed.), *Scotland and the Sea* (Edinburgh: John Donald Publishers).

Higson, A. (1995), *Waving the Flag* (Oxford: Clarendon Press).

Hill, J. (1999), *British Cinema in the 1980s* (Oxford: Oxford University Press).

McArthur, C. (1982), *Scotch Reels: Scotland in Cinema and Television* (London: BFI).

McArthur, C. (1994), 'The cultural necessity of a poor Celtic cinema', in Hill, J., McLoone, M. and Hainsworth, P. (eds), *Border Crossing: Film in Ireland, Britain and Europe* (Belfast: Institute of Irish Studies, and London: BFI), pp. 112–25.

McArthur, C. (1996), 'The Scottish discursive unconscious', in Cameron A. and Scullion, A. (eds), *Scottish Popular Theatre and Entertainment* (Glasgow: Glasgow University Library).

McArthur, C. (2003), *Whisky Galore! & The Maggie* (London: I.B. Tauris).

MacMahon, D. (2004), 'Scotland at the Smithsonian: beyond the cultural cringe?', *Scottish Affairs*, 47 (spring).

Malcolmson, S.L. (1985), 'Modernism comes to the cabbage patch: Bill Forsyth and the Scottish Cinema', *Film Quarterly*, 38 (spring): 16–21.

Milne, T. (1983), *Monthly Film Bulletin*, 52(2): 87–8.

Minh-ha, T.T. (1989), 'Outside in Inside Out', in Willemen, P. (ed.), *Questions of Third Cinema* (London: BFI), pp. 133–49.

Nowell-Smith, G. (1985), 'But do we need it?', in Auty, M. and Roddick, N. (eds), *British Cinema Now* (London: BFI), pp. 147–58.

Pendreigh, B. (2002), *The Pocket Scottish Movie Book* (Edinburgh: Mainstream Publishing).

Petrie, D. (2000), *Screening Scotland* (London: BFI).

Roddick, N. (1983), 'A light in the sky', *Sight and Sound*, 52(2): 138–9.

Smout, C. (1991), 'The Highlands and the roots of green consciousness, 1750–1990', *Occasional Paper; Scottish Natural Heritage*, no. 1.

Yule, A. (1988), *David Puttnam: The Story So Far* (Edinburgh: Mainstream Publishing Company).

Internet sources

www.geo.ed.ac.uk/home/scotland/tales/hero.html
www.scotland.gov.uk
www.scottishscreen.com
www.snh.org.uk

8

'Imagination can be a damned curse in this country':[1] material geographies of filmmaking and the rural

Andy C. Pratt

'[I'm a] nobody ... [I'm] just an extra' (Charlie Conlon, *Stones in his Pockets*, Act 1, Jones, 2000)

Introduction

Marie Jones's (2000) play *Stones in his Pockets* provides a useful introduction to both the positive and negative aspects of filmmaking in rural areas. The play focuses on two extras that have been employed to help out with a US film shoot in rural Ireland. The play, in part, points to the way that filmmakers and rural communities seek to use one another in order to achieve their own ends. For the two local protagonists the dream is of a life-change, escape and an opportunity in film (one of them has a script that he dreams of pursuing). For the filmmakers the rural is an idealised location where filming costs are reduced (but, where, from the director's point of view, the cows are not Irish enough). The village, in turn, hopes to reap income from the incomers in the few short weeks of shooting. Yet the play's title also refers to the dark side of dreams: the means of suicide of one of the villagers during the filming. Jones's play, although fictional, is set in County Kerry, in the far southwest of Ireland, near to the Blasket Islands.[2] The film in the play is *The Quiet Valley*, a not-so-obscure reference to the John Ford films *How Green is My Valley*, and *The Quiet Man*, which were filmed in this area in the 1950s. Twenty years later *Ryan's Daughter* (David Lean, 1970) made the landscape an additional draw for visitors. The Irish film industry has its roots as far back as 1916; however, despite its attractions to visiting filmmakers, it was not until 1958 that a permanent professional studio was established there (Ardmore Studios[3]), Even today Ireland lacks comprehensive post-production capabilities; work either goes to London or Los Angeles (Pratt, 1999; 2001a). From 1981 onwards the Irish Government have sought to support filmmaking (despite a reversal of policy in 1987–93). The particular use of tax incentives has made Ireland renowned for its location shooting; a notable big-budget Hollywood film shot there was *Braveheart* (Mel Gibson, 1995).[4] While there is a small and vibrant low-budget filmmaking community, major films simply use Ireland as a location shoot.

Similar stories can be found in Canada, Australia, New Zealand, Slovakia, South Africa, France, in every major city and many rural districts. It is not simply a case of stage-struck politicians but an indicator that images have become a powerful tool for localities to compete with one another in an era of increasingly mobile international investment. This chapter examines this trend and, after grounding it in filmmaking practices, evaluates the potential outcomes. The chapter picks up the theme of the tension between dreams and reality highlighted in Jones's play. In an unorthodox move the chapter considers the material practices of film making rather than dealing with its representational aspects. It also echoes the quotation in the title by adopting a rather cautionary note regarding the aspiration of rural communities to profit from film location shooting. As will be noted below, the practice of rural (and urban) communities acting as locations for film (and television) shoots is now commonplace. Moreover, many rural (and urban) communities now vie with one another to attract the next big production (Pratt, 2001a). Recent examples are the various locations in the UK in the film series *Harry Potter* (Christopher Columbus, 2001), and *The Lord of the Rings* trilogy (Peter Jackson, 2001; 2002; 2003) in New Zealand. In both cases national and local tourist offices have sought to capitalise on filmgoers' desires to visit the scenes made famous in the film. Thus, tourism is a second way in which the material intersects with the representational. Of course, one irony is that with so much digital post-production of filmmaking, the locations do not appear as they are seen in films: they can, and are, morphed into numerous forms. It raises the question of what exactly the film tourist is viewing in the countryside. However, this must be the topic of another essay. What I want to explore here concerns the material practices of filmmaking and to what extent such dreams and representations (that is, the projected benefits) are reflected in reality.

In order to explore this question I will sketch out the processes through which film is made, concentrating on the organisation of the 'back of camera' activities; I will illustrate this with some UK data on employment and exhibition. Second, I outline the changing process of film production and the rise of what has been termed 'runaway production'.[5] Runaway production is considered, on the one hand, a threat to Hollywood and, on the other, an opportunity for many global locations that hope to benefit from a migrant film industry. Finally, I explore the contradictions of location shooting for rural areas. Before this I will review some of the relevant debates in the literature.

Situating rural filmmaking

As discussed in the opening chapter of this book, the relationship between Film Studies and the other Social Sciences has been a poor one; mainly based on lack of engagement rather than dispute. Recent work in geography and sociology has reflected a closer link to more traditional socio-economic concerns with a focus on the production of film (Christopherson and Storper, 1986; 1989; Coe, 2000a; 2000b; Blair, 2001; Blair, Grey and Randle, 2001; Blair, Culkin and Randle, 2003; Scott, 2004; Kong, 2005). Much of this work has explored the development of regional clusters of film-making and the impact of labour markets, complex patterns of firm organisation, and cross-firm networking in their development. The upshot of this work is that filmmaking is an urban phenomenon. Debates that extend beyond this consider the national and international scale, often, though not exclusively, engaging with the impacts of 'runaway production' (Coe, 2001; Scott, 2002; Randle and Culkin, 2005): that is, the concern (seen from the perspective of Hollywood) that some aspect of shooting is being re-located away from Hollywood,[6] and thus leading to the dispersal of economic benefits from that place. As Christopherson and Storper (1986) noted in their study, 'runaway' production is a process of organisational change that has been experienced in many industries: the film industry moving from the 'film factory' of Hollywood to disintegrated independent companies is but another example. As Coe and others have noted (Coe, 2001; O'Regan and

Goldsmith, 2002), this opportunity is capitalised upon by cities seeking to position themselves in the film industry, though there are few examples of major cities establishing permanent new studios.[7] The slew of cities and rural areas that have attracted location shooting for a few days at a time is another issue.

The wider context of 'runaway production' is the increasing internationalisation of economic activities. Many authors have pointed to the growth of internationalisation, and to the lengths that countries will go to attract 'mobile' or 'foreign direct' investment to their locale (Harvey, 1989a; 1989b; Dicken, 2003). Specifically, a number of writers have pointed to the distortion of local priorities in order to compete in such an international 'beauty contest' (Logan and Molotch, 1987; Kearns and Philo, 1993; Hall and Hubbard, 1998). In order to compete, cities commonly adopt a number of strategies. On one hand, they are seeking more visibility through their own advertising and, increasingly, through 'appearing' on film and television.[8] On the other hand, they seek to capitalise on their 'unique selling proposition': usually built environment or cultural heritage.[9] Film, of course, offers a good opportunity to hit 'two birds with one stone' (Swann, 2001).

The major silence in this literature is of course 'rural' filmmaking. This is not to suggest that these factors do not apply in rural as opposed to urban locales; they do, perhaps even more strongly. Labour costs have traditionally been lower in rural areas, and the same would apply to the costs of renting facilities and properties. However, against this are the costs of attracting the 'talent' (actors and technicians) to a remote location, and the extra costs of accommodation. Moreover, many specialist facilities and equipment may need to be imported. As can be appreciated, many anticipated benefits to a local economy might be lost in this way.

The anticipated benefits of tourism might be expected to be more profound in a rural area; in some senses a proper legacy to the short filming presence. Even relatively small numbers of visitors may have a considerable impact. Finally, and more ambivalently, there is the question of whose representation is being 'captured'. Given the economic agenda in foreign direct investment strategies the 'image' tends to be one of an elite group and thus, implicitly, not shared by all (Pratt, 1996; Pratt, 2000). Such tensions could potentially be starker in rural areas. This assumes, of course, that viewers can, or even wish to, identify the locale in the film. In the majority of films the background is just that: background in the sense that it is 'rural' in a signifying sense rather than as a referent. Within the constraints of continuity, 'real' spaces may be mixed and matched to create the effect that the director is seeking; worse still, for the locale seeking to capitalise on its starring role, the 'actual country-side' might be digitally enhanced. Of course, the digital enhancement is part of creating the spectacle which may have bene-fits for the locale. The point, well ventilated in post-structuralist debates, is that there is no simple one-to-one relationship of coun-tryside–film–viewer as is often assumed in the place-marketing and place-promotion literature.

Film production: organisation, material production

So much for the imagined rewards of visibility on the silver screen: in order to evaluate the fantasy of recognition we need a dose of realism, or at least another perspective on what filmmaking involves. The economics and organisation of filmmaking are clearly relevant here, especially if we are to examine the regenera-tive claims of those seeking to attract filmmaking to rural areas either as part of image promotion, employment generation or tourism.

In order to review the spatial and organisational structure of filmmaking, it is useful to sketch in some of the broader context of the film industry. First, the industry is dominated by a small number of very large companies that are primarily based in the US (Aksoy and Robins, 1992). These companies control the larger-budget international films that are exhibited. However, these companies are also serviced by a large number of production companies who actually develop and make the films. In the early twentieth century, under the classic 'Hollywood system', these functions were integrated into film companies, as was distribution and exhibition (Scott, 2005). The landmark 'Paramount decision' (1948) led to a break-up of this monopoly. On one hand this was a regulatory shift, on the other it was one that made possible a number of cost savings for larger film distributors and funders who could pick and choose projects, directors and other technicians on a project-by-project basis, in effect saving on development costs and avoiding a lock-in to particular contracts. This system has been termed 'post-Fordist' in character (Christopherson and Storper,

1986; 1989). However, in recent years to all intents and purposes the 'Paramount decision' has been reversed in the courts and vertical integration has regained momentum albeit mediated by technological change (digitisation) (Christopherson, 2003). In the UK, filmmaking is concentrated in London and it is characterised by a large number of networked small production companies that are characteristically formed anew for each film around a small core of principals – usually producers and directors (Pratten and Deakin, 2000; Nachum and Keeble, 2003). Most of the employees are thus freelance or working on serial short-term contracts (Blair, Grey and Randle, 2001; Blair, 2003).

The point is that there are few film studios, and fewer post-production facilities, in rural areas; moreover, there are declining numbers of cinemas (Hubbard, 2002). The rather crude, but indicative, data that exists on employment in the film industry[10] in the UK demonstrates this (Table 8.1). Depending upon how one classifies the rural, there is something around 10 per cent of employment in the film industry in rural areas. Data on the number of screens in rural areas tells a similar story (Table 8.2). In fact, as there is a positive correlation between screen density and film admissions, the fewer screens in rural areas[11] also translates into fewer viewers per screen (Film Council, 2003: 35; Wainwright, 2004). Moreover, the programming in rural cinemas is significantly less diverse than that of urban areas (Film Council, 2003).

These crude data make the point rather forcefully that filmmaking and filmgoing is predominantly an urban activity; and in the case of the former, massively dominated by London. While we may see rural locations on screen, films are not made in rural, or indeed, most urban areas in the UK.[12] In the remainder of this section I will outline how films are made, how this relates to space, and where and how the rural enters the big picture.

Filmmaking can best be conceived of as a 'production network' whereby a number of discrete but inter-related processes must be integrated (Pratt, 2004). However, particular elements have particular location requirements, or some kind of inertia (social, political or economic). Each part of the network is not evenly balanced in terms of time, effort or expenditure. Crudely put, filmmaking can be considered as having four elements: pre-production, production, post-production and distribution. Pre-production concerns script writing and development, pre-planning and securing finance

Table 8.1　UK film screens by location 2001–3 (Film Council, 2003)

	Numbers of screens			% of screens in 2003
	2001	2002	2003	
City centre	1404	1466	1470	44.3
Out of town	1207	1199	1234	37.2
Edge of centre	410	456	464	14.0
Suburban	46	34	33	1.0
Rural	107	103	117	3.5
Total	3174	3258	3318	100.0

Table 8.2　Employment in film industry, 2002, by type of location, UK (© Nomis, 2004, with permission)

	Number in SIC: 9211	% in SIC: 9212	Number in SIC: 9212	% in SIC: 9211	Number in SIC: 9211 and 9212	% in SIC 9211 and 9212
London	10155	61	3241	74	13396	64
Other urban	4950	30	918	21	5868	28
Rural	1084	7	170	4	1254	6
Remote	478	3	53	1	531	3
Total	16667	100	4382	100	21049	100

Notes: 9211 is the industrial classification code for 'Motion picture and video production'; 9212 is the industrial classification code for 'Motion picture and video distribution'. The classification of urban, rural and remote relate to the degree of built up land use.

and legal requirements. Production usually involves the hiring of 'talent' (actors and filmmakers, as well as numerous ancillary staff too numerous to detail here, but this contributes 90 per cent of the credits that roll at the end of the typical film), plus the cost of cameras, studio-time and sets (or location costs). The post-production stage takes the film and edits it, dubs sound and adds special effects and the titles. Last, but certainly not least, is distribution. This includes making prints of the film and physically distributing them to cinemas; it involves negotiation with cinemas, marketing and promotion.

Implied in each stage is a level of infrastructure investment and the availability of a particular labour market. In the former case it may entail office space for the writers, directors and producers, a sound stage and related cameras, lights and sets, editing suites, and cinemas; in the latter case, a very specialised labour force for different stages: technicians, administrators, actors, and so forth. All of which will be employed at different stages, and for various amounts of time. The exact balance of costs varies enormously project by project, and may be different for a Hollywood blockbuster as opposed to a UK independent film, or a film that uses extensive digital effects. Furthermore, the particular organisational form within which filmmaking exists can and does change. Costs are very difficult to untangle, but the broad breakdown works out something like: 10 per cent pre-production, 40 per cent production, 10 per cent post-production, and 40 per cent distribution and exhibition. Moreover, a large proportion of production costs are tied up with camera hire and fees for the star actors, as well as the crew. To provide a sense of scale Vogel (2001: 80) notes that the average US film cost $51million to make in 1999.

Very broadly, *pre-production* work allows the team to pitch their project to a funder or a distributor. The issue of selling a script is very 'touchy feely' and commonly operates within a small community that works on a 'reputation' system (Kong, 2005). Thus, directors need to pay close attention to market trends and funders' prejudices. They also need to maintain 'visibility'. It is not difficult to see how this draws directors to a few major cities, along with other directors, funders and distributors. These locations are also close to eventual markets.[13]

Usually, if the distributor agrees, the bank lends the money. As usual it is a story of risk minimisation; just like a mortgage. The distributor is looking to the market and how many viewers they might get, as well as the deals that can be obtained with exhibitors (who may be one and the same). Upon funding, the project is realised and in *production*. Here there are a number of issues. First, there are 'script demands' suggesting a particular location. However, the director has the choice of reproducing these in a studio, or going to a location named in the script, finding a 'stand in' location, or morphing an existing studio or location using special effects. Here we get to the nub of the question about runaway production: what money can be saved? In large part, it has to be pointed out, 'runaway production' refers to re-location of a Hollywood film to be shot in (urban) Vancouver, Sydney, Prague or London. Thus, it is a process of trading off cheaper crew, more flexible union agreements, and facilities between one site and another. 'On location' shooting is different. Here one is looking for the marginal savings between studio and non-studio time. Talent and equipment are accounted for in both cases. However, equipment and talent may be more expensive to move around and accommodate for the on-location period.[14] So the potential cost-savings between 'on-location' and 'studio' shooting may be very small in the production budget, and miniscule in a whole budget. Moreover, the number of days of working on location will be very small, usually no more than four weeks, and often considerably less. The salient point here is that the key 'value added' elements of the film industry production network do not lie in location shooting; quite the opposite. To simply attract film shooting is not to cash in on the huge amounts of money that the film industry earns.[15]

Post-production may happen many thousands of miles away from the production site. However, given that the director will want to view the 'rushes', and this may affect subsequent filming, proximity is useful. Post-production facilities are very expensive; they are used for a very short time by one filmmaker, and employ very specialised technicians. Thus, there is a clear case of agglomeration economies. Post-production facilities best serve numerous filmmakers, and thus tend to gravitate to central locations. The location of *marketing and distribution* is not critical, but does relate to filmmakers and the ownership structure of exhibition spaces.

Representation, regeneration and promotion

Thus far I have presented a very negative view of the local benefits of filmmaking. These benefits, it is claimed, are a minute proportion of the total budget. Moreover, the actual location may be unidentifiable, or digitally enhanced. However, it would be wrong to write off the impact. In fact, a stronger case can be made for rural compared to urban areas on the basis that the impact could be greater in terms of a boost to a relatively smaller local economy. It would be inaccurate to imply that all filmmaking took place in studios. Initially, there were limitations due to lighting and film quality that tied films to controlled locations. With technological advances 'on-location' shots became popular. However, the possibilities were always set against the risks of bad weather or local problems that might disrupt a shooting schedule (which is very costly). The aim of this section is to review the potential benefits that rural areas may gain from filmmaking activities taking place there.

The glamour of film and local politicians is a combustible mixture. However, the estimation of direct and indirect economic benefits has created a legitimate argument to promote local filmmaking. Earlier in this chapter I discounted the possibility of film companies basing their sound stages in rural areas. Clearly, there are many traditional economic advantages to locating on the edge of urban areas when land is cheaper, but access is still easy. The exception is for small and independent filmmakers where the case may well be different. There are many areas that support a local film culture and filmmakers can benefit enormously from a reasonable sound stage. For example, the new development of a sound stage in Cornwall (St Agnes, South West Film studios[16]) has sought to capture filmmaking for Cornwall. It is claimed that 'two or three feature films would keep the studios at capacity throughout the year, supporting between 50 and 200 jobs – depending on demand – in addition to directly employing ten full-time staff'. Such employment would represent a slight boost to an economy based upon agriculture and seasonal tourism.

Clearly, the attraction of big-budget location shooting is the target of most initiatives by local communities. Here three categories of impact can be identified. Firstly, direct employment; secondly, indirect job and service creation; and, thirdly, tourism benefits. Local Screen Commissions are always happy to cite that numbers of jobs that were created during filming. Sometimes the numbers look impressive. However, they need to be treated with caution. As an example we can look at the production of *The Last Samurai* (Edward Zwiek, 2003), a substantial part of which was filmed on location in Taranaki, New Zealand (*not* Japan) in 2003 (Venture Taranaki, 2004). This was a US$170-million film, a major Hollywood production. It is claimed that 50 per cent was invested in the New Zealand economy, and 58 per cent of that 50 per cent ($50m) in the Taranaki economy. The number of jobs created locally was 616; this total includes direct jobs and those as a result of increased local trade, most likely via hotel bed-nights, transportation, and food and drink. This sounds a lot, except that the impacts were only for six months: 308 full-time equivalents on a one-off. The key point is that such development is not sustainable (unless another film of this size were to follow on), so the project was a minor salve to local unemployment. Although there are no similar details available, an interesting comparison might be with the smaller-budget *Oscar and Lucinda* (Gillian Armstrong, 1997) filmed in Grafton, New South Wales, Australia (Martin, 2001). The thirteen-week shoot generated an estimated AUS$0.75m for the local economy. If the rate of job creation was in line with *The Last Samurai* as reported above, then just four local full-time equivalent jobs might have been created; moreover, *Oscar and Lucinda* did not have a call for as many extras as *The Last Samurai*.[17]

The third category of impact is the tourist effect; there is a small body of research that tries to understand the scale and impact of film (and television) tourism. The general argument is that distinctive locations will attract visitors: 'the ultimate product placement' (Busby and Klug, 2001). However, the impact is not direct; it depends on the successful combination of additional factors. First, that the viewer recognises the location; second, that the film is sufficiently successful to attract a big audience; third, that tourists thus spurred on can actually access the site. A report notes that the *Lord of the Rings Location Guidebook* sold 70,000 copies in the seven weeks following the film release (Mintel, 2003).

In the case of *The Last Samurai*, there were some further problems given that New Zealand was acting as a 'stand in' for Japan: 'Warners [the film company] did not want the movie to look like New Zealand and does not want to promote this fact' (Venture Taranaki, 2004); this is despite the fact that 74 per cent of the film was shot in New Zealand. Another example is the remote village of Furness, Scotland; especially the phone box, which had an iconic presence in the film *Local Hero* (Bill Forsyth, 1983). A report notes that the beach used in the film is several miles away from the village, and only accessible via a poorly signed track (Alderson, 2003). On the other hand, the wedding suite in the rural hotel featured in *Four Weddings and a Funeral* (Mike Newell, 1993) was booked up a year in advance after the film was released, and visitors to Thailand in the wake of *The Beach* (Danny Boyle, 2000) were up 11 per cent overall, and 22 per cent in the case of the fifteen to twenty-four age group (Mintel, 2003).

The *Harry Potter* films are included in the British Tourist Authority's 'film location map'[18] (VisitBritain, 2004). This is a tourist strategy that seeks to 'piggy-back' on successful films and point tourists to film locations and other locations that share a similar imagery. So in the Harry Potter case links are included to a variety of steam-train attractions, as well as those featured in the film. Interestingly, in the case of Goathland Station, rural North Yorkshire – which doubles as Hogwarts station in the Harry Potter films – while visitor numbers are up, a local survey revealed that 15 per cent of visitors to the area were looking for Harry Potter locations, yet 38 per cent had been drawn by its association with an ITV television series: *Heartbeat* (Topham, 2003).

The process of attracting film shooting is increasingly becoming institutionalised; there is now an international association of screen council / film commissions,[19] whose membership worldwide is in excess of 300. This agency seeks to assist filmmakers to find the right location, and to shoot their film there. Even if successful for local agencies, the impact has a relatively small 'halo' of economic benefits that fades quickly.

In recent years the renewed concentration of film exhibition into fewer hands, and the economies of scale that can be reaped in a multiplex, has led to the decline of independent cinemas. It is perhaps ironic that in this time when rural film shooting does seem to be in ascendance it is paralleled by a decline in filmgoing by rural inhabitants, and a decline in rural screens: what the UK Film Council calls the 'screen gap'. A recent initiative utilises the possibility of digital film distribution and projection to create economically sustainable film exhibition in rural areas.

Finally, we might consider the potential for different forms of rural film production that are led by cultural rather than economic agendas. A good example in this respect is France. Many small French communities have their own film festival and screen commission, and many also offer subsidies to filmmakers. While there is little evidence on the use and take-up of these funds, their small scale and the generous film funding and distribution deals in France ensure that rural film has the potential to be enacted in different, and perhaps less obvious, ways (Pratt, 2001a). Perhaps this is one direction that other rural communities ought to explore:

to develop images and expressions of their own rather than acting as a backdrop for Hollywood. Only then, perhaps, is there a possibility of the elaboration of the multiplicity of 'rurals' rather than simply one externally imposed and idealised version (Murdoch and Pratt, 1993).

Conclusion

The film industry has an unusual structure: domination by a few trans-national companies, and a multiplicity of less powerful short-term micro-production companies. It is the production companies that actually 'make' films; to do so they have to employ a range of specialist and skilled employees for a short period of time and bring them together in one, or a number, of places to actually do the shooting. The costs at this stage are enormous, and delays, hitches and hold-ups must be avoided if the whole filmmaking machine is not to grind to a halt. Thus, using a studio, where all the variables can be controlled, has its advantages. Moreover, a location that is close to a diverse and skilled labour force helps. Location shooting can clearly add to the artistic conception and execution of the film; however, seldom is a background unique and it may be interchangeable with another, or digitally enhanced in the post-production phase. It is not clear that location shooting is done to simply save money.

The key desire of filmmakers is to 'get in', film the shots, and 'get out' as quickly as possible with minimal hassle. Rural communities would like the 'film circus' to linger as what economic gains there are to be had for the local community from filmmaking rely upon the use of local services. Secondary gains, through visibility in the final film, are neither guaranteed nor certain; however, on occasion they can be significant in the short term.

Despite the self-interested scare-mongering of Hollywood itself, film production is not departing from the major film centres yet. Moreover, as I have pointed out above, the whole production phase (including pre-, post- and production itself) may only absorb 50 per cent of a film budget; of that 50 per cent the high-value-added parts, those activities that sustain permanent employees and facilities, tend to be locked into urban locations (especially post-production and film financing), as does the whole distribution system. So, realistically, location shooting is a small-time and ephemeral activity that may produce a local bonanza once in a while. Moreover, the chances of a distinctive rural image appearing in the final film are slim: more commonly they end up on the cutting-room floor, or 'made over' in the digital post-production suite.

As I have also noted, perhaps the real crisis of rural film is going un-noticed: first, the loss of exhibition spaces; second, the rush to appear for five seconds in a Hollywood movie is perhaps under-mining more thoughtful investment in a film infrastructure, one that might be supportive of local filmmakers exploring a more variegated and diverse image of the rural. At present, economic pressures seem to be driving both local filmmaking and exhibition out of rural areas; in the process, rural areas are literally becoming a backdrop for urban film audiences. This surely has implications for how 'we' (as mainly urban-dwelling audiences) see the country-side more generally.

Aside from looking at the rise of rural film shoots and the attempts of communities to harness them to an economic end this chapter has sought to place the material practice of filmmaking centre stage. It is hoped that the overwhelming weight of analysis of images and representations of the rural might be tempered by an insight into both their means of production and their dissemina-tion. In so doing I think I have pointed to a demise of the practices of production of representations by people who have a strong connection to those places. When we think about the circulation of images, we might perhaps consider who produced them, why they were produced, and how the subjects and objects of their represen-tation might like to respond. Perhaps then imagination may not be a curse, but instead a positive asset, for rural communities.

The political economy of filmmaking is going to present some continuing challenges to rural filmmakers. In many senses rural (or, generally, non-Hollywood) filmmaking is as much of an 'extra' as the bit player who delivers the line in Jones's play quoted at the beginning of this chapter: something that can be used and abused, and discarded with little social or cultural responsibility beyond the immediate legal or contractual. More optimistically, rural film-making does create new opportunities; potentially these filmmaking events can be used like a catalyst to re-imagine the countryside and to engage with it in new ways. For rural dwellers this may also present a short-run opportunity to stimulate the local economy. In terms of film culture the real opportunities at present may be technological in nature; the cheap production possible using digital cameras, lap-top editing and digital distribution may bring filmmaking within in the grasp of more people. Potentially, this could offer a platform for rural filmmakers to pursue their craft without moving away, or having to address urban agendas, or urban representations of the rural. In the end it is this process that may offer the only way of really challenging, or at least offering some diversity to, representations of the rural in film culture.

Acknowledgements

Thanks to Galina Gornostaeva for extracting the employment data used in Table 8.1, Janet Gill for the theatre programme from *Stones in his Pockets*, and David Steele at the UK Film Council for ideas on film and tourism. The paper was based partially upon research funded by the ESRC (Grant No: RES-000-23-0653). The responsibility for the interpretation of this information lies with me alone.

Notes

1 This is a quotation Brother Gerard, Act 2, Jones (2000).
2 This paragraph draws upon Anon. (2000). The Blasket Islands, uninhabited since 1953, are now a popular subject for Irish historical writers, and temporary home to many, as well as a popular film shooting location www.blasketislands.com.
3 Located 12 miles south of Dublin: www.ardmore.ie. Ardmore is still the only fully functioning '4 wall' studio in the Republic.
4 Of course, Braveheart is a 'Scottish' film. This fact further underlines the confusion of location and narrative in the viewers' mind.
5 Runaway production is an emotive term that refers to any on location shooting (some of which may be in a remote studio). The US film industry terms it 'runaway' when shooting does not happen on US soil.
6 Plus other film centres such as Hong Kong, Mumbai and London.
7 The exceptions here are Vancouver and Sydney; and, latterly, Prague. All, in one way or another, are based upon cost savings compared to Hollywood.
8 Most of the academic work has concerned itself with print-based advertising and representations (Short and Kim, 1998).
9 Or indeed, commissioning architects to create new icons that will court controversy and attract publicity.

10   Employment data on the film industry is an underestimate due to the crude taxonomies and lack of dedicated classifications that focus only on the film industry (Pratt, 1997; 2001b).

11   Rural screens have been declining year on year, although a reverse trend occurred in 2003. However, this 13.6 per cent increase represented just 14 extra 'rural screens' (Film Council, 2003: Table 6.4).

12   This is a pattern found in most other nations: one city dominates filmmaking. Moreover, filmmaking is confined to a small number of locations in the world (Scott, 2005).

13   Proximity is not vital here, as complex – and expensive – first-screening market research is carried out, even to the extent of re-editing a film that does not play well at first screening.

14   Once again, for talent and crew, urban agglomeration effects operate. They tend to live in urban areas and thus may be able to travel to and from home daily. If they go on-location they need to be accommodated and the situation of time agreements can be complex.

15   It is significant that the film industry is one of the major contributors to US exports (just exceeded by computer games) (Siwek, 2002). Film receipts and profits go to the headquarters, not to the locations where a film is shot.

16   It claims to be the first purpose-built studio in the UK since 1923 www.southwestfilmstudios.com/ne/ne-3.html.

17   In the case of *The Last Samurai*, 280 people were contracted for the whole film and there were 400 short-term extras (mainly from Japan) (Venture Taranaki 2004). It is not only film that has an impact, but also television.

18   At the time of writing the focus was the 'The Master and Commander movie map'; previous movie-maps featured have included 'Johnny English – Mission to Britain' and 'Harry Potter – Discover the Magic of Britain'.

19   www.afci.org: Association of Film Commissioners International.

References

Aksoy, A. and Robins, K. (1992), 'Hollywood for the 21st century – global competition for critical mass in image markets', *Cambridge Journal of Economics*, 16(1): 1–22.

Alderson A. (2003), 'Hero's welcome', *The Guardian* (10 May 2003).

Anon. (2000), *Stones in his Pockets: Programme Notes* (London, New Ambassadors Theatre).

Blair, H. (2001), '"You're only as good as your last job": the labour process and labour market in the British film industry', *Work, Employment and Society*, 15(1): 149–69.

Blair, H. (2003), 'Winning and losing in flexible labour markets: the formation and operation of networks of interdependence in the UK Film Industry', *Sociology: The Journal of the British Sociological Association*, 37(4): 677–94.

Blair, H., Culkin, N. and Randle, K. (2003), 'From London to Los Angeles: a comparison of local labour market processes in the US and UK film industries', *International Journal of Human Resource Management*, 14(4): 619–33.

Blair, H., Grey S. and Randle K. (2001), 'Working in film – employment in a project based industry', *Personnel Review*, 30(1–2): 170–85.

Busby, G. and Klug, J. (2001), 'Movie-induced tourism: the challenge of measurement and other issues', *Journal of Vacation Marketing*, 7(4): 323.

Christopherson, S. (2003), 'The limits to "new regionalism" (re)learning from the media industries', *Geoforum*, 34(4): 413–15.

Christopherson, S. and Storper, M. (1986), 'The city as studio – the world as back lot – the impact of vertical disintegration on the location of the motion-picture industry', *Environment and Planning D-Society & Space*, 4(3): 305–20.

Christopherson, S. and Storper, M. (1989), 'The effects of flexible specialization on industrial-politics and the labor-market – the motion-picture industry', *Industrial and Labor Relations Review*, 42(3): 331–47.

Coe, N.M. (2000a), 'On location: American capital and the local labour market in the Vancouver film industry', *International Journal of Urban and Regional Research*, 24(1): 79–94.

Coe, N.M. (2000b), 'The view from out west: embeddedness, interpersonal relations and the development of an indigenous film industry in Vancouver', *Geoforum* 31(4): 391–407.

Coe, N.M. (2001), 'A hybrid agglomeration? The development of a satellite- marshallian industrial district in Vancouver's film industry', *Urban Studies*, 38(10): 1753–75.

Dicken, P. (2003), *Global Shift: Reshaping the Global Economic Map in the 21st Century* (London: Sage).

Film Council (2003), *Statistical Yearbook of the UK Film Council* (London: UK Film Council).

Hall, T. and Hubbard, P. (1998), *The Entrepreneurial City: Geographies of Politics, Regime, and Representation* (New York: Wiley).

Harvey D. (1989a), 'Flexible accumulation through urbanization: reflections on 'post-modernism' in the American city', in Harvey, D. (ed.), *The Urban Experience* (Oxford: Blackwell), pp. 256–78.

Harvey, D. (1989b), 'From managerialism to entrepreneurialism – the transformation in urban governance in late capitalism', *Geografiska Annaler Series B-Human Geography*, 71(1): 3–17.

Hubbard, P. (2002), 'Screen-shifting: consumption, "riskless risks" and the changing geographies of cinema', *Environment and Planning A*, 34: 1239–58.

Jones, M. (2000) *Stones in his Pockets* (London: Nick Hern Books).

Kearns, G. and Philo, C. (1993), *Selling Places: The City as Cultural Capital, Past and Present* (Oxford and New York: Pergamon Press)

Kong, L. (2005), 'The sociality of cultural industries: Hong Kong's cultural policy and film industry', *International Journal of Cultural Policy*, 11(1): 61–76.

Logan, J.R. and Molotch, H.L. (1987), *Urban Fortunes: The Political Economy of Place* (Berkeley: University of California Press).

Martin, G. (2001), 'Debate on rural and regional film industry' (*NSW Legislative Hansard*), p. 9371)

Mintel International (2003), 'Film tourism: the global picture', *Travel and Tourism Analyst*, October.

Murdoch, J. and Pratt, A.C. (1993), 'Rural studies – modernism, postmodernism and the post-rural', *Journal of Rural Studies*, 9(4): 411–27.

Nachum, L. and Keeble, D. (2003), 'Neo-Marshallian clusters and global networks – the linkages of media firms in central London', *Long Range Planning*, 36(5): 459–80.

O'Regan, T. and Goldsmith, B. (2002), *The Policy Environment of the Contemporary Film Studio* (Canberra: DCITA, Communications Research Forum).

Pratt, A.C. (1996), 'Discourses of rurality: loose talk or social struggle?', *Journal of Rural Studies*, 12(1): 69–78.

Pratt A.C. (1997), 'The cultural industries production system: a case study of employment change in Britain, 1984–91', *Environment and Planning A*, 29(11); 1953–74.

Pratt A.C. (1999), *Technological and Organisational Change in the European Audio-Visual Industries: An Exploratory Analysis of the Consequences for Employment* (Strasbourg: European Audio Visual Observatory).

Pratt, A.C. (2000), 'Cultural tourism as an urban cultural industry. A critical appraisal' in Interarts (ed.), *Cultural Tourism* (Barcelona: Turisme de Catalunya, Diputació de Barcelona), pp. 33–45.

Pratt A.C. (2001a), *Audiovisual Policy in Europe: The Regional Dimension: Report on a Four Nation Case Study (Ireland, United Kingdom, France, and Germany)* (Strasbourg: European Audiovisual Observatory).

Pratt, A.C. (2001b), 'Understanding the cultural industries: is more less?', *Culturelink*, 35 (special issue): 51–68.

Pratt, A.C. (2004), 'Creative clusters: towards the governance of the creative industries production system?', *Media International Australia*, 112: 50–66.

Pratten, S. and Deakin S. (2000), 'Competitiveness policy and economic organization: the case of the British film industry', *Screen*, 41(2): 217–37.

Randle, K. and Culkin, N. (2005), *Still 'a Perfect World for Capital'? Hollywood in an Era of Globalizing Film Production* (University of Hertfordshire Business School: copy available from authors).

Scott, A.J. (2002), 'A new map of Hollywood: the production and distribution of American motion pictures' *Regional Studies*, 36(9): 957–75.

Scott, A.J. (2004), 'Hollywood and the world: the geography of motion-picture distribution and marketing', *Review of International Political Economy*, 11(1): 33–61.

Scott, A.J. (2005), *On Hollywood: The Place, the Industry* (Princeton, NJ: Princeton University Press).

Short, J.R. and Kim, Y.-K. (1998), 'Urban crises/urban representations: selling the city in difficult times', in Hall, P. and Hubbard, P. (eds), *The Entrepreneurial City: Geographies of Politics, Regime and Representation* (London: John Wiley and Sons), pp. 55–75.

Siwek, S. (2002), *Copyright Industries in the U.S. Economy: The*

2002 Report (Washington: The International Intellectual Property Alliance).

Swann, P. (2001), 'From workshop to backlot: the Greater Philadelphia Film Office', in Shiel, M. and Fitzmaurice, T. (eds), *Cinema and the City: Film and Urban Societies in a Global Context* (Oxford: Blackwell), pp. 88–98.

Topham, G. (2003), 'Harry Potter a wizard for tourism' *The Guardian* (24 April 2003).

Venture Taranaki (2004), *Economic Impact Assessment for the Filming of the Last Samurai in Taranaki* (New Plymouth, Wellington: Investment New Zealand and New Zealand Trade and Enterprise).

VisitBritain (2004), *Movie Map* http://Campaigns.Visitbritain .Com/Moviemap/Index.Htm (London: British Tourist Authority).

Vogel, H.L. (2001), *Entertainment Industry Economics: A Guide for Financial Analysis* (Cambridge: Cambridge University Press).

Wainwright, M. (2004), 'Films fade out for country folk' *The Guardian* (3 March 2004).

9

The Lord of the Rings and transformations in socio-spatial identity in Aotearoa/New Zealand

Martin Phillips

The Lord of the Rings as films in space and spaces of film

Recent years have witnessed growing interest in what Clarke (1997) refers to as 'cinematic geographies', with much work focused on the 'spaces in films', such as 'the space of the shot, the space of the narrative setting; the geographical relationships of various settings in sequence in a film; the mapping of a lived environment on film' (Shiel 2001: 5). Shiel, however, argues that there is another cinematic geography, namely 'films in space', which involves, he argues, the study of such features as 'the shaping of lived ... spaces by cinema as a cultural practice; the spatial organization of its industry at the levels of production, distribution, and exhibition; the role of cinema in globalization' (2001: 5). In this chapter I want to draw on the notions of 'spaces of film' and 'film in space' to examine rural socio-spatial identities being performed within and around the film industry of New Zealand (or Aotearoa, to give it its indigenous title).[1]

New Zealand has had a small film industry since the early twentieth century but it has recently risen to prominence following the decision to shoot a three-feature-film adaptation of Tolkein's *The Lord of the Rings* (hereafter *LOTR*) using the physical landscape locations, studios and production personnel of the country. The films appear to have had a substantial economic and cultural impact in the country: a report for the New Zealand Film Commission, for instance, claimed that most of the films' production costs, reputed at $NZ300 million, had been spent within New Zealand (NZ Institute of Economic Research, 2002). The report argued that the films had impacted the country's film industry, significantly strengthening the production base such that 'New Zealand is no longer just a scenery-based location' and that future international productions in New Zealand were likely to be 'denser in local content' and less reliant on imported film crew (2002: vii). It was also claimed that the films had left 'a unique and lasting footprint' on the country's economy and culture: 'It leaves significant intellectual property and human capital gains. It has changed the way the film world views New Zealand, our capabilities and the risk of doing business here. It has given New Zealand a stunning new profile in our key tourism markets' (2002: iv).

Other 'international productions' have indeed been shot in New Zealand including *The Last Samurai*, *Boogeyman*, *Antarctic Journey*, *Sylvia*, *King Kong* and *The Chronicles of Narnia*. The degree to which these productions are denser in local content and less centred on New Zealand scenery is perhaps questionable, given that the films are all ostensibly located elsewhere than New Zealand and, in the first and last case, clearly make much of the country's scenery. In *The Last Samurai* the choice of location was clearly connected to the presence of Mount Taranaki to act as a simulation of Japan's Mount Fuji, while in *The Chronicles of Narnia* New Zealand stands in, as with *LOTR*, for a mythical landscape bearing the hallmarks of Europe.

The Chief Executive of the Film Commission claimed that the study of the impacts of *LOTR* 'demonstrates clearly the benefits of a creatively-driven film industry' and that the films 'originated in New Zealand' being 'pre-produced, produced, filmed and postproduced' in the country (2002: iv). The films' producer, Peter Jackson, was born in New Zealand and the films' scripts and design work, as well as filming, editing and special effects, were done in New Zealand though a series of inter-linked companies (see Table 9.1). However, the New Zealandness of the film can be questioned. Not only are the films based on a book long identified as a canonical text in English and European literature – and its leading actors came largely from Britain, Australia and the USA – but the films were financed and distributed by New Line Cinema, one of the 'Big Ten' Hollywood-based film studios and owned by Time Warner, reputed to be the world's largest media company, with the corporate motto 'The world is our audience'. *LOTR* may well be described as a 'runaway' or 'internationally mobile' production (NZ Institute of Economic Research, 2002: iv), partic-

Table 9.1 Selected list of companies involved in the production of *The Lord of the Rings* film trilogy

Stage of production	Company	Involvement in the films	Locational centre	Corporate links
Pre-production	Miramax	Funded initial development work but pulled out because of cost of project	New York, USA	Subsidiary of Walt Disney
	New Line Cinema	Took over financing films after withdrawal of Miramax	Los Angeles, USA	Subsidiary of Time/Warner
	Weta Workshop	Undertook initial design work	Wellington, New Zealand	Part-owned by Peter Jackson
Production	Three Foot Six Limited	Company set up and contracted to New Line Cinema to oversee film production	Wellington, New Zealand	Owned by Peter Jackson
	Weta Workshop	Undertook costume and set design and construction	See above	See above
Post-production	Weta Digital	Created digital special effects	Wellington, New Zealand	Off-shoot of Weta Workshop
	The PostHouse New Zealand	Undertook digital colour gradings of films	Wellington, New Zealand	Office of Hamburg-based firm, set up specifically to undertake work on the films
Distribution	New Line Cinema	Distributed films	See above	See above
	New Line Entertainment	Distributed video and DVD	Los Angeles	Division of New Line Cinema
	Weta Limited	Produces and distributes merchandies related to *The Lord of the Rings*	Wellington, New Zealand	Off-shoot of Weta Workshop
	Electronic Arts	Design and distributed computer games based on films	Redwood City, San Francisco, USA	–

ularly given that Jackson has admitted that Canada was also considered as a potential location for the films' production (Wakefield, 2001).

Although assertions as to the New Zealandness of *LOTR* are contestable, it is clear that the films have had economic and cultural impact (although see Pratt, this volume, Chapter 8). The report to the Film Commission, for instance, claimed that the films had three long-term impacts. First, the films produced significant increases in intellectual property and human capital through 'up-skilling' the film and associated industries at both technical and management levels and through fostering creative entrepreneurship. Second, international perceptions of the New Zealand industry were changed, raising the profile both of New Zealand film-writers and producers, and of the country's production and post-production facilities and expertise. Third, they argued that it was likely to stimulate significant tourist spin-offs through enhancement of 'Brand New Zealand' and the establishment of new tourist attractions and merchandising opportunities.

The third set of effects is very clearly evident. While tourism in many areas of the world suffered decline following 9/11, New Zealand saw an increase in overseas tourist visitors of almost 23 per cent between 2001 and 2004 (Statistics New Zealand, 2005). During this period, New Line Cinema had pursued a two-year marketing deal with Air New Zealand in which the airline branded itself as 'The Airline to Middle Earth' (Figure 9.1) as well as participating with governmental ministries and agencies to promote New Zealand as the 'Home of Middle Earth' through advertising campaigns (for example, see www.newzealand.com) and the creation of an interactive online map (www.filmnz.com/map.html). A series of promotional identities were also established by central and local agencies, including New Zealand as 'Best supporting country', 'Aotearowood' and 'Wellingwood'. Furthermore, as Jones and Smith (2005: 938) comment, local tourist businesses were also 'quick to respond', establishing a series of 'LOTR-themed packages and attractions' in an attempt to attract so-called 'filmatic tourism' (Tooke and Baker, 1996), while a location guidebook to the films (Brodie, 2002) became the country's fastest-selling book.

Jones and Smith (2005: 927) suggest that the films are seen to have produced a 'tsunami of spin-offs' (see also Tzanelli, 2004),

The movie is fictional. The location isn't.

MIDDLE EARTH is New Zealand.

9.1 New Zealand as Middle Earth

although they note that not all the claimed impacts have materialised, nor indeed are welcomed by everyone. They also note that the impacts have not been exclusively economic in character, suggesting that the films have become part of a re-working of national identities, an argument also made by the Chief Executive of the New Zealand Film Commission:

> Film is important not just as a potent advertising medium for New Zealand; not just as a way of creating and personifying our country as a brand in all its diversity; not just as a high growth, high margin knowledge based business. It is all of these, but it is also a statement to ourselves. (Ruth Harley, quoted in Jones and Smith 2005: 932)

Such claims, and the debates surrounding the economic impacts of the films, highlight Shiel's argument that films are situated in space. In this chapter I wish to sketch out aspects of both the economic and cultural dimensions of *LOTR* 'films in space', and also explore the 'spaces in the films', most particularly its rural spaces.

Rural space in *LOTR* films

Hobbiton, the Shire and the ruralities of England and New Zealand

According to commentators, much of the appeal of the original *LOTR* books stemmed from their portrayal of place. Helms (1974: 7), for instance, has argued that Tolkein 'created an imaginary world so compelling, so real, that hundreds of thousands of people have entered it not just once but several times', whilst Garth (2004: 35) claimed that a particular 'spirit of place pervades much of Tolkein's work: human variety is partly shaped by geography'. While discussions of film adaptations do not necessarily need to address literary precursors (see Turner, 1993) it is both clear that for audiences, producers and critics, fidelity to Tolkein's literary constructions of place figures prominently (Chin and Gray, 2001; Tzanelli, 2004; Jones and Smith, 2005), and also significant that Mathijs (2004: 14) sees Tolkein's books as relating quite directly to the author's 'concern at the erosion of a (romanticized) English rural life within which he grew up'.

Such claims are reproduced clearly in the filmatic and literary texts associated with the films, which, as Jones and Smith (2005: 934) argue, frequently employ a 'genealogical rhetoric' in which the films are positioned as 'authentic' because they accurately represent Tolkein's work and/or 'the historical pasts which are claimed to lie behind it'. They suggest, however, that this rhetoric of authenticity lies in tension with other claims being made about the films, namely that they reflect the land and culture of New Zealand (see also Tzanelli, 2004). New Zealand has in the past been described as 'Britain's Farm' (see Cook and Phillips, 2005) and it may well be that the imagined geographies of the rurality of New Zealand and England are for many people not as distinct as their spatial differentiation might suggest. Early sequences of *LOTR* can, for instance, be seen to perform many of the 'figurative nuclei of rurality' previously identified within British television dramas by Phillips *et al.* (2001). Hence the filmatic images of Hobbiton and the Shire present views of gently undulating open spaces littered with signifiers of agriculture such as people tilling the fields of crops, scarecrows and windmills. These figurative elements are all far from modernistic, an issue clearly considered significant by one of the conceptual artists involved in the films' production: 'To me ... Hobbiton felt like what England would be if you had never seen England ... I wanted Bag End to be the English manor house, more luxurious and refined than the homes of his rustic neighbours, but still totally "Olde Worlde" – with the e's on the end of course' (John Howe in Sibley, 2002: 54).

This quotation also raises issues related to social content in that Hobbiton was clearly seen as modelled on images of the English countryside marked by class distinctions, a viewpoint reiterated in *National Geographic*'s (2001) portrayal of 'the realities' behind *LOTR*. In this production Peter Jackson, for instance, states that Tolkein started formulating ideas for *LOTR* whilst serving at the Battle of the Somme in the First World War, and that the central characters of Frodo and Sam reflected Tolkein's experiences of 'the rigid class boundaries separating English officers and their subordinate officers' and a perception that these tended to 'evaporate amidst the horrors of war' (National Geographic, 2001; see also Garth, 2004).

Allusions to class differences figure clearly in *LOTR* novel: 'the poorest Hobbits', for instance, were described as 'living in burrows of the most primitive kind' (Tolkein, 2003: 6), while others were presented as living in large and 'luxurious' tunnel complexes. A third group were portrayed as living above ground and characterised by Tolkein in ways which have clear resonances with historical descriptions of the English 'middling' sorts, ranks or classes: 'there were many houses of wood, brick or stone ... specially favoured by millers, smiths, ropers, and cartwrights, and others of that sort ... accustomed to build sheds and workshops' (Tolkein, 2003: 6).

The film and books also make considerable play on notions of community in which socio-economic differences are seen as inconsequential in comparison with relations of kinship and friendship nurtured through extended habitation of a common space.[2] Early in *LOTR*, for instance, Tolkein described Hobbits as living 'quietly in Middle Earth for many long years' and being 'clannish' in nature, drawing up 'long and elaborate family trees with innumerable branches', such that 'In dealing with Hobbits it is important to remember who is related to whom, and in what degree' (Tolkein, 2003: 6). There are clear parallels here with academic constructions of rural communities drawing on the work of Tönnies (1957) and his conception of *Gemeinschaft*, which explicitly constructed communal culture as being bound 'by blood' and 'locality ... established through ... the common bond ... [of] friendship' (1957: 47–8).

As noted in Phillips (1998), Tönnies' writings resonate with the language of 'retrospect to an "organic" or "natural society"', features which are clearly evident in *LOTR*, which sets up Hobbiton as a place of ecological harmony immunised from modern developments:

> Hobbits are unobtrusive but ancient people ... for they love peace and quiet and good-tilled earth: a well-ordered and well-farmed countryside was their favourite haunt. They do not and did not understand or like machines more complicated than a forge bellows, a water-mill, or a hand-loom ... Hobbits ... lived quietly in Middle Earth for many long years before other folk became even aware of them. (Tolkein, 2003: 1)

The opening sequences of the film enact many of these elements: mention has already been made to the presence of tilled fields and windmills, and signifiers of social harmony and bountiful nature also abound. The whole community is, for instance, represented as coming together to celebrate Bilbo Baggins' birthday, and fields, gardens and tables all appear laden with produce. Pathways and

homes also appear set into the landscape, arguably implying continuity of dwelling and harmonious relations with nature as well as
enacting notions of nucleated rural settlement '"nestling" within a
wider space of the country' (Phillips *et al.*, 2001: 7).

For Garth (2004), Tolkein's literary constructions of Hobbits
and Hobbiton were drawn directly from experience, a view that
was reproduced in interviews with those involved in creating the
films: '[t]he hobbits are actually quite close to the people that
Tolkein grew up with as a child in the rural area just outside
Birmingham, and he kind of treasured memories of the more
simple folk and he recreated them in the hobbits' (Alan Lee in
National Geographic, 2001). For four years at the close of the nineteenth century and beginning of the twentieth Tolkein had lived in
Sarehole, which at the time was a small village close to Birmingham
(although now long incorporated into the city's suburbs). For
Garth (2004: 11) this brief period in a 'rural idyll' exerted a
profound impact on Tolkein with 'the climate and character of this
older world' becoming 'etched ... in the young John Ronald's
heart'. Garth himself clearly employs a rural retrospect in this
comment, constructing the countryside as an 'older world', a view
which Tolkein also arguably shared in that he spoke of 'a particular love of what you might call central Middle English countryside,
based on good water, stones and elm trees and small, quiet rivers
and ... rustic people' (Tolkein, quoted in Garth, 2004: 11). Indeed,
he apparently argued that Hobbiton was 'more or less a
Warwickshire community of about the period of the Diamond
Jubilee [i.e. 1897]' (Garth, 2004: 307).

Tolkein's experience of rural Warwickshire had actually been
relatively limited, having moved into the city of Birmingham when
he was eight. His views on the countryside may well be a reflection
of much wider influences. Tolkein was formulating *LOTR* during
a period which has been identified as witnessing rising interest and
concern over the state of the British countryside (see Miller, 1995;
Matless, 1998). Indeed, Matless links Tolkein to organicist visions
of the English countryside promoted by the likes of H.J.
Massingham and Rolf Gardiner, suggesting that while there is no
evidence of direct personal influence, 'organicists must have felt at
home in the agricultural and spiritual climate of the Shire'
(Matless, 1998: 134).

Matless (1998: 134) also argues that while the English organicists of the period between the wars and during the Second World War had 'little policy or popular impact' their ideas appear quite familiar to people now as they bear 'resemblances to current Green thinking'. Matless' focus is on England, but the folding of Tolkein, organicism and contemporary environmentalism may be equally pertinent to New Zealand. As Bell (1996), Cloke and Perkins (1998), Cook and Phillips (2005) and Coyle and Fairweather (2005) have all observed, New Zealand has come to be marketed at least from the mid-1980s as an unspoilt, unpolluted, 'clean green' environment. The imagery of the Hobbiton and the Shire quite clearly resonates well with this imagery, although interestingly it is rather wilder landscapes that tend to figure most prominently, and it is to these that attention now turns.

Wild country in *LOTR*

Wright (2000) has highlighted how New Zealand has been promoted as 'the world in one country' (Film New Zealand, 1999), the country's landscapes and natural features used to represent such places as the Italian lake district, the American northwest, Nevada and Kansas, the Scottish highlands, Norwegian fjords, and coastlines in the USA, Korea, Ireland and Greece. Wright adds, however, that the appeal of New Zealand may lie less in its ability to act as a stand-in for other places but rather in the capacity to represent 'other worldiness', a place of 'untouched beauty and adventure' (Wright, 2000: 52) which appears dislocated from and other to the audience's everyday environments. New Zealand is hence used as wilderness, as a space which is remote from and untamed by the modern world; a space of a primordial natural space which is 'bigger than us, older than us and remains uncontainable' (Wright, 2000: 53). She points to how a series of television series shot in New Zealand in the 1990s – *Hercules: the Legendary Journeys*, *Xena: Warrior Princess*, *The New Adventures of Robin Hood*, *The Legend of William Tell* and *Dark Knight* – whilst ostensibly portraying worlds ranging from Ancient Greece to medieval England and early modern Switzerland all make extensive use of this imagery, as did the George Lucas film *Willow*, in which, she suggests, New Zealand is 'framed' such that its 'scale and immensity ... overwhelms both the actors, and also the audience' (2000: 57). She also adds that given such a cultural construction of New Zealand, '[I]t is little surprise ... that New

Zealand was also chosen for the setting of Peter Jackson's ... film trilogy' (2000: 54). Expansive landscapes with seemingly miniscule human presence are certainly very evident within these films.

It could be objected that there are many other areas which have been similarly coded as pristine wilderness and that a series of other conditioning factors were at work in the selection of New Zealand as the location for *LOTR*. Peter Jackson has, for instance, claimed that the films would not have been shot in New Zealand if New Line Cinemas had not been able to exploit a tax loophole (Wakefield, 2001). However, I wish to pursue a different question: namely, how do presentations of wilderness, and indeed other constructions of rurality such as pastoralism, act in these films? *LOTR* can be seen as essentially located in rural space, or rural spaces, with there being relatively few passages set in towns or cities, and even when urban-like spaces do make an appearance, they are very much constructed as fortress settlements set within wider landscapes.

LOTR and movement through rural spaces

As Mathijs (2004) highlights, there is considerable debate about the literary and filmatic genres that might be applicable to *LOTR*. Amongst the descriptors commonly placed on both the book and films is that of 'adventure': Peter Jackson, for instance, has described how the film reflected his 'lifelong passion to make a fantasy adventure film' (Fischer, n.d.), whilst Petty (1979) argues that both *LOTR* and its precursor novel *The Hobbit* enact the narrative structure of the 'mythic quest' in which an unlikely hero is called to partake in adventure and, despite an initial refusal, comes to depart from a place of well-being and travel into spaces of danger, overcoming various trials to bring about a return to a situation of well-being.[3] Petty undertakes a highly structuralist analysis derived from Propp (1970) but there are also clear parallels with the more post-structural and explicitly geographical analysis of Phillips (1997: 22), who argues that adventure stories map, naturalise and normalise 'constructions of identity and geography'. He highlights how adventure stories commonly involve spatial movement from a home environment which is 'domestic, civilized, mappable space' (1997: 29) into a distant, unknown and life-threatening environment which, after much struggle, becomes known, domesticated and civilised.

Adventure stories set up quite particular constructions of space, and also imply movement through and transformation of space. Phillips employs both generic notions of place – writing for instance of the employment of a 'dialectical geography of home and away' (Phillips, 1997: 22) – and quite specific constructions, as in the 'Hudson Bay Company Territories' in northern Canada and 'the bush' of South Australia. These places might all be seen as rural, although not embodiments of the rurality of Hobbiton and the Shire discussed earlier. Rather, these places, at least as constructed in the adventure stories Phillips is studying, might be characterised as wilderness, or wild places. Hence the adventure narrative can be seen as revolving around home environments and wilderness, and to involve movement from home into the wilderness. Furthermore, the practices of both fearing and then mapping, domesticating and civilising these spaces as identified by Phillips may be seen as enactments of what Short (1991) has described as the 'classical attitude' to wilderness.

Short identifies the eighth-century poem *Beowulf* as a clear illustration of the classical attitude, which is particularly significant in the present context given that Tolkein was a leading authority on Beowulf (Tolkein, 1936; 1937), as well as on many other epic poems which had their origins in northern Europe. According to commentators such as Helms (1974: 11), Tolkien's academic studies were closely linked to his fictional writing, influencing the development of characters, plot lines and lines of critical justification. Many of the wild places present in Beowulf, such as high moors, forests, underground caverns, mountains and marshland, also figure in *LOTR*, and, as in the epic poem, dangerous creatures and spirits are seen to lurk within them.

While this landscape may be seen as simply the product of adaptation of the literary landscapes of Tolkein, it may also have some other sources of influences, notably what has been described as the New Zealand, Kiwi or Antipodean Gothic (for example Tincknell, 2000; Conrich, 2005). These phrases refer to films which configure New Zealand not as a place of some pastoral idyll, nor indeed as a place of untouched beauty, but rather as a place where danger and horror lurk around every corner, in any person, and likely to make an appearance at the most unlikely of occasions.

Peter Jackson is often cited as a producer of Kiwi Gothic – his early films such as *Bad Taste* (1987) and *Braindead/Dead Alive* (1992) and even his more popularist 1994 film *Heavenly Creatures* all being quoted as illustrative examples. *LOTR* might, however, be seen to align more closely in style with European gothic rather than with Antipodean variants, which have been identified as having as a hallmark 'dark, inward comedy' (Dermody and Jacka, 1992: 51). Jackson, for instance, explicitly remarked that *LOTR* has 'a certain darkness' and that 'We didn't want to undermine the action with humour, and make it very campy like Hercules and Xena – we wanted to steer ours more towards Braveheart' (Peter Jackson in Wakefield, 2001).

Places of wilderness were clearly constructed as a gothic and classical wilderness: a rural anti-idyll (Bell, 1997) to fear and if possible tame or at least subdue. One of the actors in the film is presented describing how Peter Jackson creates 'extraordinarily well' a 'cinematic landscape of darkness and fear' (Sean Astin in New Line Cinema, 2001a) and there are parallels to be drawn here with Helms' (1974: 94) comments of the literary landscapes of *LOTR* and how good and evil are 'manifested in the various aspects of weather and atmosphere of Middle-Earth, in the air and the sky', and also in the land, with the area of Modor in particular being presented as a bleak, desolate and despoiled landscape.

LOTR is also, as Helms (1974) and Wright (2000) both note, replete with images of wilderness as places of beauty and hence corresponds rather more closely with Short's (1991) concept of a 'romantic' attitude in which wildness is a place to be valued and even revered. Indeed it is these images, often also configured as moving spectacle or 'accelerated sublime' (Bell and Lyall, 2001), which figure strongly in the promotion of the films and associated marketing (see Figure 9.1). However, in the films themselves there is a general movement from romantic spectacular wilderness into more classical, gothic images of wilderness as a place of danger and horror, interspersed with brief stays in places such as Rivendell and Lothlórien, which correspond more closely to the contours of the 'home environment' of the Shire in that they are presented as places of harmony, contentment and ecological balance.

The narrative significance of these places has been discussed by Petty (1979: 53), who argues that they acts as points of initiation and complication as well as providing momentary glimpses 'of paradise and hope' with a 'path of darkness and dread'. The significance of their idyllic qualities and notions of ecological balance or harmony are also very evident in the commentaries provided on the construction of the models and sets used in their filmatic presentation:

> For much of the movie, the hobbits find themselves in the wild, in the dark, with fear all around them. Amongst so many inhospitable places, I wanted Rivendell to be a safe-haven, an oasis of beauty. (Chuck Shuman in Sibley, 2002: 71)

> We wanted to make the buildings to sort of fit around the trees so that we would have to have too much of an impact on the landscape as the Elves would have done. (Alan Lee in New Line Cinema, 2001b)

In the next section I will consider the presentation of nature in these spaces of refuge, and in other parts of the *The Lord of Rings*. If the films enact an imaginative geography involving movement through differing constructions of rural space, they also very much enact movement through various imaginative geographies of nature as well.

Imaginative geographies of nature in *LOTR*

As Gregory (2001) has commented, the concept of 'imaginative geographies' has spawned a wide range of studies within and without the discipline of geography, most of which have interpreted the term in a highly spatial, indeed arguably 'geometrical', manner. In the context of film studies, the concept of imaginative geography in this sense can be seen as equivalent to Shiel's notion of 'spaces in film'. Gregory argues, however, that a more expansive sense of geography is required, one which includes nature as well as spatiality.

It has indeed been argued by Petty (1979) that nature is an important 'character' in *LOTR*, being represented an immanent force drawn upon by agents of good and whose destruction is sought by agents of evil. Petty, for instance, remarks on how at the very moment when the Ringwraiths look likely to catch Frodo 'the magic immanent in nature comes to the rescue: the River awakens' and pursing riders and horses are washed away by a torrent of water which takes the form of 'white riders upon white horses with frothing manes' (Tolkein, 2003: 209). The refuges of Rivendell and Lothlórien likewise enact much of the organicism identified in the portrayal of Hobbiton, being represented as places cut off from the ecological ravages of the rest of the world and acting as oases where the recuperative powers of nature are recognised and realised.

The destruction of nature by agents of evil is clearly represented by the transformation of Isengard, which appears fleetingly in the first two films as an open and verdant space bordered by distant mountains. These shots are followed by a much more extensive series of images detailing environmental destruction which are quite directly linked with industry and warfare through the accompanying dialogue: 'The old world will burn in the fires of industry, the forests will fall, a new order will rise. We will drive the machine of war with sword and spear and the iron fist of the auk' (Sarumen, in New Line Cinema, 2001c).

As with the representation of Hobbiton, two lines of questioning have emerged around the representation of environmental degradation. First, commentators such as Garth (2004) and National Geographic (2001) have linked it to Tolkein's own biographical experiences, both with regard to his brief period of residence in the rural settlement of Sarehole and also to his period of serving in the British Army in the First World War. Tolkein himself in the foreword to the second edition of *LOTR* remarks that the book reflect in some part his own experiences, although not so much those surrounding the onset of the Second World War but 'much further back' in his childhood, when he supposed that the countryside 'was being shabbily destroyed'.

A second line of 'criticism' is undertaken by Cubitt (2005; 2006), who considers how *LOTR* links to contemporary representations of New Zealand as a place of unspoilt nature. Interestingly, some of the films' 'ancillary materials' (Barker, 2004) represent the films' production as environmentally sensitive:

> 'What you have to remember is that this was a New Zealand production: the Maori and all New Zealanders have a strong respect for the land: an early connectness, so it wasn't difficult to convince people to be careful ... to leave everything as they found it'. There was a phrase that became a watchword on the film: 'All that we ever leave behind are footprints'. Yet quite often, thanks to the painstaking level of post-filming restoration, there weren't even any footprints! (Sibley, 2002: 36)

Such representations can, however, be critiqued in the sense that no mention is made for instance, of the amount of fuel consumed in the movement of cast and crew to distant location and in the production of the aerial fly-overs which figure prominently in the films and may be seen as key ingredients in the constitution of their 'accelerated sublime'. Cubitt (2005) also makes reference to the presence of bounded spaces in *LOTR* – places such as Rivendell, Lothlórien or Osgiliath are all enclosed with barriers to keep out elements from other, different worlds – and suggests that these chime with contemporary highly political concerns related to biosecurity and migration. In other words, the imaginative geographies of space and nature in *LOTR* have parallels, and perhaps even some diffuse connections, with the spaces, and natures, in which these films are produced, circulated and consumed. However, before considering such issues of the 'spaces (and natures) of film', it is important to note that the imaginative geographies of *LOTR* do not simply involve environmental destruction but that, as one might expect in a story of good and evil, see good nature come to defeat the evil agencies of industry and war.

So, for instance, while the forces of evil are embodied and personified in Sarumen, the forces of nature are, as Helms (1974: 93–4) notes, personified in Treebeard, an animate tree which acts as a shepherd to the trees in the forest of Fanghorn, and through whose agency the trees are, as Helms puts it, 'roused' so that 'nature crushes its offender Sarumen'. Once again there are clear contemporary resonances in that the destruction of Isengard and Sarumen by the trees of the forest can be seen as a clear enactment of notions of the 'revenge of nature' espoused within many contemporary 'deep green' ecocentric perspectives (see Phillips and Mighall, 2000).

LOTR films in the spaces of Aotearoa/New Zealand

As previously mentioned, Shiel (2001) argues that attention should not only be paid to the roles of space within films, but also to the presence and effects of films within extra-filmatic spaces such as lived and economic space, and to processes such as globalisation. In this final section I want to briefly address these issues, linking *LOTR* films both to spaces and processes highlighted by Shiel and to the concepts of social and spatial 'imaginaries' as outlined by Dermody and Jacka (1992) and Larner (1998) respectively.

Larner's notion of spatial imaginaries is framed in the context of discussions of economic globalisation and the integration of Aotearoa/New Zealand into this space-economy. She argues that globalisation has involved shifts in the objects of economic governance and that these in turn are predicated on shifts in spatial imaginaries, or imaginative geographies. In particular she argues that there has been a shift in how New Zealand has been perceived by governmental and business policymakers with the country becoming increasingly portrayed from the early 1990s as a 'node in the flows and networks of the Pacific Rim' (Larner, 1998: 599; see also Cook and Phillips, 2005).

Larner makes no reference to either the film industry or to the impact that films might make on the spatial imaginaries of New Zealand. Shiel (2001: 10), however, argues that films and cinema may be seen as central to globalisation, not only being 'one of the first truly globalized industries in terms of its organization' but also at 'the cutting edge of globalization as a process of integration and homogenization'. Mention has already been made to the distributed/networked character of *LOTR* films' production, which despite protestations as to its New Zealandness is clearly a globalised production in terms of its production, distribution and consumption.

Given its globalised features, it is easy to dismiss protestations about localness as ideological misrepresentation and/or wishful fantasy. However, not only might this ignore the degree to which particular places and people may be able to accrue some, albeit perhaps quite temporary, benefit from involvement in film production and cinematic representation (see Pratt, this volume, Chapter 8), but it also arguably fails to recognise the complex effects of film within lived spaces. It is in addressing these issues that the notion of social imaginaries as outlined by Dermody and Jacka (1992) appears useful.

Dermody and Jacka focus on Australian cinema, where they use the concept of 'social imaginaries' as an 'intermediary' or 'mediating' term between studies of cinematic production and film 'texts', national socio-cultural and economic histories, and subject formation and spectatorship. They argue that Australian film industry, like the New Zealand one, 'exists in an environment strongly conditioned and even regulated by the norms established by Hollywood' (1992: 13) but that it has also played a significant part in projections of Australian national identity. Australian cinema, they argue, is a 'doubled industry', caught between a series of contradictory and changing influences and pressures. They identify two contrasting productive responses to these dilemmas, creating films which 'package carefully selected and marketable common-places of Australian "national type" . . . and "colourful locale"', or alternatively, 'by effacing . . . Australian character . . . and searching . . . for good "universal" stories and genre elements abstracted from their cultural origins' (1992: 14).

These categories may be quite readily applied to New Zealand film production, with films such as *Once Were Warriors*, *The Piano* and *Whale Rider* being placed in the former category and films such as *LOTR*, *Sylvia*, *King Kong* and *The Chronicles of Narnia* into the latter. Many films in the second group are not only internationally produced but also present images which are abstracted or, as Wright (2000: 52) puts it, 're-placed and dis-located' from New Zealand. However, as Jones and Smith (2005) have highlighted, in *LOTR* such processes of production and symbolisation are accompanied by attempts to establish a national connection to the films, attempts which I would suggest connect closely to Dermody and Jacka's analysis of social imaginaries implicated in the production of Australian films, and in particular their claim that these are both conditioned by and seek to repre-sent, in one of three ways, a 'peripheral sense of loss over who we [Australians] are, and how we should be' (Dermody and Jacka, 1992: 325).

Dermody and Jacka suggest that one widespread response has been a sense of 'anguish about the uninterpreted nature' of Australia which often manifested through representations of 'lone figures, lost in a landscape' (1992: 21); imagery which not only resonates strongly with my earlier analysis of the space in *LOTR* but also may be seen to connect with Wright's (2000: 55) claim that there are striking parallels between *LOTR* and a belief that New Zealand is 'a country of adventure . . . where a pioneering spirit is sustained'.

The pioneering imagery, whilst a feature of many Australian and New Zealand films, has been the subject of considerable commen-tary and critique, particularly with regard to its deployment of gendered and colonial identities. Margolis (2000b: 16), for instance, claims that the 'man-alone theme is not unique to Aotearoa New Zealand, but its importance for the film industry of this country is exceptional'. Her comment points to the masculini-ty and, by reference to the Maori name for the country, the colonial relations performed in representations of the pioneer. She adds, '[n]o plot could be further from the general interests of either the Kiwi female or Maori film-makers, as their words and films attest' (2000b: 17), suggesting that Maori and women producers' films tend to eschew the man-alone theme in favour of a focus on community and family relations.

Whilst not necessarily fully endorsing Margolis' arguments, they do raise important questions with regard to presence and effects of *LOTR* within Aotearoa/New Zealand. As Margolis outlines, the country saw an emergent bi-culturalism and a re-invigoration of feature-film production in the 1980s, with many films explicitly seeking to address questions of gender, colonialism and racial/ethnic identity (for example Lee Tamahori's *Once Were Warriors* and its sequel, Ian Mune's *What Becomes of the Broken Hearted?*, Jane Campion's *The Piano*, Peter Jackson's *Heavenly Creatures*, and most recently Niki Caro's *Whale Rider*). Whilst being far from immune from feminist and post-colonial criticism (see Margolis, 2000a; Matahaere-Atariki, 1999), these films contrast strongly with *LOTR* which can be read as, to borrow Phillips' (1997) phrase, 'mapping men and empire'. Not only are the central characters in the films all male adventurers travelling into and taming the wilderness, they are also all played by white Anglo-Americans. Furthermore, while Maori did feature in the cast and crew, and in some of the associated film and touristic texts, these were clearly not the bodies given filmatic prominence: 'When we ran out of blond, blue-eyes extras for the men of Rohan, we would have to cast brown-skinned, brown-eyed Maori boys, stick wigs on them and try to hide them in the background' (Sibley, 2002: 111).

The second response identified by Dermody and Jacka is a sense of inhabiting a 'second-rate' culture which does not live up to that of 'the metropolitan centre', which in Australia's case, as with New Zealand, has long been seen as Britain and Europe, but may now also encompass the United States of America (see Watson, 2001; Malouf, 2003) and, with the reconfiguration of the spatial imaginaries identified by Larner, even Japan and other Asia nodes within the Pacific Rim. Studies of New Zealand film and television, for instance, have argued that production within the country has been hampered by a so-called 'cultural cringe' whereby domestically produced products are seen as inherently inferior in quality to overseas productions (Lealand, 1988; Perry, 1994; Phillips, 2003;

Dunleavy, 2004). Much of the positivity in response to *LOTR* films within New Zealand might be ascribed to a feeling that these films have dealt a blow against the cultural cringe: the previously mentioned report to the country's Film Commission claimed that the films had both changed the way the film world viewed New Zealand and its film industry and also 'engendered a new self-confidence' in the country's 'writers, directors, producers' (NZ Institute of Economic Research, 2002: 36; see also Jones and Smith, 2005).

Classic cited illustrations of cultural cringe include the television series *Hercules: The Legendary Journeys* and *Xena: Warrior Princess*, although Naismith (2002) argues that the latter series represent an example of Perry's (1998) concept of 'antipodean camp' whereby cultural cringe is transformed into ironic parody which anticipates, internalises and immunises itself from cultural criticism. For Perry, antipodean camp represents a post-colonial strategy of resistance by 'dominion subjects' who are ambiguously positioned between the identities of coloniser and colonised. *LOTR* appears to make no use of such a strategy of resistance, although as Jones and Smith (2005) note, repeated references are made in associated promotional materials to notions of 'Kiwi ingenuity', an ability to 'make do and mend' and 'get things done against the odds'. They suggest that the films hence enact and become emblematic of a national patriotism which is widely seen as exemplified in the character and dress of the film's producer, Peter Jackson, who is 'still the idealized Kiwi guy. He wears shorts and jandals and doesn't flaunt his wealth' (quoted in Jones and Smith, 2005: 933).

Dermody and Jacka's (1992: 21) third response is a feeling of having a 'second-hand' culture which is always 'not quite our own'. In both Australia and New Zealand colonial connections to Britain still exert a powerful cultural influence, while concern has also long been expressed over the Americanisation of culture (Lealand, 1988; Perry, 1994; Phillips, 2003). Whilst claims have been made about *LOTR* films creating 'new Hollywood – New Zealand relationships' (Jones and Smith, 2005: 930) whereby Hollywood has come to Aotearoa/New Zealand, concerns continue to be expressed about the size and future of country's film industry and about the economic and cultural impacts of internationally mobile productions:

> *The Lord of the Rings* – possibly the largest film production
> anywhere to date – was 'made in New Zealand' ... but despite the
> perseverance and creativity of Peter Jackson and his team, and the tax
> break provided by the New Zealand Government to ensure produc-
> tion stayed here, the majority of revenues from the intellectual
> property flow to the United States. (Screen Production Taskforce,
> 2003: 28–9)

Britain can also be seen as exerting an influence on the films'
production and reception. References have already been made to
claimed fidelity to Tolkein literary work and to its embedment in
British and European culture and experience. Connections to
Britain may also have acted as a source of authenticity for a New
Zealand location: '[t]he historical links that New Zealand has with
Britain, and "beyond" Britain to an Anglo-Saxon cultural imagi-
nary gives a kind of cultural plausibility to the choice of New
Zealand as Middle-earth' (Jones and Smith, 2005: 934; see also
Tzanelli, 2004 on perceived repression of Englishness).

The three senses of national culture, and their associated
concerns and dilemmas, are far from static, hegemonic or entirely
complementary. Jones and Smith (2005), for instance, highlight
how notions of 'Kiwi ingenuity' are being re-worked alongside
notions of technological expertise and cultural creativity.
References have previously been made to how notions of wilderness central to the 'man alone' thematic identified by Margolis
(2000a) conjoin in *LOTR* with environmentalist concerns and
with performances of an 'accelerated sublime' which in turn
connect to the branding the country as 'young, fresh and innova-
tive' (see Cloke and Perkins, 1998). Concerns over British and
American filmatic 'cultural imperialism', whilst still acting to
challenge the promotional hype associated with the films, also, as
Jones and Smith (2005) note, work to foster new visions of
nationhood centred on an emergent 'postcolonial confidence',
although they add that this has yet to displace long-established
notions that the country's identity lies in nature rather than
culture. Indeed, while Jones and Smith link *LOTR* to the affirma-
tion of re-worked concepts of nationhood, it is also possible to see
the three cultural responses identified here as all embodying well-
rehearsed rural identities, such as the coloniser of the wilderness,
the green pastoralist exercising careful stewardship over nature,
and the rustic happy to forgo the sophistications of the metropol-

itan cultures in favour of the simple pleasures of an outdoors lifestyle.

Conclusion

This chapter has explored the rural spaces of *LOTR* films and the *LOTR* films in the space of Aotearoa/New Zealand, a space that is itself widely identified as rural in character despite the country having one of the most urbanised populations in the world, as marked by the proportion of people living in spaces designated as urban. The chapter has highlighted how the films enact many of the figurative nuclei of rurality identified with a pastoral idyll, but also draw strongly on classical and romantic constructs of wilderness. The significance of movement through these spaces of rurality was highlighted, as was the presence of anti-idyllic constructs of wilderness. The chapter also highlighted two ways in which the constructions of rural space are often read: first were genealogical readings which move from the films to the precursor text of Tolkein's book and then, in some cases, to the lived spaces inhabited by the author at some point in his life; second were what might be seen as more synchronic readings which move from the films to contemporaneous texts in circulation in the spaces which the films might be seen to inhabit now, or Shiel's 'spaces of film'. As Tzanelli (2004: 24) has argued, with films such as *LOTR*, people are presented not with a singular symbolic product to consume but rather with a 'cluster of signs' involving a series of hermeneutic encounters, including, but not only, those 'by filmmakers (of novels), by audiences (of films) and by holiday providers (of audiences' film reading)'.

The final section of the chapter explored one particular space of film by considering the economic and more particularly the cultural impacts of the film in Aotearoa/New Zealand. The chapter has posited three ways in which responses to the films – which although in many ways have little connection to the space of Aotearoa/New Zealand in that they are 'based on an explicitly English text, and financed by Hollywood' (Jones and Smith, 2005: 928) – connect to, and thereby potential reveal much about, the social and spatial imaginaries of the nation and its countrysides. It has been suggested that *LOTR* is situated within and connects to masculinist/ colonial, and indeed now highly commercialised

(Cloke and Perkins, 1998; Tzanelli, 2004), spatial imaginaries of New Zealand as a space of adventure and conquest, as well as pastoral and ecological imaginaries of clean and green New Zealand and attempts to engender post-colonial and globally oriented national self-confidence. Tzanelli (2004: 38) has indeed suggested that the production of *LOTR* signals the dawn of a new national identity for New Zealand, one which 'stands poles apart' from its prior ruralised identity as a land of 'the dull sheep farmer'. This chapter suggests, however, that the reconfiguration of identities associated with the films is much more complex than this, not least because *LOTR* as both a space in film and a space of film has drawn upon and continues to foster a range of rural imaginaries.

Notes

1   Note should be made of the debate surrounding the appropriate use of the two names (for example Berg, 1994; Berg and Kearns, 1996; Lees and Berg, 1995; McClean *et al.*, 1997). In the context of the present paper I decided to make general use of the term 'New Zealand' but switch to using 'Aotearoa/New Zealand' at the start and end of the paper, contexts where I was explicitly seeking to raise issues surrounding the representation of Maori.

2   Although Tolkein's dual emphasis on class distinction and the irrelevance of class seems contradictory it may be seen as quite characteristic of Eder's (1993) 'individualistic class ethos', which adopts a socially conservative politics of identity whereby socio-economic inequalities are naturalised and emphasis is given to retaining established lines of social differentiation (Phillips, 2001).

3   One of the interesting contrasts between the book and the films is that in the former Frodo returns to home to Hobbiton to find it 'all ruined', transformed by Saruman into a place of 'filth and disorder' (Tolkein, 2003: 994), with industry and industrialisation very clearly presented as agents of destruction. The omission of this part of the book from the film may well be explicated with reference to audience tolerance over film length and narrative clarity, but it also raises interesting issues relating to the film's reproduction of notions of 'clean green' New Zealand.

References

Barker, M. (2004), 'News, reviews, clues, interviews and other ancillary materials', *Scope*, February (www.nottingham.ac.uk /film/scopearchive).

Bell, C. (1996), *Inventing New Zealand* (Auckland: Penguin Books (NZ)).

Bell, C. and Lyall, J. (2001), *Accelerated Sublime* (Westport, CT: Greenwood Press).

Bell, D. (1997), 'Anti-idyll: rural horror', in Cloke, P. and Little, J. (eds), *Contested Countryside Cultures* (London: Routledge), pp. 94–108.

Berg, L.D. (1994), 'Masculinity, place and a binary discourse of "theory" and "empirical investigation" in the human geography of Aotearoa/New Zealand', *Gender, Place and Culture*, 1: 245–60.

Berg, L.D. and Kearns, R.A. (1996), 'Naming as norming', *Environment and Planning D* 14: 99–122.

Brodie, I. (2002), *The Lord of the Rings Location Guidebook* (Auckland: HarperCollins).

Chin, B. and Gray, J. (2001). '"One Ring To Rule Them All": pre-viewers and pre-texts of the *Lord of the Rings*', *Intensities: Journal of Cult Media* 2 (www.cult-media.com).

Clarke, D. (ed.) (1997), *The Cinematic City* (London: Routledge).

Cloke, P. and Perkins, H. (1998), '"Cracking the canyon": representations of adventure tourism in New Zealand', *Environment and Planning D* 16: 185–218.

Conrich, I. (2005), 'Kiwi Gothic', in Schneider, S. and Williams, T. (eds), *Horror International* (Detroit, MI: Wayne State University Press), pp. 114–27.

Cook, D. and Phillips, M. (2005), 'People in a marginal periphery', in Phillips, M. (ed.), *Contested Worlds* (Aldershot: Ashgate) pp. 353–402.

Coyle, F. and Fairweather, J. (2005), 'Challenging a place myth', *Area*, 37: 148–58.

Cubitt, S. (2005), *EcoMedia* (Amsterdam/New York: Rodopi Press).

Cubitt, S. (2006), 'The fading of the elves', in Mathijs, E. and Pomerance, P. (eds), *From Hobbits to Hollywood* (Amsterdam /New York: Rodopi Press), pp. 65–80.

Dermody, S. and Jacka, E. (1992), *Anatomy of a National Cinema* (Sydney: Currency Press).

Dunleavy, T. (2004), 'Made in New Zealand', in Horrocks, R. and Perry, N. (eds), *Television in New Zealand* (Melbourne: Oxford University Press), pp. 203–21.

Eder, K. (1993), *The New Politics of Class* (London: Sage).

Film New Zealand (1999), *The Production Guide to the World in One Country* (Wellington: Film New Zealand).

Fischer, P. (n.d.), '"Hobbit man" talks Tolkien', *iofilm* (www.iofilm.co.uk).

Garth, J. (2004), *Tolkien and the Great War* (London: Harper Collins).

Gregory, D. (2001), '(Post) colonialism and the production of nature', in Castree, N. and Braun, B. (eds), *Social Nature* (Oxford: Blackwell), pp. 84–111.

Helms, R. (1974), *Tolkein's Worlds* (London: Thames and Hudson).

Jones, D. and Smith, K. (2005), 'Middle-earth meets New Zealand', *Journal of Management Studies*, 42: 923–45.

Larner, W. (1998), 'Hitching a ride on the tiger's back', *Environment and Planning D* 16: 599–614.

Lealand, G. (1988), *A Foreign Egg in our Nest?* (Wellington: Victoria University Press).

Lees, L. and Berg, L.D. (1995), 'Ponga, glass and concrete', *New Zealand Geographer*, 51: 1–41.

Malouf, D. (2003), 'Made in England: Australia's British Heritage', *Quarterly Essay*, 12.

Margolis, H. (ed.) (2000a), *Jane Campion's* The Piano (Cambridge: Cambridge University Press).

Margolis, H. (2000b), '"A strange heritage": from colonization to transformation?', in Margolis, H. (ed.), *Jane Campion's The Piano* (Cambridge: Cambridge University Press), pp. 1–41.

Matahaere-Atariki, D. (1999), 'A context for writing maculinities', in Law, R., Campbell, H. and Dolan, J. (eds), *Masculinities in Aotearoa/New Zealand* (Palmerston North: Dunmore Press), pp. 104–18.

Mathijs, E. (2004), 'Where is Middle Earth?' Paper presented to the International Association for Media and Communication Research Conference 2004, Porto Alegre.

Matless, D. (1998), *Landscape and Englishness* (London: Reaktion Books Ltd).

McClean, R., *et al.* (1997), 'Responsible geographies', *New Zealand Geographer*, 53: 9–15.

Miller, S. (1995), 'Urban dreams and rural reality: land and landscape in English culture, 1920–1945', *Rural History: Economy, Society, Culture*, 6: 89–102.

Naismith, G. (2002), 'Locating the local(e) in Xena Warrior Princess', *Metro*, 129/130: 217–21.

National Geographic (2001), *Beyond the Movie: The Lord of the Rings The Fellowship of the Ring* (Carlshalton: Quandrant Video).

New Line Cinema (2001a), 'Passage to Middle Earth: the making of Lord of the Rings', in New Line Cinema (ed.), *The Lord of the Rings DVD* (Los Angeles: New Line Cinema).

New Line Cinema (2001b), 'Rivendell: the Elven Refuge', in New Line Cinema (ed.), *The Lord of the Rings DVD* (Los Angeles: New Line Cinema).

New Line Cinema (2001c), 'Fellowship of the Rings', in New Line Cinema (ed.), *The Lord of the Rings DVD* (Los Angeles: New Line Cinema).

NZ Institute of Economic Research (2002), *Scoping the Lasting Effects of The Lord of the Rings* (Auckland and Wellington: NZ Institute of Economic Research).

Perry, N. (1994), *The Dominion of Signs* (Auckland: Auckland University Press).

Perry, N. (1998), *Hyperreality and Global Culture* (London: Routledge).

Petty, A. (1979), *One Ring to Bind them All* (Tuscaloosa: University of Alabama Press).

Phillips, M. (1998), 'The restructuring of social imaginations in rural geography', *Journal of Rural Studies*, 4: 121–64.

Phillips, M. (2001), 'Class, collective action and the countryside', in Gyes, G., de Witte, H. and Pasture, P. (eds), *Can Class Still Unite?* (Aldershot: Ashgate), pp. 247–74.

Phillips, M. (2003), 'Dramatic ruralities in a changing society', in Gao, J., Le Heron, R. and Logie, J. (eds), *Windows on a Changing World* (Auckland: New Zealand Geographical Society), pp. 257–61.

Phillips, M., Fish, R. and Agg, J. (2001), 'Putting together ruralities', *Journal of Rural Studies*, 17: 1–27.

Phillips, M. and Mighall, T. (2000), *Society and Exploitation through Nature* (Harlow: Prentice Hall).

Phillips, R. (1997), *Mapping Men and Empire: A Geography of Adventure* (London: Routledge).

Propp, V. (1970), *Morphology of the Folktale* (Austin: University of Texas Press).

Screen Production Taskforce (2003), *Taking on the World* (Wellington: New Zealand Trade and Enterprise).

Shiel, M. (2001), 'Cinema and the city in history and theory', in Shiel, M. and Fitzmaurice, T. (eds), *Cinema and the City* (Oxford, Blackwell Publishers), pp. 1–18.

Short, J.R. (1991), *Imagined Country* (London: Routledge).

Sibley, B. (2002), *The Lord of the Rings: The Making of a Movie Trilogy* (London: Harper Collins).

Statistics New Zealand (2005), *Tourism and Migration 2004* (Wellington: Statistic New Zealand/Te Tari Tatau www.stats.govt.nz/tables/tables-tourism-2004).

Tincknell, E. (2000), 'New Zealand Gothic?', in Conrich, I. and Woods, D. (eds), *New Zealand: A Pastoral Paradise?* (Nottinham: Kakapo Books), pp. 107–22.

Tolkein, J.R.R. (1936), 'Beowulf, the monsters and the critics: Sir Israel Gollancz Memorial Lecture', *Proceedings of the British Academy*, 22: 245–95.

Tolkein, J.R.R. (1937), *Beowulf: The Monsters and the Critics* (London: Humphrey Milford).

Tolkein, J.R.R. (2003), *The Lord of the Rings* (London: HarperCollins).

Tönnies, F. (1957), *Community and Association* (London: Routledge & Kegan Paul).

Tooke, N. and Baker, M. (1996), 'Seeing is believing', *Tourism Management*, 17: 87–94.

Tzanelli, R. (2004), 'Constructing the "cinematic tourist": the sign industry of *The Lord of the Rings*', *Tourist Studies*, 4: 21–42.

Turner, G. (1993), *National Fictions* (St Leonards: Allen and Unwin).

Wakefield, P. (2001), 'Directing the three Ring circus', *On Film* (December), p. 3.

Watson. D. (2001), 'Rabbit syndrome: Australia and America',

Quarterly Essay, 4: 54–5.

Wright, A. (2000), 'Realms of enchantment', in Conrich, I. and Woods, D. (eds), *New Zealand: A Pastoral Paradise* (Nottingham: Kakapo Books), pp. 52–60.

Part III

Identity and difference

10

Idylls and othernesses: childhood and rurality in film

Owain Jones

'What would we do? Live in a council flat? At least we have the countryside here' (The mother, *Will it Snow at Christmas?*, Veysset, 1996)

Introduction: rurality, childhood and film

The initial premise of this chapter is simple. If there are discourses of rural childhood and rural childhood idyll in literature, music, art, advertisements and so forth, then it can be expected that these will have extended into the realms of television and film as they have risen to cultural pre-eminence throughout the twentieth century. The questions remain; in what ways has this occurred, and in what ways does the medium of film itself develop, intensify and/or subvert the discourses of rurality and childhood it carries?

Social construction is practised through discourses, which 'structure both our sense of reality and our notion of our own identity' (Mills, 1997: 15). They not only *carry* meanings and values through cultures, they are bound up in the creation and maintenance of meaning and values in close relation to ideology and power. This is about the production of knowledge, meanings and value through language *and* social practice (Hall, 1992). Film and television now play an important part in this, and the meanings they make do not remain in the imagined, virtual realm alone. They become enacted, performed and materialised. For example, discourses of rural idyll (Rose, 1996) are played out in processes of counter-urbanisation and middle-class colonisation of the countryside (Boyle and Halfacree, 1998; Murdoch and Day, 1998).

There is a long tradition of studying the nature and consequences of discourses of rurality, and rurality in relation to urbanity, in written and static visual texts of various kinds (Keith, 1975; Williams, 1985; Mingay, 1989; Bunce, 1994). By doing this, not only do we continue the work of understanding the evolution and life cycle of these discourses that are at the heart of powerful social constructions, but we also start to account for the differing articulations of discourse these media produce, particularly in terms of the articulation of imagined landscapes. Inevitably, attention is now being paid to rurality as depicted in television (MaCeachern, 1993; Phillips *et al.*, 2001) and, now, film.

Within discourses of rurality, childhood has often been a particular focus (Williams, 1985; Bunce, 1994). Colin Ward's (1990) book the *Child in the Country* is replete with literary references. Ward observes that constructions of 'the country child' have in large part been propagated through literary discourses. These discourses of country childhood are potent forces and are closely related to the wider idea of idyll (Jones, 1997; 2002). The countryside as idyll was very much a romantic creation which centred on nature. Modern notions of childhood were also romantic constructions, again with nature at their core. Inevitably, then, notions of childhood and the rural were in harmony. The specialness, purity and naturalness of childhood merited a special, pure natural space to be in – the countryside. This always worked in tandem with the notion of the vexed presence of the romantic, Apollonian child (Jenks, 2005) in the demonic cities of nineteenth-century England (Jones, 2002).

As notions of idyll have emerged in filmic expression, so too have notions of rural childhood idyll. As I will show in the first section, some films do indeed portray the rural as a (childhood) idyll. In both films *for children* and films *about children*, their harmonious relationships are depicted and developed. I will briefly look at films made for children and at filmic realisations of famous literary portrayals of children in the countryside and unashamedly idyllic depictions of rural childhood, which deliberately play upon romantic notions of the rural as an ideal childhood environment.

But I want to go beyond this initial and probably quite obvious point to explore two other aspects of childhood in the cinematic countryside. Firstly, heeding Little's (1999) concern about the whole notion of idyll (see also Cloke *et al.*, 1995), I consider films which go beyond obvious ideas of idyll in two ways. The first are films which show the other side of idyll, or life behind the 'façade' of idyll, raising issues of poverty, but also oppression through patriarchal power, and other harsher realities of children's lives. The second way is films which explore what I have termed 'the otherness' of childhood (Jones, 2002; 2003).

In the penultimate section I briefly consider two films which 'play' with the interface between town and country, which offer a particularly telling way of looking at discourses of childhood, the countryside, nature and the city in a filmic context, as children move across boundaries between these symbolic and material spaces. And finally, I offer some thoughts on children, rurality and dwelling.

The rural childhood idyll in films

In much children's literature the rural has featured as both setting and narrative focus (Hunt, 1995; Jones, 1997; Horton, 2003). This continues in films made for children, thus reflecting and developing adult discourses which link childhood, nature and the countryside. The rural is presented as a suitable imaginative destination for children. This also, at the same time, peddles certain discourses about the rural to children (and to parents). Bunce (1994) makes the point that adult discourses of rurality begin when images and descriptions of rurality are absorbed in childhood through exposure to children's books. He argues that 'given the formative experience of the early years, exposure to even small amounts of children's literature must result in the subconscious absorption of stereotypically perceptions of rurality' (2003: 23). This seems convincing, and Bunce (1994; 2003) and Horton (2003) do excellent jobs in delving into the vast range of children's texts in which the countryside is embedded as either a setting and/or subject of narration in some or other way. Horton (2003) importantly begins to also consider television. Many famous children's stories with a rural inflection, such as *Winnie the Pooh* and *Thomas the Tank Engine*, are now to be seen as powerful global brands, which occupy a broad spectrum of media, ranging from books to television, films and products. Even now, these quaint Edwardian tales with their innocent, bucolic British rural settings are consumed on a vast global scale.

Three points can be made about television and film products such as these (and others) as a medium for discourses. Firstly, children can watch films and television before they can read, and thus can assimilate such images at a very early age. Secondly, it would seem that many children watch television/video for many more hours than they read. Thirdly, television and film can be a very intense experience for children (this is not to say reading is not, but reading is hard at first, while pictures and sounds are more accessible). Our children, and many others I have witnessed, watch TV with an attention and absorption that is utter, and are happy to watch favourite programmes and films many times over. So the question of how television and film have become the peddlers of discourses is important.

Inevitably, many of the classics of childhood literature have been turned into films. As this cannon has been reworked in moving images, and new filmic additions made to it, the rural inflection continues and is re-rendered in visualised idyllic terms (even if it is beset by oppression in one way or the other) as in Walt Disney's *Robin Hood*. Classic rural childhood adventures such as *The Railway Children*, *The Secret Garden*, and *The Wind in the Willows* now persist in film as well as print.

The geographical imaginations of the original stories (often visualised in illustrations) is inevitably visualised in a much more complete sense in film. In animated films where designers, animators and background painters can create whole worlds, it is possible to see highly distilled visions of the countryside rendered for childhood consumption. It is easy to decry Disney for its mawkishness, its sometimes dubious political complexion (on and off screen) and, latterly, its status as one of the big bad transnational corporations pushing a certain and corrosive form of cultural/economic globalisation, but its rise to prominence was, in part, built on an ability to take popular geographical imaginations and distil them into incredible, 'high art' renditions. For example, in *The Jungle Book* (watched until the tape wore out in our house) – which may be a rendition of colonial notions of food, nature and the 'the other' (Cook *et al.*, 2004) and a natural space for male childhood where the arrival of the female means the end to the idyll (Jones, 1999) – the drawings of the jungle are quite wondrous distillations of the myth of jungle as an exotic, beautiful paradise. The same can be said of wild Africa in the *Lion King* and pre-European-colonised North America in *Pocahontas*. But these perhaps are more wilderness than countryside. In Disney's *101 Dalmatians* the English countryside is rendered in a way that crystallises the (English) rural idyll into a complete and highly seductive visual form.

The film of Raymond Briggs's classic children's book *The Snowman* continues this tradition of highly rarefied renditions of the English countryside. Typical of Briggs, however, there is a depth and poignancy to the story, so although the boy lives in a ravishingly beautiful rural location, he is lonely, has no one else to play with in the snow, and so he finds a new friend, and they fly off together. The opening sequence, the scenes where he and the snowman ride a motorbike around the woods and fields, and then the key scene when they take off and circle and swoop over the countryside, heading for the coast, all portray a vision of 'perfect English rurality'. The countryside is a pattern of hedges, woods and small hamlets. Animals – owls, rabbits, a fox, a horse – all hove into view. The boy gazes around in delight. As in the animated *101 Dalmatians*, the snowfall renders this perfect countryside white rather than green, thus deepening its purity to a poignantly beautiful pitch.

Live-action film adaptation of children's classics such as *The Railway Children* and *The Secret Garden* could be seen as doing little more than visualising the imagined landscape of their parent books. But the interesting thing is that – with a bit of location research, shot framing and prop and scenery manipulation – the countryside can be easily reconstructed to provide suitable settings for these stories. There is a kind of spiralling logic at work here in which discourses build up momentum. The books were inspired by writers' observations/imaginations of the countryside, which are then rendered in the rarefied imaginative forms that good writers can generate. These books become classics and then are made into films, and filmmakers go back to the countryside to find locations in which to visualise these stories. The countryside is of course an intensely visual discourse: from the paintings of Constable to the evocative covers of the Batsford guides, to acts of walking, driving or riding through the countryside, the visual is the pre-eminent sense. The ubiquitous format of the cinema screen is landscape (not portrait). Film is obviously a visual artifice where scenes of landscape and people in them are produced, ready made then to articulate landscapes of rurality and idyll.

Perhaps one of the most unashamedly idyllic view of country childhood is the home life of the children in *Chitty Chitty Bang*

Bang. Here they live on a hill with an eccentric father and grand-dad, free from rules and school. It is pastoral and sunny (most of the time). The only things missing are a mother – and success for the dad. The magic car delivers both in the end, of course, but only after they have all been to a bad foreign place where children are, in stark contrast, locked away, and strays are caught by the terrifying child catcher on the prowl in the town square. These filmic extensions of the canon of children's literature have inevitably extended the discourse of the rural as an idyll, and as a childhood idyll, and in doing so, through the needs and techniques of film production, have conjured even more rarefied notions of such imagined spaces as the English countryside (and beyond).

Other films (for adult audiences) depict rural childhood as idyll. This again continues a dominant tradition in literature in the most immediate way in so far as iconic books, such as Laurie Lee's *Cider with Rosie* (1962), have been turned into films. These, like the books before them, are more about adult longing and adult assumptions about what it is to be a child. These again involve taking geographical imaginations and rendering them in apparent reality, generating visual realisations of adult discourses. This idea of film constructing childhood in rural space to meet the needs of adult ideals is very well illustrated by the home movies Chislett made of family holidays (Nicholson, 2001) in which rural childhood idyll is constructed: 'Chislett constructs scenes of idealised childhood and family life ... [I]mages of childhood innocence in a rural setting unsullied by war. Mythic visions of an unchanging countryside and the romanticised, self-indulgent scenes of carefree play, echo earlier and enduring conventions in child representation' (Nicholson, 2001: 132).

Nicholson points out that not only were these 'non-fiction' films highly contrived by shot selection, but the holidays themselves and the family itself stage-managed to generate such rarefied images. But it is a complex form of construction in which the living out of the ideal and the desire to record it are in an interdependent escalating relation. In contrast, Chislett later shot films for charity organisations, of children in urban environments where 'the film portrays children as poignant images of urban deprivation [and] victims of the urban environment' (Nicholson, 2001: 132).

These home and amateur movies well illustrate how film can be used to articulate and perpetuate discourses of adult expectations.

This goes for films such as *Cider with Rosie*, where, despite scenes of poverty, hardship and violence (in both book and film), the idea of childhood idyll predominates. Now we turn to films where this relationship is inverted and/or the notion of idyll is lost to other discourses.

Beyond ideas of idyll: oppressions and the otherness of childhood

Behind the mask of idyll

Some studies have focused on children's lives beyond the facade of idyll in the countryside (for example Davis and Ridge, 1997). Some notable films have also shown children's lives in a similar vein in different national contexts, depicting a variety of hardships, but, somehow, the notion of idyll is not always entirely eradicated.

The French Film *Will it Snow at Christmas?* by Sandrine Veysset (1996) is a powerful story of a mother with seven children living and working in poverty in rural southern France in the early 1970s. The film portrays hard, manual horticultural work in the production of crops such as radishes, lettuces and leeks. The seasons play their full part bringing heat, torrential rain and finally snow as the life on the farm unfolds. The mother and children are ruled over, and put to work, by a lover/father who has another, legitimate, family elsewhere. His visits mean even harder work for the older children, brief moments of affection for the younger children, and sexual demands alongside small amounts of tenderness and money for the long-suffering mother. However, childhood does find time and space. The opening scene is of the children playing chase, crawling through straw/hay bales in the barn. They build model farms and houses in the dirt and disused corners of the yard; they sail home-made boats down the irrigation channels built to carry water the fields in summer. The countryside is open yet unremarkable. The children are outside a lot, in the yard in the sun, with dogs roaming amongst them, or playing chase at night. At one point they are told they are lucky to live where they do. The idea of idyll is overshadowed by the oppressions of poverty and child labour, the corrosive patriarchal power, and the predatory sexual aggression of the father, which leads to conflict. This builds to the point where the dedicated mother struggles to keep the family together. I won't give away the ending (I recommend you see it if you haven't). However, despite all, the notion of rural idyll persists. As Holden (1997) says, it depicts life as 'nasty, brutal and idyllic'. Nature is redemptive, as the mother says at one low point 'at least we have the countryside'.

In *Will it Snow at Christmas?*, to an extent, and more so in the very successful pair of films *Jean de Florette* and *Manon des Sources*, which depict rural communities (and therefore children in wider family/community narratives), there seems to be an adult longing for the lost space and time of authentic rurality, where not only childhood, but community and humanity belonged, or dwelt, in landscape and locality. This is a theme to which I return later.

A chapter on childhood, film and rurality should make some reference to the films *The Night of the Hunter* directed by Charles Laughton, and *Ivan's Childhood* The first is a bit of an oddity; it was not initially that successful, critically or commercially, and was therefore the only film that this great English actor directed. It is now regarded as classic, and one of the great American movies. The plot, in essence, is that of two young children, – a brother, aged nine, and a sister, aged six – on the run from a profoundly disturbing character – a fire-brand preacher who is also a serial killer – who suspects the children know the whereabouts of money stolen by their now dead father. The children flee down the Mississippi encountering grotesque visions, wildlife and characters, until taken in by a kind old lady – who is handy with a shotgun. It is a kind of darker, Gothic version of the great America rural childhood books by Mark Twain – almost a rural horror film.

But it is different to the rural horror that David Bell (1997) considered through films such as *Deliverance*. In that film, of course, a child famously appears playing the banjo, and 'duels' with one of the tourists on their canoeing trip which goes so horribly wrong. This child, 'inbred, retarded, autistic' (Bell, 1997: 103) 'is a product of a society at the end of its existence', and communities which seem idyllic but which are in fact 'malignant'. In *The Night of the Hunter* the children are innocent yet also worldly (by necessity). The horror follows them into and through the rural landscape. The American countryside in the post-civil-war era (as in *Huckleberry Finn* and *Tom Sawyer*, books which have been filmed and serialised on television), and in the agricultural depression (as filmed in *The Grapes of Wrath*) seems not only much vaster than the more pastoral, rustic British countryside, but also wilder and unsettled, as populations of settlers, slaves, refugees and the dispossessed are on the move. This offers the children challenges, independence and adventure, in a way reflecting the American frontier sprit.

Ivan's Childhood opens with a lyrical scene of child in nature as Ivan – beautiful, fresh faced, full of wonder – apparently flies through treetops, sees animals, hears a cuckoo, meets his pretty, happy mother in the woods and drinks clear clean water from her bucket, like a young animal. Then he wakes in the war-torn countryside of the Second World War Eastern Front. Further flashbacks of innocence, companionship and nature contrast with the barren, bitter landscape and life of Ivan's present as he works (in this instance) as a child spy for the Russian forces. The connections between nature and childhood are darkly inverted as it is revealed that Ivan uses berries, fir cones and differing types of leaves to record German troop positions and armour. The end scenes, as flashbacks, return Ivan to nature and happiness, although the war has had its inevitable consequence for him.

What these above films present is the idea that childhood in the countryside can be tainted and oppressed by adult geographies. The countryside as space of labour exploitation and poverty – of family conflict and gender inequalities – or as a space of war. Children are victims (with agency) in the face of such unsympathetic, indifferent or hostile adult striations of space. War seems the starkest corruption of space. The film *Turtles Can Fly* (Bahman Ghobadi, 2004) depicts the life of village children in Iraq before and during the 2003 invasion. The children seem to have established a moral (and fiscal) economy of their own, and are very much at large in the countryside. But the currency is munitions left over from previous conflicts, and much of the (possibly beautiful) countryside is laced with land mines – perhaps the ultimate adult striation of (rural) space in terms of hostility to childhood. *Ararat* by Atom Egoyan (2003) also shows a brutal inversion of any idea of the country childhood idyll in the scene where a child sits under a wooden hay cart, holding hands with his Armenian mother as she is raped by a soldier on the boards above.

The acclaimed film *Tree of Wooden Clogs* (Ermanno Olmi, 1978) bears some similarities with *Will it Snow at Christmas?* Set in Bergamo, Lombardy, Italy in the 1900s it depicts the poor, rural, working-class life of five families living in a farmstead in rich detail (and employed local people to play parts in the film). Here, again, there is disquieting hardship and oppression, in this instance in the form of harsh terms of tenancy and rule of overseers. The film takes its title from a scene when a father cuts down a tree to make his son a new pair of clogs, and despite their efforts to disguise the 'theft', harsh retributions follow for the entire family. But also like *Will it Snow at Christmas?* there is an underlying theme of rural authenticity and dwelling, and an attachment between people and nature and the land, a theme to which we will return. The children in the farmstead are often the focus of the camera, working with the family in the barns and fields, playing (sometimes), and living with nature in terms of the landscape and farm animals.

The 'otherness' of childhood

In the film *Whistle Down the Wind* (Bryan Forbes, 1962) three children living in a farmhouse in north Lancashire find a man in a barn, who, for various reasons, they consider to be Jesus Christ. It's a secret. A series of comings and goings between the farmhouse, barn and local school take place with a slowly increasing number of children being in on the secret. All the while the audience, but not the children know the man is a dangerous fugitive.

From the opening scene with the three children secretly following the farm hand, to the last extraordinary shots of two other young children looking up into the camera and then turning and walking away, the whole film is premised on the apparently complete, independent spatial freedom of the children to roam in the countryside. The film visually plays with ideas of childhood, idyll and nature. Children are framed as small figures moving through large vistas, and the plot is partly driven by the children's affinity with animals.

Most of all, though, the film is notable for the extent to which it effectively depicts the children's other world and its emotional economy. Their world is depicted as separate from that of the adults. This separateness is achieved partly through their independence, partly through the children's subterfuge and lies (the everyday lies all tell), and partly through adult indifference and disdain. Their otherness is shown through the solemnity and matter-of-factness with which they deal with confronting and then caring for 'Jesus Christ'. Their own worlds of conflict, secrecy from each other, dealing with sibling jealousies, bullies at school, and betrayals are all carefully presented by the camera. This is not so much idyll, as a space in which children's lives unfold in becomings of fullness and otherness remote from the surveillance of adults.

Etre et Avoir, by Nicholas Philbert (2003), was a surprise success not only in its home country in France, but in the UK and elsewhere. Rarely does a quiet documentary film end up competing with Hollywood blockbusters on general release. This film depicts life in a small, one-class infant school in the village of Puys-de-Dome, in Auvergne, South West France. The story follows the class and its one teacher through a year of schooling. It picks up on minor (to us) dramas in the classroom and playground, and shows glimpses of some of the children's (rural) lives beyond school. It also has the storyline that the skilful and seemingly endlessly patient teacher is heading for retirement. Nature again is articulated as a real presence, through outdoor walks, the changing seasons, and through one powerful shot where the screen fills with trees near the school billowing in a storm. The glimpses of life beyond school show a poor farming community. One child, not very capable at his lessons, is seen working at home on the farm, expertly driving a tractor. The film is notable for the un-patronising, non-judgemental depiction of the everyday lives of the children. They are not treated as beings-in-waiting (although the question of their future in the 'big school' in a town some distance away is raised). Again, their becoming, their joys and pains are taken seriously. Idyll is not the major theme. The viewer is a witness to a scene in the playground where a small injustice occurs because the teacher did not see what happened but the camera did.

To me these films are more centred on the children themselves than on adult discourse of what childhood is and where it should be; idyll, or anti-idyll for that matter, are not very meaningful constructs for children. What matters to them are the practices of everyday life in family, friends, community and landscape. This emotional ecology of being depends on much, and is experienced in ways we cannot fully know, but can observe.

I have argued elsewhere that there is an otherness to childhood to which adult knowledge cannot fully return. This raises questions about research aims, ethics and methodologies. The camera can be a frank and illuminating eye. Sensitive filming of children as in *Etre et Avoir* can show the otherness of childhood at work, as, say, a sequence of fleeting expressions of concern, interest, frustration and anger flits across the face of a child doing some task in class. We cannot know fully what these experiences are, but we can see that these experiences are real and deep and relevant, even if the child is involved in what might be seen as a trivial and ephemeral task.

Films featuring children and childhood nicely point out the deep complexity of adulthood–childhood relations. Adult constructions of childhood by adults are in many ways more about the aspirations, desires and fears of adulthood than they are about the lived experiences of children themselves (Higonnet, 1998). In film, the image of the child, in the country, or anywhere else, becomes more 'real' as child actors or actresses appear on the screen. The adult construction becomes 'flesh' and can be framed and set in carefully selected settings and actions. Thus, while childhood on screen looks more real as it is embodied and performed by children, it can be, in fact, one of the most complete adult constructions of them all, as adult discourses – manifested through film writers, directors and cinema photographers – get to manipulate the body of the child as well as the image and idea of a child in the rendering of their discourses.

The edge of the countryside

If the urban has a fringe then it stands that that which it meets has a fringe too (that is, the rural fringe). This border territory offers a chance for narratives of childhood including those by filmmakers to play with, or explore, crossings of children/childhood between the town and the country. A notable example of this is the film *Kes* by Ken Loach. In the novel upon which the film is based by Barry Hines (1969), the hero, Billy, moves between his home and school in a northern town and the surrounding countryside. Home, school and town represent bullying, humiliation and often despair. When, in the novel, he first moves from the housing estate and out into the country the sense of release is palpable:

[He is running, having thrown some pebbles at a window from which he had been shooed away from by the mother of a friend]

he ran back across the estate and straight down the avenue ... He cut down a snicket between two houses, out into the fields leaving the estate behind him.

The sun was up and the cloud band in the east had thinned to a line on the horizon. The air was still and clean, and trilling of larks carried far over the fields of hay, which stretched away on both sides of the path. Great rashes of buttercups spread across the fields, and amongst the mingling shade of yellow and green, dog daisies showed their white faces, contrasting with the rust of sorrel. All underscored by clovers, white and pink and purple, which came into their own on the path sides where the grass was shorter, along with daisies and the ubiquitous plantains.

A cushion of mist lay over the fields. Dew drenched the grass, and the occasional sparkling of individual drops made Billy glance down as he passed. One tuft was a silver fire. He knelt down to trace the source of light. The drop had almost forced the blade of grass to the earth, and it laid in the curve of the blade like the tiny egg of a myth-ical bird. Billy moved his head from side to side to make it sparkle, and when it caught the sun it exploded, throwing out silver needles and crystal splinters. He lowered his head and slowly, very carefully touched it with the tip of his tongue. (Hines, 1969: 23–4)

This is a startlingly lyrical excerpt from a novel known for its dour grittiness. The sense of space opening out after passing through the last houses is more than empirical, it is a scene of the child soul opening up to beauty and to nature – the romantic discourse holding firm. The water droplet is a promise of the kestrel to come and Billy even connects with its purity by touching it with his tongue.

How, it is interesting to ask, is this pivotal moment in the book rendered in the famous film made of *Kes*? My overriding memory of the film is Billy out on moorland, with Kes, above the city with many of the shots showing this boy in nature with a wild creature and the grey town as a contrast and backdrop. Indeed, when I watched it again, shots which looked through the town into the country, and vice versa, are a common theme. Billy is framed in them on a number of occasions. What I didn't remember were the other children populating the streets, in a classic vision of pre-car-dominated urban street life. When Billy enters the fields in the same point of the story the scene is very different. The pastoral, favourable mood is established by music, but Billy is not finding wonder in a drop of water refracting light, rather he is swishing at branches and stinging nettles with a stick. He throws a lump of wood into a pond. This is much more the child as other than child as natural innocent. However, the romantic sensibilities are not entirely abandoned. The film instead makes the flight of the kestrels, hunting in and out of their nest in the ruin of the barn, the moment of lyricism. Billy, framed in black shadow, watches, and the screen is then filled with sky, as the camera follows the bird in flight, hovering then moving on. The music trills. Here is the moment of connection with nature, the redemption of Billy, a boy who, a few scenes earlier, had been seen stealing and lying as he made his way around town.

Ratcatcher (1996) by Lynne Ramsey is a powerful exposition of ideas of urban childhood distopia (but not straightforwardly so). It is set on a poor Glasgow housing estate in the 'Winter of Discontent' (1978–79). There is a strike by refuse collectors so the streets in which many children sit around, play and fight are strewn with rubbish. The film starts with a strange, disturbing image of a child apparently being wrapped in some material and spinning around. This, it turns out, is James spinning himself around in his mother's net curtains before he is shooed out to play. The urban is actually depicted as a semi-wilderness, much action taking place in an overgrown wasteland with a canal running through it. James witnesses another boy drowning in the canal and this remains a dark secret. He has built an idea that he wants to move to new houses being built on the edge of the city and there is a break in the naturalistic tenor in the film when, in a pivotal magical/fantasy sequence, he is running through the fields on the edge of the city, a reference to the rightness and hope of nature as child environment.

These films, then, rather reinforce the country childhood idyll idea. But idyll is not to be seen as some simple surfacy space/place which is fun and free for children, it is about profound, deeply embedded concern and aspiration for individual and collective life in modernity.

Conclusions. The persistence of idyll: childhood and dwelling

Bunce (1994; 2003) discusses in convincing detail 'the depth and durability of the rural idyll as a cultural construction which has evolved with the rise of anti-urbanism' (2003: 22–3; see also Lowe *et al.*, 1995). It is clear that such discourses of the country as a space for children and country childhood idyll are easily identified in filmic output. Films have become very powerful purveyors of cultural discourses. In the nature of films and television, discourses that were once a matter of text – and isolated, static images – are realised in apparent 'real life' in terms of spaces, bodies and movements. But films have also, at the same time, developed, intensified and challenged this.

The notion of idyll maybe questionable in many ways, but I feel it is the discourse that haunts the films discussed. So having tried to go beyond the idyll I am forced back to it. Not only are notions of childhoods and rurality inflected with romantic sensibilities, so too are wider constructions of the condition of humanity, which sees the industrial revolution, the growth of modern capitalism, urbanism, science, liberalism and secularism as highly problematic. The rural, against all the odds and all evidence, remains a place partly outside this process (most obviously outside urbanisation), and thus a refuge not only for the romantic child, but romantic society.

Films are important in this respect in two ways. Many of the films discussed, notably *Will it Snow at Christmas?* and *The Tree of Wooden Clogs* have been credited as notable artistic achievements. They are thus not to be taken lightly in terms of peddling cheap or shallow renderings of rural authenticity and, within that, country childhood discourses. The complexity, the difficulties and the otherness of children's varying experiences are depicted with subtlety and insight. The experiences in *Will it Snow at Christmas?* and in *Tree of Wooden Clogs* are often far from idyllic. But despite this, somehow the idea of the rural as a natural, good place for childhood sustains.

These films depict – to an extent at least – what could be seen as dwelling as famously set out by Ingold (1993; see also Macnaghten and Urry, 1998). Dwelling is, in one sense, about an authentic and fulfilled pattern of collective living. It is about communities enduring over time and space and about connectiveness with landscape and nature; children are a key element in this (Bahktin, 1981). Dwelling is about trying to achieve this within the modes of social reproduction that people inevitably find themselves enmeshed.

But this is not really so much about the rural *per se*, or the rural idyll – it is about (urban) modernity as the absent other. Although this begs a number of questions, the predominantly technological and urban conditions of modernity have made any notion of dwelling as originally set out by Heidegger impossible (that's why he set out his vision of peasant rurality when seeking out an expression of this idea). Ingold's (1993) dwelling example is also a traditional rural vision. As Macnaghten and Urry (1998) suggest, dwelling in a landscape becomes compromised by the speed and mobility of modern practices (for example the car); it feels as if modernity *has* produced the non-places that Auge (1995) discusses. These are the apotheosis of globalisation's impact on authentic, or at least meaningful, places, and are the culmination of this eradication of dwelling by modernity. Although these films portray hardship and oppression, they still resonate with a nostalgia and longing for authentic community in touch with place, landscape and nature. The films are not simply an assertion of the countryside as context for community and childhood. They are a sort of assertion that all people, communities, families, and children within them, were better off, at some deep level, in these authentic, dwelt lives. To put it simply, to be poor and oppressed in an authentic rural landscape is better than being poor and oppressed in an urban setting. In the former, attachment of place, nature and landscape and the depth of belonging in community gives you something; in the latter, all that is swept away by the mobility and anonymity of life. This is the anti-urban/modernism which has been a driving force in Anglo-centric culture (Lowe *et al.*, 1995). Childhood has its place in the imagined city and in the imagined country, and the (rural) idyll persists as an idea, but can be corrupted by the horrors of the world.

References

Auge, M. (1995), *Non-Places: Introduction to an Anthropology of Supermodernity* (London: Verso).

Bahktin, M.M. (1981), *The Dialogic Imagination* (Austin: University of Texas Press).

Bell, D. (1997), 'Anti-idyll: rural horror', in Cloke, P. and Little, J. (eds), *Contested Countryside Cultures* (London: Routledge), pp. 94–108.

Boyle, P. and Halfacree, K. (eds) (1998), *Migration into Rural Areas: Theories and Issues* (Chichester: John Wiley and Sons).

Bunce, M. (1994), *The Countryside Ideal: Anglo-American Images of Landscape* (London: Routledge).

Bunce, M. (2003), 'Reproducing the Idyll', in Cloke, P. (ed.), *Country Visions* (London: Pearson Education), pp. 14–30.

Cloke, P., Phillips, M. and Thrift, N. (1995), 'The new middle classes and the social constructs of rural living', in Butler, T. and Savage, M. (eds), *Social Change and the Middle Classes* (London: UCL Press).

Cook, I., Crang, P. and Thorpe, M. (2004), 'Tropics of consumption: "getting with the fetish" of "exotic" fruit', in Hughes, A. and Reiner, S. (eds), *Geographies of Commodities* (London: Routledge), pp. 173–92.

Davis, J. and Ridge, T. (1997), *Same Scenery, Different Lifestyle: Rural Children on a Low Income* (London: The Children's Society).

Hall, S. (1992), 'The rest and the west: discourse and power', in Hall, S. and Gieben, B. (eds), *Formations of Modernity* (Cambridge: Polity Press), pp. 291–5.

Higonnet, A. (1998), *Pictures of Innocence: The History and Crisis of Ideal Childhood* (London: Thames and Hudson).

Hines, B. (1969), *Kes* (Harmondsworth: Penguin Books).

Holden, S. (1997), 'Nasty, brutish and idyllic, review of *Will it Snow for Christmas?*', *New York Times* on the Web, www.nytimes.com (accessed May 2006).

Horton, J. (2003), 'Different genres, different visions? The changing countryside in postwar British children's literature', in Cloke, P. (ed.), *Country Visions* (London: Pearson Education), pp. 73–92.

Hunt, P. (1995), *Children's Literature: An Illustrated History* (Oxford: Oxford University Press).

Ingold, T. (1993), 'The temporality of landscape', *World Archaeology*, 25: 152–74.

Jenks, C. (2005), *Childhood* (London: Routledge) (second edition).

Jones, O. (1997), 'Little figures, big shadows, country childhood stories', in Cloke, P. and Little, J. (eds), *Contested Countryside Cultures* (London: Routledge), pp. 158–79.

Jones, O. (1999), 'Tomboy tales: the rural, nature and the gender of childhood', *Gender, Place and Culture*, 6(2): 117–36.

Jones, O. (2002), 'Naturally not! Childhood, the urban and romanticism', *Human Ecology Review*, 9(2): 17–30.

Jones, O. (2003), '"Endlessly revisited and forever gone": on memory and emotional imaginations in doing children's geographies. An "addendum" to "'To Go Back up the Side Hill': memories, imaginations and reveries of childhood" by Chris Philo', *Children's Geographies*, 1(1): 25–36.

Keith, W.J. (1975), *The Rural Tradition: William Cobbett, Gilbert White: And other Non-fiction Prose Writers of the English Countryside* (Brighton: Harvester Press).

Lee, L. (1962), *Cider with Rosie* (London: Penguin).

Little, J. (1999), 'Otherness, representation and the cultural construction of rurality', *Progress in Human Geography*, 23: 437–42.

Lowe, P., Murdoch, J. and Cox, G. (1995), 'A civilised retreat? Anti-urbanism, rurality and the making of an Anglo-centric culture', in Healey, P., Cameron, S., Davoudi, S., Graham, S. and Madani-Pour, A. (eds), *Managing Cities: The New Urban Context* (London: Wiley).

MaCeachern, C. (1993), 'Time and the significance of the rural in a British soap opera', *Time and Society*, 2(1): 7–28.

Macnaghten, P. and Urry, J. (1998), *Contested Natures* (London: Sage).

Mills, S. (1997), *Discourse* (London: Routledge).

Mingay, G. (ed.) (1989), *The Rural Idyll* (London: Routledge).

Murdoch, J. and Day, G. (1998), 'Middle-class mobility, rural communities and the politics of exclusion', in Boyle, P. and Halfacree, K. (eds), *Migration into Rural Areas: Theories and Issues* (Chichester: John Wiley and Sons), pp. 186–99.

Nicholson, H.N. (2001), 'Seeing how it was? Childhood geographies and memories in home movies', *Area*, 33(2): 128–40.

Phillips, M., Fish, R. and Agg, J. (2001), 'Putting together ruralities: towards a symbolic analysis of rurality in the British mass media', *Journal of Rural Studies*, 17: 1–27.

Rose, G. (1996), 'Place and identity: a sense of pzfclace', in Massey, D. and Jess, P. (eds), *A Place in the World* (Oxford: Oxford University Press), pp. 106–18.

Ward, C. (1990), *The Child in the Country* (London: Bedford Square Press).

Williams, R. (1985), *The Country and the City* (London: The Hogarth Press).

11

Deviant sexualities and dark ruralities in *The War Zone*

Michael Leyshon and Catherine Brace

Introduction

This chapter brings together recent work on rural landscapes and identity, the lives of young people in rural areas and the representation of rural youth in fiction to construct a critical analysis of Tim Roth's film *The War Zone* (1998). Based on the novel by Alexander Stuart, first published in 1989 (Stuart, 1999), *The War Zone* tells the story of Tom's traumatic adolescence, the discovery of his sister, Jessie's, incestuous relationship with their father and the subsequent melt-down of the family. Set in north Devon, the film reconfigures the rural as aberrant, heteroclitic and sinister in several linked ways. First, it challenges the lay discourse which positions the countryside as a safe place in which to grow up by portraying it as alienating and marginalising. Second, it resists the popular image of rural sexuality as playful, innocent fumbling in a hayloft by foregrounding Tom and Jessie's exploration of their (deviant) sexual identities. Finally, by using as its setting the bleak landscape of north Devon, it envisions a contemporary alternative to a historically constituted version of rural England as a green and pleasant land. Taking these three themes as its focus, this chapter will explore both the production of the film and the alternative ruralities within it.

Plot synopsis

The War Zone was released in 1998 by Film Four.[1] It was the directorial debut of the actor Tim Roth and was based on the novel of the same name by Alexander Stuart, who also wrote the screenplay. In a film characterised by silences, meaningful looks, mute insinuations, incriminating body language and stillness punctuated by violent accusations, a synopsis of the action is, of necessity, short and tricky.

The family have moved from London into an isolated cottage in north Devon. After a car crash in the country lanes, Mum's baby is delivered at the crash site. Whilst Mum and the baby remain in hospital, Dad and the others get on with life in the cottage. Tom exhibits a clumsy but burgeoning sexual attraction to their cleaner, Lucy. He also discovers his father and Jessie sharing an illicit bath together. Tom confronts Jessie in private, but she calls him sick. Later in the pub, Tom notices his dad's possessive response when Jessie hooks up with a local lad, Nick. Tom sits forlornly on the beach while Jessie and Nick find a quiet spot to have sex in the dunes. When Tom and Jessie arrive back at the cottage, Dad looses his temper, slapping Jessie in a jealous rage. Later, Tom goes through Jessie's private possessions until he finds several polaroids of her naked, including one of Dad holding her breasts. Deranged with anger and confusion, he attacks Jessie in her bed. Jessie tries to turn Tom's accusations back on him by pointing out that he is obsessed with sex. As Tom leaves, Jessie cries herself to sleep. Tom discovers that Jessie is using a deserted wartime bunker on the cliffs to have sex with Nick and Dad. When Jessie and Dad leave the house separately on apparently different errands, Tom follows them to the bunker and films them having sex. Later, Tom again challenges Jessie who allows Tom to deliberately burn her breasts with a cigarette lighter in a twisted challenge to his feelings. On a trip to London with Dad, Jessie persuades her friend Carol to have sex with Tom to keep him happy. There are hints that Jessie is in a lesbian relationship with Carol. When they return to Devon, baby Alice falls ill and has to be rushed to hospital. On a visit to the hospital, Tom, now deranged and incomprehensible with rage, confusion and unhappiness, tells Mum not to trust Dad and that she must keep him away from the baby. When he arrives back at the cottage, Dad is raging that Mum won't see or speak to him. Jessie is sobbing at the kitchen table. Tom accuses Dad of incest and Dad attacks him before storming out to go to the hospital. When Dad arrives back, Tom and Jessie jointly confront him. When Dad tries to turn the accusations back on his children, Tom stabs him and flees. In the final scene, Tom is joined by Jessie in the bunker. They sit quietly, unspeaking, and Tom closes the door, shutting them both in.

Imagining young people in the countryside

Research on rural youth continually runs up against and attempts to destabilise popularly held views on what it must be like to be a young person in the countryside, in particular the notion that rural youth are harmoniously embedded into the daily routines and practices of countryside living. Valentine (1997), in her study of parents living in the countryside, illustrates this point by showing how they construct an anti-modernist idyllic discourse around their children, and discussed them in terms of innocents who need protection from the vagaries of contemporary society. Through raising their children in the countryside parents believe that their children can feel a sense of belonging and that the countryside and their physical distance from urban spaces does protect them, to a certain degree, against urban vice. This discourse of rurality is predicated on the construction of a 'purified' naturalised space of the countryside (Sibley, 1995), in which home and community are created as safe, inclusive, wholesome and, importantly, distant from the abject, marginalising and dysfunctional spaces of the city (Jones, 1995). This discourse works in two interrelated ways on young people: firstly, positioning young people as bound to nature/countryside suggests they are intrinsically 'good'; secondly, for raising the 'good young person' the 'privileged' spaces (Takahashi, 1998) of the countryside need protecting and the borders patrolled from urban incursions (both literally or imaginatively) (Cloke *et al.*, 2000). However current research by Leyshon (2003) and Matthews *et al.* (2000) contend that young people's experience of rural living is incongruous with notions of the rural idyll by illustrating that they are paradoxically situated within the countryside. Leyshon (2003) argues that young people are often seen as a problem rather than contributory members of their community, and as such their activities and spaces become regulated. Parents often resolve this paradox by dividing young people into their own and the *others* (Aitken, 2000). Thus, parents strive to limit their children's interaction with other young people.

The War Zone is part of a contemporary discourse on rural youth which constructs a dark alternative to a popular ideal characterised by the carefree adventures of Arthur Ransome's *Swallows and Amazons* (1928) or examples of Enid Blyton's enormous output including the Famous Five, Adventurous Four, Secret Seven and *The Children of Cherrytree Farm* (1940). In their research on the vicarious constructions of childhood in children's literature, Jones (1997) and Kent (1999) identify how early twentieth-century cultural texts, such as Laurie Lee's (1959) *Cider With Rosie* and Flora Thompson's (1945) *Lark Rise to Candleford*, present powerful evocations through recollected childhoods that celebrate the countryside as a rural idyll. Similar images can be found in Denton Welch's (1945) book *In Youth is Pleasure* and Herbert Asquith's (1950) poems *Youth in the Skies*, in which rural youth are seen to belong in and be part of the countryside. Matthews *et al.* (2000: 2) claim that the overwhelming image of these texts is 'of a glorious place where children can grow up safely' in a well-organised pastoral-agricultural environment. Although, as Valentine (1996) suggests, these images serve to reinforce the parental attitudes that growing up in the countryside is safe and therefore good for their children, *Cider With Rosie* is far from a celebration of the rural idyll, but is rather a very sinister novel portraying the countryside, in Bell's (1997) terminology, as an 'anti- or dark-idyll'. However, the popular mythology surrounding texts such as *Cider With Rosie* is more powerful than the actual textual images of murder, planned and attempted rape, bestiality and animal cruelty that Lee describes in some detail.

The War Zone has to be understood in the context of an alternative vision of the rural based in contemporary film and literature. *Morvern Callar* (2002),[2] for example, is a hedonistic, dark and disturbing portrayal of a young woman in a remote Scottish town. Morvern is a supermarket stacker who on Christmas morning discovers her boyfriend has committed suicide in their kitchen, leaving his novel and credit cards. His death signifies her liberation and release from a mundane, routinised and sterile rural life. She spends her dead boyfriend's money on clubbing, drugs, alcohol and a Mediterranean holiday before returning home. In part the movie draws on stereotypical images of rural youth as Morvern is presented as a bored and vulnerable young woman, distant from, but longing for, excitement and stimulation in the form of music and youth culture. However, more darkly, she is also portrayed as a cold and amoral opportunist, who uses the remoteness of the

Scottish Highlands to avoid the gaze of suspicion as she steals her boyfriend's identity for her own financial gain and then engages in the grotesque act of amputating and then burying his body parts. The film works as a succession of moments in Morvern's life in which the narrative tempo swings from high velocity infused with pounding club music to stillness and silence when Morvern cuddles up to the corpse, lit intermittently by flashing Christmas tree lights. They are moments that succeed each other in a kind of narrative weightlessness: an extra-temporal sequence of events in which the rural is juxtaposed with a dysfunctional antithesis. Whilst this is not realism, the film attempts to convert the size and shape of the 'real' world of a rural youth into something subtly, yet radically and disturbingly, strange.

Youth stylised novels from the late twentieth century such as James Hawes' *A White Merc With Fins* (1996) also present a rather different vision of what it is like to live and grow up in the country-side. Hawes depicts rural young people as being bored and boorish, and perhaps tipsy on half a pint of cider outside the village hall. Indeed, their only redeeming feature appears to be their ability to dream of escape to the city, where presumably their desires and aspirations can be satisfied. Hawes' account of rural youth is not an isolated one. Indeed, amongst the recent proliferation of stylised youth novels which are primarily situated in urban contexts – such as Rebecca Ray's (1998) *A Certain Age*, Irvine Welsh's (1993) *Trainspotting* and Krissy Kays' (1997) *Wasted* to name but three – can be found similar terse statements deriding the lives of rural youth. Their shock value lies in locating in the countryside a group of young people who are consumption-oriented, and into sub-cultural styles founded on drugs, music and urban living. Tim Roth's film *The War Zone* (1998) and *A White Merc with Fins* (1996) portray a very bleak image of what it is like to grow up as a rural youth and detail, albeit at differing scales, the decline of the English countryside. The prognosis of the countryside is so bleak that in Christopher Hart's *Harvest* (1999) (set in the Wessex down-lands), the lead character Lewis Pike, when faced with the prospect of being forced to leave the village in which his family have lived for generations, commits suicide on the altar of the parish church. Burgess' *Junk* (1997) is no less desolate as the two sixteen-year-old main characters leave the fictitious rural town of Minely-on-Sea in the hope of a better life in Bristol. Their travels and encounters in

Bristol result in their decline into drugs and prostitution as they lack the social skills to negotiate the city and its people. Pears' *In the Place of Fallen Leaves* (1994) presents an image of the countryside as populated by at best eccentric and at worst dysfunctional local families at odds with incomers from nearby cities.

Contemporary films and recently published novels on rural youth depict young people's lives in the countryside being at odds with the early literary projections of a happy, innocent and carefree time. The young characters' personal voyages of discovery are mirrored in discussions on the condition of the countryside. Authors and directors extract dramatic tension from juxtaposing the idea of the countryside as a moral repository of order, aesthetic harmony, nationhood and identity with the transitory, abject and deviant behaviour of young people living there. The films and novels mentioned here portray young people's lives in a way that punctures the hermetic seal of the rural idyll. Through focusing on the social, political and cultural nexus of a single location, these stories bring a sense of a differentiated world in the countryside; young people are positioned as included or excluded depending on changing circumstances. Such writing and the motifs used serve to challenge the early twentieth-century conception of a coherent 'universal' childhood of innocence, vulnerability and happiness without responsibility. Images of rural youth portrayed in *The War Zone* and *Morvern Callar* suggest that there can be no return to the past and a golden age as represented by competing discourses of nostalgia. The central message these stories relay is that 'identities are embedded, recreated and sustained through specific practices and milieu' (Crang, 1999: 448), but once these practices are challenged from perceived external sources something 'real' is lost forever (Brace, 1999a).

As well as contesting the youthful idyll of the imagination, the books and films mentioned here also force us to ask searching questions about how to define 'youth'. Youth as a category is understood to be the gap between being a child and an adult, but this deceptively simple statement hides quite a complex debate about whether youth 'starts' at a certain age. This effort to order youth into a specific age bracket only works if it is based on the understanding that there is a condition between childhood and adulthood, a liminal period of transition, from innocence and immaturity to awareness and maturity. But this recognition of a condition between childhood and adulthood also, paradoxically, *frustrates* attempts to decide on an age-bracket, for it is virtually impossible to know when an individual has 'arrived' at adulthood. Further, the credibility of an age bracket becomes questionable when everyone clearly does not 'arrive' at adulthood at the same time. *The War Zone* complicates attempts to categorise youth by constructing the teenage Jessie as worldly, sexually experienced, experimenting with different sexual and sensual possibilities such as pain, incest, casual heterosexual sex and gay sex. Tom is her antithesis: he is clumsy and virginal, inexperienced in sexual politics and transfixed by Jessie's sexual poise and maturity beyond her years.

The War Zone destabilises the idea of the innocent rural childhood and youth in a number of ways. First, and most evidently, the grey, dank winter of north Devon runs counter to the eternal summerland of happy youth, long summer holidays and innocent outdoor adventures that characterises the rural in early twentieth-century popular fiction and film from Enid Blyton to *The Railway Children* (1970). The use of winter in the film is an interesting departure from the book which, like many other rites of passage novels about young people, is set in an unnaturally hot summer. In his film notes, Stuart reflects that 'summer was really important to me in the novel – the idea of a really hot, unusual, primal English summer, with Devon as almost a jungle: nature gone crazy' (Stuart, 1999: 305–6). The unpredictability of the English summer for filming and Stuart's enjoyment of the Cohen brothers' film *Fargo* (1996), set in the frozen winter, convinced him to go with 'a far bleaker natural backdrop' for the screenplay. He noted that 'this seemed to fit absolutely with Tim's thinking – he was already talking very precisely about how he'd like to shoot the film, using a widescreen format and powerful Turneresque landscapes' (Stuart, 1999: 306).

The second way in which the film upsets the iconic construction of growing up in the countryside lies in Tom's own reaction to Devon. Tom's troubled adolescence is not smoothed by his encounter with rurality. He is not remade by contact with nature and the outdoors. On the contrary, he is moody, resentful and uncommunicative. The third challenge to the innocence and adventure of a youth spent in the countryside lies in the suggestion that Dad moved the family to Devon to continue his incestuous relationship with Jessie, hidden in an isolated cottage away from friends, neighbours and colleagues in London. Some of these points are explored further below. However, this chapter now turns to a detailed consideration of sexuality in *The War Zone*.

Rural sexualities

The sexualities on display in *The War Zone* are complex, fluid and on the move. The boundaries around appropriate sexual behaviour are continually transgressed in unexpected ways by the revelation that Jessie might have instigated a sexual relationship with her father and by Tom's tortured complicity in the relationship. Tim Roth and Alexander Stuart play on assumptions about the nature of sexuality in the rural to add weight to their portrayal of incest and abuse. Whereas in the popular imaginary the city can be readily associated with sexual deviance, the rural is associated with innocent, roll-in-the-hay sex without the carnality. Little (2003: 403) has argued that this popular construction of rural sexuality serves to naturalise heterosexual normalcy and affirms 'the idea of procreative sex as the quintessential sexual act'. In this way sex is, according to Hubbard (2000), de-eroticised because sexuality is in the service of a higher purpose. Sex is defined through popular discourses of morality that serve to naturalise the view that sex must be based on an exchange that is meaningful both materially and emotionally and is based on procreative sexual intercourse. Sex for any other purpose is thus seen as deviant. The performance of rural sexuality is therefore immersed in power-relations that define gender roles and the appropriateness of sex in the country-side (Little and Leyshon, 2003).

Tom has reached a point of maximum adolescent awkwardness: spotty and solemn, chronically inept in attracting Lucy, the local girl who cleans for the family, and incapable of preventing himself from noticing his sister and his mother in a sexual way. He is riveted by the site of his mother's breasts after she has fed the baby, and he snatches glances at Lucy's breasts wobbling braless under her t-shirt. Yet what should be a period of sexual exploration and awareness for Tom is fundamentally altered by his discovery of the relationship between his dad and his sister. Having accepted that the incest exists, Tom struggles to apportion blame. Even here, though, his assumptions that Dad is to blame are countered by the suspicion that Jessie might have instigated the relationship. Even as he is overwhelmed with fear and disgust, he is also drawn in and becomes complicit. He could stop it with a word to his Mum, but instead he finds himself unable to look away. In his attempts to gather 'evidence' using his video camera at the bunker he becomes a terrified voyeur, engrossing himself by pressing his face closer and closer to the slit to see what is going on. He ends up flinging the video camera over the cliff.

Jessie's own sexuality is complex and ambiguous. There is a suggestion of a lesbian relationship with her friend in London, Carol. Jessie is portrayed as a sexual predator who has recently come to learn the power of her own sexuality over others and in particular the power of her sophisticated, urbane brand of sexuality over the local country boys. This is contrasted with Lucy, who holds an unsophisticated rosy-cheeked, rustic appeal to Tom. The contradictions and ambiguities that surround Jessie's relationship with her father are many: it is never clear who began the sexual relationship, but Jessie sees sex with her father as a form of adventure and power. She has a hedonistic urge to experience danger and pain. Her secret knowledge of the relationship alters her relationship with her mother, who becomes a rival as well as a source of maternal comfort. Though seeking empowerment through sex with her father, Jessie is also damaged by it. When he wants anal intercourse at the bunker she asks him 'why don't you do it like you do it with Mum?' to which he replies 'I mustn't do that'. The experience is far from pleasurable for Jessie who sobs openly throughout. In the film's penultimate scene in which Jessie and Tom confront Dad, Jessie's casual sophistication and hardened indifference are stripped away by Dad's denials.

Sexual behaviour and flows of power in the film are structured around relations of looking. The film's dialogue is sparse. Characters stare at each other knowingly, try to avoid each others' eyes, refuse to see, let their eyes slide over each other, are incriminated and attempt to avoid incrimination through the mechanism of the gaze through which knowledge and power flow. Two key shots indicate the importance of these relations of looking. The first is the opening shot in which the coastal landscape is glimpsed through the look-out slot in the bunker. The slot both enables and constrains sight, framing a restricted view in concrete. The viewer sees some things and interpolates others, imaginatively filling in the blanks beyond the concrete walls. The counterpoint of this shot, which looks *out* of the bunker, is a shot of Tom looking *in* through a smaller slit at his sister and Dad having sex. Only his eyes are visible, filling the slit as the slit fills the screen. He no longer needs to imagine and interpret; what he knows and has been told is now visible. But he is not liberated by this knowledge, but sucked in, unable to look away, disgusted and enthralled, amazed and aroused by the sight of two people having sex, repulsed by the fact that the two people are his Dad and his sister. Critically, Dad does not have sex with Jessie in a position that allows him to look her in the eye with all the appeal to honesty and directness that this entails. Ultimately, Dad does not want to see that it is his daughter with whom he is having sex rather than a willing teenager.

In his film notes, Stuart recalled that he and Tim Roth talked about 'how *The War Zone* should play on looks and gestures as much as dialogue – on the emotions and small moments that run through a family, especially in the early scenes' (Stuart 1999: 308). In order to achieve this, Stuart returned to silent movie scripts to evaluate the way screenwriters communicated emotion on screen without words. The relations of looking that structure the film are communicated through both scenes in which characters look at and between each other and through close-up headshots through which anxiety, distress, anger, struggle, ambiguity, ambivalence, jealousy and lust are expressed. Tom is alerted to his father's sexual jealously by the intensity of the glare that Dad fixes on his love-rival Nick after Jessie directs a defiant glance at him. Jessie also gives her mother contemptuous, surly looks from beneath knitted brows.

The only character who, critically, seems unable to either discern or interpret the relations of looking that are gradually exposing the incest is Mum. Here Bruce Chatwin's concept of a dark light[3] is a useful explanatory metaphor. Chatwin argues that the angle and diffusion of a dim light in a confined space can serve to cast other spaces of the room into a contrasting darkness, thereby obscuring the space's shape and form and rendering objects blurred to the eye. What is seen depends on the position of the viewer in relation to the dark light. Paradoxically, the closer one stands to the light the less becomes visible. A dark light, then, does not render visible a space, rather it focuses our gaze towards the light and thereby makes other, close, spaces indistinct. In this way things that are near can seem *other/invisible*. Hence in *The War Zone* mundane family life and the new baby combine to produce the dark light that serves to obscure from Mum the incest and the mounting anxiety and anger of her son. Visually, this is conveyed by shots of the shadowy interior of the cottage, dimly lit with inadequate lights which deepen the gloom gathering in the corners of the room. This is not the sophisticated mood lighting of an urbane hideaway but that of a old tasselled standard lamp with a low-watt bulb casting a sepia glow that mutes colours, emphasises clutter, blurs the details, conceals truths. If the light in the cottage gets in the way, the lighting of the bunker leaves nothing to the imagination. Lit by an invisible source off set, the bunker's grey interior lays bare the nature of Dad and Jessie's relationship. Looking in, Tom is literally, figuratively and emotionally enlightened with all the tragic consequences this entails. As well as calling attention to the link between looking and illumination, the key interiors of the cottage and the bunker provide reference points to a dysfunctional rurality, to which this chapter now turns.

Dark ruralities

Writing about his choice of *The War Zone* as his directorial debut, the director Tim Roth noted, 'I believe in the importance of images. A story on film must be told not through dialogue, like a play, but with what you see' (Stuart, 1999: 294). *The War Zone*'s contemporary alternative to the historically constituted green and pleasant land revolves around a landscape scarred by the violence of natural processes. Static, disorganised piles of rocks, jagged cliffs, inhospitable windswept beaches and the cataclysmic geology of north Devon form the context for the film. Nature is used explicitly as an external marker of internal tumult, violent thoughts and confusion. The slippages between book and film are interesting here, for they expose the way in which Tim Roth relocates the story for increased dramatic effect. Whilst the book was originally set near Sidmouth in south Devon, the film is set in the altogether harsher and austere landscape of north Devon in winter.

The opening sequences establish the atmosphere of chilly bleakness that characterises the mood of the film. As the title credits fade out, they are replaced by the shot through the slit of a wartime coastal defence bunker mentioned above. We then see Tom cycling along a deserted lane. The light is dark and wintery and the bleakness is emphasised by a leafless, twisted tree sculpted by the prevailing wind. Tom races down hill then stands on his pedals to tackle the next uphill. These shots parody an iconic childhood freedom – whizzing around the countryside on a bike. Tom turns onto a muddy track and we get the first glimpse of the family home. It is so remote that not even the track appears to lead to it. The opening sequence ends with the shot of the cottage that Roth uses again and again – square on but with darkened windows. The home as the iconic site of familial tenderness and support is destabilised by the film which places the violence, uncertainty, jealousy and tension firmly inside its walls. The symmetry of the house belies the a-symmetrical family relationship that exists inside.

This opening sequence is laden with symbolic meanings that structure the film as a whole. Of particular significance is the bunker which operates to support the relations of looking which we discussed previously. It marks the boundaries between inside and outside as the site at which the deviant sexual relationship between sister and father is carried on, watched by Tom who finds himself not only on the outside of the bunker but on the outside of normal familial relationships. Its historical associations with shelter and defence are reconfigured into a contemporary association with hidden deviance, attack and distress. Jessie's sobs are drowned out by Dad's coital grunting and when it is over, she sits huddled up, with her head bowed, weeping. The bunker's brutal concrete silhouette gives material form to both the brutality of the act that has occurred and to Tom's sense of isolation and alienation. The bunker anchors both ends of the film. The opening shot, with the camera looking out across the coast, seems to symbolise both Tom's sense of entrapment within his own feelings and in the circumstances of his family life. But at the end, the bunker is the place to which he and Jessie retreat, barricading themselves in against the crisis that has enveloped them.

In his film diary, Stuart noted that he chose a war-time bunker because 'I wanted a space that would be horrific and memorable ... the art department's version on the rocks here looks ... desolate, yet with a kind of vast, Turneresque seascape behind it that locates our characters firmly in a very primal Britain' (Stuart, 1999: 324). This idea of a primal Britain is worked through the film in many ways. There is a sense in which the family, having removed themselves from London, have also removed themselves to an earlier era.

In the opening sequence this is communicated through absences – there are no cars, no pylons, no farm machinery or buildings to locate north Devon temporally in a particular era. Early on, scenes in the living room and the kitchen show old-fashioned furniture, dim lighting and muted colours. When Dad comes in from work, Mum helps to scrub him at the kitchen sink in scene that owes more to a Catherine Cookson novel than a film set in the later years of the twentieth century. When Tom and Mum talk over his problems, they are seated in a café that sports art deco signage and a distinctly antiquated air.

The film draws on a popular conception of the countryside as somehow old fashioned and anti-modern. There is a long provenance in countryside writing of identifying in the rural relict elements of a simpler life in order to mount a criticism of contemporary living (Brace, 1999b). However, in *The War Zone* the powerful thread of anti-modernism is used to suggest backwardness, boorishness and the stubborn refusal to engage with contemporary life. Like the film *Withnail and I* (1987), in which black humour is drawn from an encounter with rustic ways, *The War Zone* uses rusticity to foreground the primitiveness of rural life. The family are shown to be isolated spatially and temporally from the moral structures that might contain their deviant behaviour.

Conclusion

After his first meeting with Tim Roth, Alexander Stuart noted that the director wanted to 'make an uncompromising film about abuse – something which will confront the audience, let them feel the pain' (Stuart, 1999: 301). It does so in part by chipping away at the lay discourse of the countryside as the repository of the best of human nature. Indeed, *The War Zone* forms part of a broader discourse of the anti-rural that denies both the relevance and credibility of traditional views of the countryside. It revels in its imagining of an aberrant other countryside in which incest can continue under the noses of frankly indifferent villagers and locals. The rural does not redeem in the way it does in, for instance, Pat O'Connor's *A Month in the Country* (1987). Tom is out of place, mute and emotionally incapacitated in an environment which should nurture and protect him. In this way, Tom is denied the smooth transition into adulthood popularly portrayed in youth stylised novels as he becomes disillusioned with the certainties of family life that cushion childhood.

The film also questions the existence of youthful innocence uncontaminated by deviant sexual desire and unequal power relationships. It deliberately locates the performance of its complex sexual politics in the rural, making an explicit challenge to the pervasive myth of rural sex as innocent, romping fun. Power is exchanged through sex. Sex is heteroclitic; conducted in strange places, fuelled by inappropriate desires, wreaking damage on everyone in the end. Importantly, whilst the film deploys a conventional narrative device portraying a family unravelling, the film's dénouement leaves many questions unanswered. In particular, there is no hint of forgiveness, explanation or justification. The fate of the characters is unknown: will Dad die? Will Mum leave? Will Jessie and Tom be arrested? Will anyone survive the emotional wounds that have been inflicted upon them? In short, the film rejects reconciliation as an appropriate end point.

In as much as sex is bestial, driven by desires that are unmoderated by social expectations and mores, the landscape of the film is also primal. Used explicitly as an external marker of internal and familial turmoil, the rural landscape of the film owes more to the blasted moorland of William Wyler's 1939 film *Wuthering Heights* than the cosy rusticity of *Darling Buds of May* (ITV, 1991–93). Ultimately, this is a film which offers no tidy resolutions to the monstrous acts it explores. The unexpected juxtaposition of the abusive and dysfunctional family with a chaotic, bleak, inhospitable rurality restructures our thinking about both rural sexualities and rural idylls, proffering a particularly dark vision of contemporary ruralities.

Notes

1 The principal characters are Dad (Ray Winstone), Mum (Tilda Swinton), and their older children: Jessie (Lara Belmont) and Tom (Freddie Cunliffe). Finally, Lucy, the young local girl who cleans for the family is played by Kate Ashfield.

2 Directed by Lynne Ramsey and based upon the novel of the same name by Alan Warner.

3 Chatwin's obsession with the paradoxical extended to his desire to own a 'dark lamp' made by his friend and artist David King. The 'dark lamp' was a black wood column, approximately 2m high and 30cm square, with a 25–watt bulb sunk into the top. The lamp emitted a light so faint that it was difficult to know where it was coming from (cf. Clapp, 1997).

References

Aitken, S. (2000), 'Fear, loathing and space for children', in Gold, J. and Revill, G. (eds), *Landscapes of Defence* (Harlow: Prentice Hall).

Bell, D. (1997), 'Anti-idyll', in Cloke, P. and Little, J. (eds), *Contested Countryside Cultures* (London: Routledge).

Brace, C. (1999a), 'Finding England everywhere: regional identity and the construction of national identity, 1890–1940', *Ecumene*, 6(1): 90–109.

Brace, C. (1999b), 'The door is ajar: the use of the past in constructions of English national identity', *Journal of Historical Geography*, 25(4): 502–16.

Clapp, S. (1997), *With Chatwin: Portrait of a Writer* (London: Jonathan Cape).

Cloke, P., Widdowfield, R. and Milbourne, P. (2000), 'The hidden and emerging spaces of rural homelessness', *Environment and Planning A*, 32: 77–90.

Crang, M. (1999), 'Nation, region and homeland: history and tradition in Dalarna, Sweden' *Ecumene*, 6(4): 447–70.

Hubbard, P. (2000), 'Desire/disgust: mapping the moral contours of heterosexuality', *Progress in Human Geography*, 24(2): 191–217.

Jones, O. (1995), 'Lay discourses of the rural: developments and implications for rural studies', *Journal of Rural Studies*, 11(1): 35–49.

Jones, O. (1997), 'Little figures: big shadows: country childhood stories', in Cloke, P. and Little, J. (eds), *Contested Countryside Cultures* (London: Routledge), pp. 158–79.

Kent, A. (1999), '"At the far end of England ...": constructions of Cornwall in children's literature', *The Cornish Banner*, 98: 16–21.

Leyshon, M. (2003), *Youth Identity, Culture and Marginalization in the Countryside*. Unpublished PhD, University of Exeter.

Little, J. (2003), '"Riding the rural love train": heterosexuality and the rural community', *Sociologia Ruralis*, 43(4): 401–17.

Little, J. and Leyshon, M. (2003), 'Embodied ruralities: developing research agendas', *Progress in Human Geography*, 27(3): 257–72.

Matthews, H., Taylor, M., Sherwood, K., Tucker, F. and Limb, M. (2000), 'Growing-up in the countryside: children and the rural idyll', *Journal of Rural Studies*, 16(2): 141–53.

Sibley, D. (1995), *Geographies of Exclusion* (London: Routledge).

Stuart, A. (1999), *The War Zone* (London: Black Swan).

Takahashi, L. (1998), *Homelessness. AIDS and Stigmatization: The NIMBY Syndrome at the End of the Twentieth Century* (Oxford: Oxford University Press).

Valentine, G. (1996), 'Children should be seen and not heard: the production and transgression of adults' private space', *Urban Geography*, 17(3): 205–20.

Valentine, G. (1997), 'A safe place to grow up? Parenting perceptions of children's safety and the rural idyll', *Journal of Rural Studies*, 13(2): 137–48.

12

Feral masculinities: urban versus rural in *City Slickers* and *Hunter's Blood*

David Bell

This chapter builds on my previous interests in the cinematic countryside and in constructions of urban and rural masculinities (Bell, 1997; 2000). It seeks to make a modest contribution to the growing body of work on gender and the rural, and more specifically on the relationships between rurality and masculinity (for an overview, see Little, 2002). My aim (to borrow from Rachel Woodward [2000: 645]) is to examine 'the ways in which ruralities and masculinities connect or bounce off each other'. To do this, I want to explore how the urban/rural binary is figured in selected cinematic texts through the lens of masculinity – with the countryside being seen as either the site of pre-cultural, animalistic 'wild' masculinity, or imagined as a regenerative resource for the reclaiming of a 'natural' masculinity. In both cases, country men are seen as the embodiment of particular modes of masculinity, seen as the opposite of an urban masculinity constructed as effete and feminised. Urban men come to the country, and are either remasculinised by contact with raw nature (and raw natural men) or are further feminised through their encounter with rural masculinity. In these films, I also want to track, as Mark Lawrence (2003: 93) does in his essay on Jane Austen films, how rural locations are used 'to enervate particular kinds of interaction between … characters'. Ultimately, I want to explore how the narratives of the films rest on a restatement of the essential connection between masculinity and nature, and stage a critique of the emasculating effects of urban life.

The formulation of the city as feminising and the rural as (potentially) masculinising is, of course, context-specific. It is based on the notion of the 'crisis of masculinity' in which contemporary urban, white, middle-class Western men are considered to have experienced a series of emasculations as a result of transformations in their social and economic roles. The 'feminisation' of work (through its white- and pink-collarisation), consumer culture, the impact of the women's movement and feminism, changes in the role of men in family life, and a whole host of other factors are attributed with having provoked this 'crisis' in what being a man means (Whitehead, 2002). Of course, this formulation is neither universal nor uncontested; in other contexts, the rural (as nature) is coded as feminine (Strathern, 1980). Nevertheless, it holds an important symbolic power in terms of representations of 'crisis-masculinity' which, I want to argue, spills over into representations of urban and rural masculinities.

I have chosen to focus this chapter on two films, which can be seen to be very different in terms of genre, production values and intended audience, but which nevertheless share certain thematics; most notably, in their depictions of urban and rural men. The films are the comedy *City Slickers* (Ron Underwood, 1990), and the horror movie *Hunter's Blood* (Robert Hughes, 1986). *City Slickers* is a big-budget Hollywood comedy which draws heavily on certain conventions of the classical Western. In part a vehicle for its wise-cracking star, Billy Crystal, the movie did very well at the box office. It also belongs to a genre (if we can call it that) labelled by Fred Pfeil (1995) the 'sensitive-guy film'. Other films in this genre or cycle that Pfeil discusses include *Regarding Henry*, *The Doctor*, *The Fisher King* and *Hook*. These films share a central theme, summarised by Pfeil in this way:

> [The] protagonists undergo conversion to sensitivity in the course of [the] film; each does so as the culmination of a passage through trials and suffering, on the other side of various terrifying and redemptive encounters with sundry Others, and, correspondingly, via so many humiliating and purgative abjections of the Self. (Pfeil, 1995: 38)

One element of the film that Pfeil neglects to dissect is *City Slickers'* setting in the 'wild west', and the ways in which modes of masculinity in the movie are explicitly connected to urban and rural habitats (a surprising omission, perhaps, given that Pfeil also discusses the men's movement in his book, and there are clear connections to make there, as I will endeavour to show).

Hunter's Blood, by contrast, belongs to a genre I have previously named 'hillbilly horror' (Bell, 1997). In fact, the film is routinely dismissed as a low-budget schlocker, and a poor *Deliverance* copy. And in some senses, it is; it certainly borrows heavily from the motifs of Boorman's definitive hillbilly horror film, and from other staples in the genre, such as *Southern Comfort*. But I think the movie is worth more than dismissal, in that it stages an encounter between urban and rural men that, while consistent with the genre, brings out some interesting and useful issues. (Or, in the words of a particularly vocal but insightful review, from the Brainsonfilm website [n.d.]: 'Some may say derivative, but I say fuck you, *Hunter's Blood* takes a not so new theme and puts a decent turn on it.') The film can also be slotted into another genre which is important for framing my analysis; that is the 'humiliation–redemption' movie, discussed by Annalee Newitz (a genre which includes, for her, films like *The Sadist*, *The Hills Have Eyes* and *Kalifornia*). Newitz sees these films as depictions of class-based white-on-white violence in which the white 'underclass' is racialised and abjected, and I shall be drawing on her excellent analysis in this chapter. But first, I want to sketch very briefly the two movies.

'You city folk, you worry about a lot of shit'

City Slickers opens in Pamplona, Spain, during the famous 'Running of Bulls' in La Fiesta De San Fermin, much beloved of Hemingway. The central character, Mitch (Billy Crystal), and his sidekicks, Ed and Phil, are in the crowd, running with the bulls – Mitch gets butted into the air by a bull. The three men, and their partners, are there on holiday – the latest in a series of 'adventure holidays' the men have been taking, each one upping the ante from the last.

Back in New York, Mitch is seen commuting to work; the city is depicted as boring, crowded. It is Mitch's thirty-ninth birthday, and we are firmly in mid-life-crisis territory. He hates his job, selling advertising airtime for a radio station; or, as he puts it in a talk at his kids' school, 'I sell air'. He is emasculated by his boss, unhappy and unfulfilled. Phil is equally emasculated; he has an overbearing wife, and works for her father, managing a supermarket. 'At this age, where you are is where you are', he says rather gloomily. It turns out he has got a checkout girl pregnant, and so loses his job and his marriage. Ed, meanwhile, is depicted as a serial philanderer, but he is trying to settle down with his 'trophy wife'.

Ed and Phil have booked the three of them on a 'dude ranch' trip (though the ranch owner emphasises it is *not* a dude ranch) as a birthday present for Mitch. He says he can't go, but his wife persuades him, saying he should 'go and find your smile'. So, off they go, to New Mexico. Their fellow trippers are a father-and-son couple of African-American dentists, a Ben-&-Jerry-style pair of ice-cream makers, and a (conveniently) single woman, Bonnie. The ranch owner explains their itinerary, that they'll be driving cattle accompanied by 'real' cowboys: 'You came out here city slickers; you're going to go home cowboys.' At the ranch, two of the 'real' cowboys start hassling Bonnie; Mitch intervenes ineffectually, and the mysterious head cowboy, Curly (Jack Palance), finally steps in, lassoing one cowboy. Ed says of Curly: 'This guy's a cowboy – one of the last real men. A mustang. We're trained ponies.'

After a send-off hoedown, the cattle drive begins. Curly gruffly refers to the three guys as 'girls'. First morning on the range, Mitch brings out his battery-powered coffee grinder – an urban luxury – which sets off a stampede (replaying the Pamplona sequence). Curly halts all the cows with a gunshot, muttering 'City folk' sneeringly. Curly takes Mitch off from the group, to retrieve strays; they camp out together – 'Oh God! It's *Deliverance*' says Mitch, but the two bond, singing campfire songs. Mitch tries to talk personal stuff with Curly, about his lack of fulfilment; Curly curtly responds: 'You city folk, you worry about a lot of shit.' The two bond even more when Mitch helps Curly birth a calf. Curly has to shoot the mother; Mitch adopts the calf, which he names Norman. They rejoin the group, triumphant.

Next day, Curly dies, sat on his horse! They bury him on the range, and Mitch delivers his eulogy. The cook drowns his sorrows, and wrecks the camp with the chuck wagon. He's hurt, so some of the city folk agree to take him off. The two 'real' cowboys get drunk, too, and start messing with Norman, goading Mitch (revenge for an earlier scene back at the ranch), calling him 'pansy-assed bastard' and 'shit-nosed little faggot'. A fight ensues, which the city guys win – Phil becomes very aggressive, but then has a mini-breakdown about his wasted life.

The 'real' cowboys flee, leaving the three city slickers to bring in the herd. They have to cross a river, swelled by a sudden storm. This really tests them. Ed says they *must* attempt to cross: 'A cowboy doesn't leave his herd', to which Phil responds 'You're a sporting goods salesman'. 'Not today!' is Ed's reply. The crossing is a key scene; the guys start to enjoy it – Mitch exclaims, happily, 'I'm thirty-nine and I'm saying "Moo cow" in a river!' – but then Norman gets swept away, and Mitch swims to save him, nearly drowning. Finally, they get the cattle across, and bring in the herd. At the ranch, however, they are told the herd's going to be sold off for beef; the city guys are very glum about this, Mitch lamenting 'These cows trusted us'.

Final scene, at the airport back in New York. Mitch has found his 'one thing' (Curly has earlier said that you need to find 'one thing' that'll be the secret of your happiness) – that one thing is his family and his 'normal' life. So, Mitch returns realigned, midlife crisis over, but ... he has brought Norman with him, to be the family pet.

'Maybe they's the breed that don't abide female poontang?'

Hunter's Blood opens on a decrepit hunting lodge, with shadowy figures scuttling about, and shots of traps and meat. It cuts to the smart city apartment of the central character, David (Sam Bottoms), a medical intern. His girlfriend, Melanie, tries to tempt him back to bed, but he is off on a hunting trip with his father, Mason, and some other city guys: Al, the driver/leader, his cousin Ralph, and Ralph's pal Marty: a novice hunter, an attorney and a Yankee. They set off in Al's big new SUV; the talk is all hunting bravado and guns. They're off to Arkansas, to hunt some woods recently bought by Al's company.

They stop for gas at Tobe's Gas Stop; David calls Melanie, and arranges to meet her there the next night. The guys talk about rednecks, jokily. Al persuades them to stop at a ramshackle bar, to buy beers. Outside, two rednecks are at a barbecue. Marty takes photos of them, saying 'These guys look like they're something out of *National Geographic*'. The rednecks turn hostile; the guys go into the bar. David spins a line to the barmaid that he's Bruce Springsteen's cousin; when she realises it's a joke, she calls him 'city cock sucker', and the local boys in the bar come over all threatening, demanding $50 'deposit' for the beer. Mason steps in, humiliating the rednecks (clearly modelled on Burt Reynold's *Deliverance* character Lewis, Clu Gulager's Mason has an air of 'deep masculinity' about him). They are chased by some rednecks in a beat-up station wagon. Al relishes this, driving his Bronco crazily, going off-road, easily out-running the rednecks.

The guys make camp in an idyllic setting (lots of shots of wildlife, and so on). Two go off hunting; the others play poker. The hunters meet two game wardens, who seem very edgy. They warn of a gang of poachers in the woods: 'A lot of people come a-missing hunting round here.' Al embellishes the warning, with campfire tales of an 'inbred barbarian tribe' reputedly living deep in the woods.

In the first night at camp, Al talks about the machismo of hunting: 'A man's gotta feel his balls ... He needs to go hunting.' Marty concurs, in a somewhat urban lexicon: 'The act of hunting brings out a rapport with a certain ... forgotten part of you'. They talk, drink, smoke weed – then Ralph gets out a ghetto blaster, and starts blasting out disco music (contrast to the country music in the redneck bar, and on the soundtrack). Al yells at him: 'Cut it out – you're bringing the city out into the woods.'

Later that night, Mason and David get up, having heard something, and go off to look. Meantime the poachers come to the camp; one of them pisses on Ralph in his sleeping bag, then spits on him; they goad the city guys, especially the Yankee Marty – lots of references to homosexuality: 'Maybe they's the breed that don't abide female poontang?' Mason and David return, and after a stand-off the poachers retreat, but leave saying 'We're gonna get ya!'

Next morning, after Marty fails to shoot a buck (despite having an over-the-top hunting rifle), the guys come across the poachers' camp; a fight ensues, then the wardens arrive, and take away the poachers in a chain gang. However, they haven't got the whole gang, and other poachers come to the rescue, shooting the wardens. The guys later find one warden butchered and strung up. They decide they need to get out the woods, and try to aim for the highway. They find the head of the second warden hanging from a tree ... They're really spooked now. The poachers ambush them, shooting Ralph dead and wounding Mason.

Melanie arrives at Tobe's Gas Stop for her romantic liaison with David. It turns out that Tobe is the redneck Mason humiliated in the bar. He spins her a line about going to meet the hunting party, offering her a lift – in a van marked Razor Back Meat Co.

Back in the woods, David stays with Mason while the others try to make for the highway. David knifes a redneck, looks horrified at his hands, but soon starts shooting poachers, though he too gets injured. Eventually, the following morning, David finds Al's Bronco, but there's a poacher laying in wait. David beats him, escapes again, only to get caught in a snare.

Back at the poachers' camp, some of the rednecks discuss how they are paid for the meat they kill in girls, that they hope they'll soon get a new delivery as the current ones are 'all used up' – though one poachers tells the other, 'They last longer if you feed 'n' water 'em.' Cut to the other hunters: Marty breaks down crying, in a classic scene of urban sissydom.

At the lodge, David is tied up like a deer. Melanie is tied up inside, too, and the poachers goad them both, calling David 'Buck' and talking about butchery. An escape–fight–get captured–escape–fight scene ensues, Melanie stabbing a poacher with some antlers from the wall, David strangling another (again, he looks in horror at his killing hands). Finally, David and Melanie make their escape and, finding the railroad, jump in a wagon. The other hunters are in there, too. They kill one last redneck, then sigh with relief and exhaustion. The camera pulls back to show the wagon bears a familiar emblem: Razor Back Meat Co.

Modes of masculinity

Having outlined the plots of my two films, I now want to pick out some of the key issues. First, and most important for my analysis, are the modes of masculinity on display here. There are the urban men – professionals with problems, if you like. *City Slickers* is, in a way, a mid-life-crisis movie, or a masculinity-in-crisis movie. It's also a movie about city men searching for kicks; kicks they hope will help give them a sense of purpose or realignment. And, like the hunting trip for the guys in *Hunter's Blood*, they turn to the wilderness as the site for that realignment. So, in one sense, both groups of urban men are 'adventure tourists', that growing breed of travellers who seek out thrills, and who can be found bungee jumping, white-water rafting, not to mention hunting and cattle-running, in tourist locations throughout the world (Cloke and Perkins, 1998; Cater and Smith, 2003). The adventure tourism experience, Cloke and Perkins (1998) argue, evidences a new set of embodied tourist practices, supplementing (and maybe even superseding) the previously dominant tourist gaze: instead of contemplating nature, adventure tourists must *experience* it bodily. Moreover, as Cater and Smith (2003: 213) say, the 'consumption of the countryside in terms of adventurous activity has profound impacts for the understanding of society's relationship with the natural environment' – an impact figured in these films in terms of conflict, as we shall see.

I think it is important to see adventure tourism as a liminal experience, staged to produce exactly the kind of realignment that Mitch and David (and their respective sidekicks) are seeking. Crucially, the experiences they are hoping to get seem to me, perhaps most explicitly in *City Slickers* given the way Mitch, Ed and Phil are depicted, to be about a realignment of their masculinity. The *City Slickers* trio all feel emasculated, either by their jobs or by their relationships, and their quest for thrills clearly embodies their desire to 'find themselves' – and to find themselves *as men*. Their admiration for the country men, most notably Curly, is equally important here. While adventure tourism offers a relatively 'safe', commodified encounter with the rural – which denies some realities of rural life, as in the fate of the cattle in *City Slickers* – there is clearly a sense that even a time-limited recreational experience can produce this realignment or rediscovery of being-a-man. The 'safe risks' offered by adventure tourism contrast with the 'real risks' of the rural, here depicted as the risk of encountering forms of wild masculinity, rather than the wilderness itself.

In the case of *Hunter's Blood*, the act of hunting – clearly framed as an instance of adventure tourism – is obviously seen by the city guys as a way of reconnecting with their 'real' masculinity, with 'feeling your balls' or finding that 'rapport with a certain forgotten part of you'. As Brian Luke (1998: 630) writes, 'one of the most common arguments used to justify hunting is that men who hunt today are expressing a deeply ingrained instinct'. But it is important to note that *Hunter's Blood* stages a conflict over the right of *different kinds of men* to hunt: the hunting trip by the city men is for recreational purposes, and is legitimised in the way that Luke suggests. However, the rural men are cast as poachers, as illegitimate hunters, despite the fact that hunting for them is an economic activity (admittedly, a debased one, given that they are paid in girls for the meat they kill). In this way, hunting is seen as a right for urban men – who are the owners of the land, and come to hunt for fun – but denied as a right to the people eking out a very marginal existence on that same land, which they inhabit 'illegally'. This formulation inverts the construction of rural hunting for food as legitimate and urban recreational trophy hunting as illegitimate (Bye, 2003). For the city guys in *Hunter's Blood*, the rural is seen as a site for leisure or consumption, rather than as a site of production – a familiar motif in discussions over the 'post-productivist' countryside and in the reconfigurations of the rural idyll (Bunce, 2003; Bell, 2006). In *City Slickers*, too, the economic activity of raising cattle is remade as a leisure activity, but this jars with the re-commodification of the cattle as beef. This point, too, will be picked up again later.

As well as adventure tourism, there are clear connections to be made here with other contexts in which rurality is seen as a resource for masculinity. These include the mode of 'military masculinity' discussed by Rachel Woodward (1998; 2000), negotiations over male farmers' identities, seen in work by Brandth (1995), Saugeres (2002) and others, some branches of the men's movement (Pfeil, 1995; Bonnett, 1996; Collier, 1996), and perhaps the most significant and enduring representation of men in the wilderness, the Western (for a useful discussion, see Hatty, 2000). Briefly, in each of these contexts we can track the interplay of what Hugh Campbell and Mike Bell (2000) call 'the masculine rural' and 'the rural masculine' – ways in which the rural is seen as 'male space' and in which men are seen as 'in place' in the rural, and ways in which certain kinds of men (and certain kinds of manly pursuits) are seen to belong in the rural.

Woodward's work on military masculinity, for example, shows how practices such as training exercises repeatedly connect being a man – in the guise of the 'warrior hero' – with 'possess[ing] the abilities to conquer hostile environments, to cross unfamiliar terrain, and to lay claim to dangerous ground' (Woodward, 2000: 644). Work on farmers' masculinity shows complex negotiations of gender identity as farming practices change (importantly, this includes the increasing use of technology and its effects on notions of what a farmer does and is). Farming men are also shown to occupy a position of closeness to nature but also mastery over nature – an interesting paradox I shall pick up again later (for an overview, see Little, 2002). The men's movement, at least in its 'mythopoetic', *Iron John* articulation, sees the wilderness as the stage for the recovery of 'deep masculinity' and the healing of 'male wounds' (Bonnett, 1996). And the Western literary and filmic genre, of course, places rural men in country settings as their 'natural' home, and as the perfect backdrop for staging performances of 'natural' masculinity, which notably include naturalised and redemptive violence (Hatty, 2000).

But before we get ahead of ourselves, we need to look briefly at the depiction of rural men in the films. In *City Slickers*, there are two archetypes. One is embodied in Curly, the 'noble savage', the true man, the cowboy. He is mysterious, deep, wise – but wise in a wilderness way, not in a bookish way. He might be dismissive of city folk, but he is honourable. Then there are the other cowboys, who play only one pivotal role, in being not-Curly (and also not-Mitch). They are closer to the redneck or hillbilly stereotype. While skilled in their work, they are ignorant, boorish, uncivilised – not to mention unreliable and ultimately cowardly. They harass Bonnie, harass Mitch and Norman the calf, get drunk and abandon the city slickers. So here we see two modes of rural masculinity at work: one noble, even enviable, the other uncivilised.

Hunter's Blood is, in some senses, much more straightforward about rural masculinity: the hunting trippers appear almost wholly disparaging of the rural men they encounter, whom they immediately categorise as rednecks or hillbillies. And quite rightly, given the way in which the poachers and the barflies in the film are depicted firmly in line with the core set of hillbilly stereotypes – feral, savage, dirty, in-bred, animalistic (these stereotypes are laid out and explored in detail by Williamson [1995]; though *Hunter's Blood* merits only one mention, in a footnote on *Deliverance* derivatives). Marty kind-of celebrates the hillbillies as he photographs them at the beer joint, saying they are 'savage and weird' – but this is clearly in an 'othering' manoeuvre, celebrating them *as rednecks*, given his quip about *National Geographic*. I shall return to the cultural work done by this rural stereotype later in the chapter. As already mentioned, the character that embodies 'deep masculinity' in *Hunter's Blood* is Mason, though the back-story for this is never really spelled out. Nevertheless, it is an important point to remember for later.

The films also raise the issue of the relationship between masculinity, technology and rurality. In *Hunter's Blood*, this is encapsulated in the SUV, Al's Bronco; in *City Slickers*, perhaps the most significant piece of technology is, somewhat ironically,

Mitch's battery-powered coffee grinder. The SUV, or four-wheel drive (4WD), has been described by Peter Bishop (1996) as reconfiguring the encounter with the wilderness. Bishop, writing about Australia, dubs this the 'high-tech outback', and details the ambivalence that technologically mediated contact with wilderness provokes. For some, the 4WD offers only an inauthentic experience. However, masculine mastery of technology is also seen to enable masculine mastery of nature, again producing 'safe risks': 'High tech becomes part of the frame by which wilderness has its imagining and its experiencing' (Bishop, 1996: 269). This is clearly the encounter that the hunting trip provides, as vividly depicted in the scene where the guys off-road to escape the rednecks. But, of course, the SUV is ultimately rendered useless, and even becomes a trap – when David returns to it, he is ambushed by a waiting poacher, who has also disabled the vehicle. Reliance on high-tech equipment is, therefore, both positively coded (it grants access to wilderness) and negatively coded (without it, the men are lost, and it can also be used against them). And remember that David and Melanie end up killing in very low-tech ways: David with his hands; Melanie using antlers.

Mitch's coffee grinder in *City Slickers* offers a more throwaway comment on technology, maybe: he has brought it with him on the trip, as a distinctly urban luxury (he shows it off to his sidekicks, who eye it admiringly). However, when he uses it, its noise causes the stampede pivotal to the plot. Nevertheless, this brief scene says something about urban masculinity's relationship to technology – here depicted as *domestic* technology, with codings about urban and urbane taste and sophistication (and also feminisation). The coffee grinder is clearly out of place on the cattle run, to catastrophic effect. A man who needs nice coffee in the morning is clearly not a real man; moreover, Mitch's inappropriate use of out-of-place technology evidences his lack of connection to 'rural reality', in his failure to foresee the consequences of its use. There are echoes here of Brandth's (1995) work on representations of technology and farming in Norway, and her work with Haugen on Norwegian forestry (2000). In both cases, masculinity proves elastic enough to cope with the increasing technologisation of rural work – like the positive coding of the 'high tech outback' in Bishop's reading, the technology is itself coded masculine, and being a rural man comes to be about use of particular forms of machinery to further men's mastery of nature. However, the coffee grinder is beyond that elasticity, and serves to further undermine Mitch's masculinity. Having traced these connections between the narratives of my two films and other bodies of work on the rural, I now want to return to my principal concern: the ways in which *City Slickers* and *Hunter's Blood* articulate different modes of masculinity, in relation to rurality.

Sensitive savages?

My analysis here draws on two essays already flagged: Fred Pfeil's (1995) 'The year of living sensitively', from his book *White Guys*, and Annalee Newitz's (1997) 'White savagery and humiliation, or a new racial consciousness in the media', from the collection *White Trash*. As already sketched, Pfeil tracks a cycle or season of sensitive-guy films emanating from Hollywood in the early 1990s, and provides a detailed reading of their common motifs. Newitz's focus is on the depiction of 'savage whiteness' in films which pitch middle-class whites as victims of lower-class white humiliation and violence. Both writers are concerned with the seemingly redemptive quality of the encounter between middle-class white protagonists and their Other, shown to be increasingly framed as rednecks or hillbillies. The central character undergoes trials and violations through his contact with the white Other, and emerges kind-of changed but also reaffirmed. To their analyses, I want to add a socio-spatial dimension, to show how my chosen films work this narrative through in terms of the urban versus the rural.

Key to Pfeil's essay is the role of what he names the 'unconventional male' character, embodied in *City Slickers* in the 'real cowboy' Curly, but rather differently in *Hunter's Blood* by Mason, David's father. These men give the protagonists access to some 'real truths' and to their 'real self'. This access is enabled by being in the wilderness setting: only by being out of place can Mitch take a real look at his life and, armed with the wisdom of Curly, re-enter his normal life changed for the better. This is one place where *City Slickers* and *Hunter's Blood* apparently diverge: in the case of the latter, no such resolution is offered. David is clearly changed by his encounter with rural men, but changed for the worse – witness the shots of his horror-filled face each time he kills one of the poachers (and remember he's a medical intern, trained to save life rather

than take it). And, of course, the film ends not with escape and re-
entry into normal life, but with the prospect of the hunting trippers
being returned to the hell they have fled, courtesy of the Razor
Back Meat Co's train. But Pfeil rightly points out that the neatness
of the resolution to the sensitive-guy film is also somewhat
disavowed at the end of *City Slickers*:

> [W]e see the minivan carrying Mitch, his wife, and his newly expand-
> ed family, now including Norman the calf, over the Triboro Bridge to
> the Bronx, with the blue skyscape of Manhattan standing in for that
> of the Rockies, the Western music on the soundtrack only emphasis-
> ing how far we are from that other landscape of heroic quest and
> fulfilment, and how ludicrous it is to expect either for Norman to
> survive or for Mitch's new-found ... vocation to re-enchant his life
> here. (Pfeil, 1995: 52)

So this scene, made chiefly for comic effect admittedly, nonetheless
raises troubling questions: has Mitch changed, and if so, how?
Does this scene ultimately show the futility of trying to change?
Both Pfeil and Newitz suggest that these films are basically restat-
ing the legitimacy of white middle-class privilege, even if
attempting to suggest that that power can be deployed differently:
'the point is not to give up power, but to emerge from a temporary,
tonic power shortage as someone more deserving of its possession
and more compassionate in its exercise' (Pfeil, 1995: 49).

Newitz lays out this reading perhaps even more explicitly, seeing
her chosen humiliation–redemption movies as a way to sidestep
issues of white power and middle-class domination: 'the victimisation of middle-class whites becomes their redemption' (Newitz,
1997: 141). Moreover, the protagonists who survive and get
redeemed can only do so by becoming savage themselves – as
vividly played out by David in *Hunter's Blood*, and in a lighter
mode by Mitch's discovery of his 'inner cowboy'. What this move
does, Newitz suggests, is to confess:

> [T]hat, in spite of white middle-class education and cultural hegemo-
> ny, whites are only a few steps away from becoming amoral, rural
> savages who kill each other with their hands ... [T]he idea that
> middle-class whites need to become savages to defend themselves is a
> perfect excuse for the middle classes to behave in outrageously cruel
> ways towards the lower classes. (Newitz, 1997: 144)

This theme is also picked out in an essay on 'redneck discourse' by

Lucy Jarosz and Victoria Lawson (2002). Their concern is with the 'disembedding' of redneck discourse, and how the image of the redneck now stands in for a particular stereotype of the white, rural working classes in the USA. Crucially, they observe that 'rednecks' as an essentialised group – a political, ideological cipher and cliche – become a foil for white, liberal, middle-class guilt' (Jarosz and Lawson, 2002: 11). This is achieved by re-imagining class as purely a matter of social mobility and lifestyle choice, so the rural poor are naturalised as merely too lazy or stupid to better themselves. Moreover, rednecks become the site of white-supremacist racism, thereby further 'obscuring the dynamics of liberal, middle-class privilege and guilt' (2002: 16).

Reading *City Slickers* and *Hunter's Blood* in tandem, there are clear divergences that emerge; the former is more firmly in the sensitive-guy film mould, while the latter belongs more squarely with the humiliation–redemption set. Nevertheless, I have purposely pulled these two films together, because I think that they present us with a series of contrasting codings of masculinity that ultimately, and only when read together, say something about the relationship between masculinity and rurality. First there are the urban middle-class men; the key characters of Mitch and David, plus their assorted sidekicks. By and large, they are depicted as out of place in the rural, even though they might confidently want to claim a right to be there (albeit temporarily). They come to the country in search of recreation, but also regeneration – but neither of them really finds it, given *City Slickers*' ambivalent ending, and *Hunter's Blood*'s no-escape denouement. The exception, of course, is Mason, David's dad in *Hunter's Blood*. He is an urban man, but he isn't out of place on the hunt – until, at least, he gets wounded. He is Pfeil's 'unconventional male', but he comes from the urban group, perhaps suggesting that some city men can buck the stereotype as effete and ineffectual. But what's his secret?

Then there are the two types of rural men: Curly, the noble savage, the unconventional male, the container of rural wisdom and skill; and the 'real cowboys' and the poachers, clearly in the redneck mould – boorish, animalistic, backwards. As Newitz says, these depictions are at once repulsive and fascinating (see Marty's photo-op), and their portrayal of feral masculinity shows what happens when men go wild. Crucially, this formulation inverts the equation of man with culture and woman with nature, highlighted by Marilyn Strathern (1980) among others. As Strathern notes, this inversion can be traced in the 'ideology of the American western frontier', which 'includes the notion of women as "culture"-bearing or civilising agents, who eventually subdued those rowdy anti-social males who tended to revert to nature' (Strathern, 1980: 183). Reverting to nature means becoming savage, conjuring a powerful image of what 'natural masculinity' is.

Clearly, then, these movies stage an ambivalent relationship between rurality and masculinity, in which the rural is potentially the site to recover a lost natural masculinity, but is equally the site where masculinity turns wild. While the aim might be to produce a new version of masculinity for our protagonist, one which represents, as Pfeil (1995: 45) puts it, 'a synthesis of his recovered child-self with selected aspects of what he has learned from [the unconventional male] and some of the manly authority and confidence of his first, empowered yet insensitive self', this imperative – which also drives participants in the men's movement out into the woods – is doomed to disappointment and failure. Rewriting Newitz's take on this, we could say that these films instead show that all men are 'only a few steps away from becoming amoral, rural savages', and that those steps get ever closer when men – even, or perhaps *especially*, when 'civilised', middle-class urban men – encounter the masculine rural and the rural masculine.

References

Bell, D. (1997), 'Anti-idyll: rural horror', in Cloke, P. and Little, J. (eds), *Contested Countryside Cultures: Otherness, Marginalisation and Rurality* (London: Routledge), pp. 94–108.

Bell, D. (2000), 'Farm boys and wild men: rurality, masculinity, and homosexuality', *Rural Sociology*, 65: 547–61.

Bell, D. (2006), 'Variations on the rural idyll', in Cloke, P. Marsden, T. and Mooney, P. (eds), *Handbook of Rural Studies* (London: Sage), pp. 149–60.

Bishop, P. (1996), 'Off road: four-wheel drive and the sense of place', *Environment & Planning D: Society & Space*, 14: 257–71.

Bonnett, A. (1996), 'The New Primitives: identity, landscape and cultural appropriation in the mythopoetic men's movement', *Antipode*, 28: 273–91.

Brainsonfilm (n.d.) '*Hunter's Blood*', www.brainsonfilm.com /index.html (site accessed 6 January 2004).

Brandth, B. (1995), 'Rural masculinity in transition: gender images in tractor advertisements', *Journal of Rural Studies*, 11: 123–33.

Brandth, B. and Haugen, M. (2000), 'From lumberjack to business manager: masculinity in the Norwegian forestry press', *Journal of Rural Studies*, 16: 343–56.

Bunce, M. (2003), 'Reproducing rural idylls', in Cloke, P. (ed.), *Country Visions*, (Harlow: Prentice Hall), pp. 14–30.

Bye, L. (2003), 'Masculinity and rurality at play in stories about hunting', *Norwegian Journal of Geography*, 57: 145–53.

Campbell, H. and Bell, M. (2000), 'The question of rural masculinities', *Rural Sociology*, 65: 532–46.

Cater, C. and Smith, L. (2003), 'New country visions: adventurous bodies in rural tourism', in Cloke, P. (ed.), *Country Visions* (Harlow: Prentice Hall), pp. 195–216.

Cloke, P. and Perkins, H. (1998), '"Cracking the canyon with the awesome foursome": representations of adventure tourism in New Zealand', *Environment & Planning D: Society & Space*, 16: 185–218.

Collier, R. (1996), '"Coming together?": post-heterosexuality, masculine crisis and the new men's movement', *Feminist Legal Studies*, 4: 3–48.

Hatty, S. (2000), *Masculinities, Violence, and Culture* (London: Sage).

Jarosz, L. and Lawson, V. (2002), '"Sophisticated people versus rednecks": economic restructuring and class difference in America's west', *Antipode*, 34: 8–27.

Lawrence, M. (2003), 'The view from Cobb Gate: falling into liminal geography', in Cloke, P. (ed.), *Country Visions* (Harlow: Prentice Hall), pp. 93–115.

Little, J. (2002), *Gender and Rural Geography: Identity, Sexuality and Power in the Countryside* (Harlow: Prentice Hall).

Luke, B. (1998), 'Violent love: hunting, heterosexuality, and the erotics of men's predation', *Feminist Studies*, 24: 627–55.

Newitz, A. (1997), 'White savagery and humiliation, or a new racial consciousness in the media', in Wray, M. and Newitz, A. (eds), *White Trash: Race and Class in America* (New York: Routledge), pp. 131–54.

Pfeil, F. (1995), *White Guys: Studies in Postmodern Domination and Difference* (London: Verso).

Saugeres, L. (2002), 'The cultural representation of the farming landscape: masculinity, power and nature', *Journal of Rural Studies*, 18: 373–84.

Strathern, M. (1980) 'No nature, no culture: the Hagen case', in MacCormack, C. and Strathern, M. (eds), *Nature, Culture and Gender* (Cambridge: Cambridge University Press), pp. 174–222.

Whitehead, S. (2002), *Men and Masculinities* (Cambridge: Polity Press).

Williamson, J.W. (1995), *Hillbillyland: What the Mountains Did to the Movies and What the Movies Did to the Mountains* (Chapel Hill: University of North Carolina Press).

Woodward, R. (1998), '"It's a man's life": soldiers, masculinity and the countryside', *Gender, Place & Culture*, 5: 277–300.

Woodward, R. (2000), 'Warrior heroes and little green men: military training, and the construction of rural masculinities', *Rural Sociology*, 65: 640–57.

Part IV

Mediating experience and performing alternatives

13

Amateur film and the rural imagination

Mark Neumann and Janna Jones

During the summer of 1916, in the seaside community of Blue Hill, Maine, F.B. Richards, a retired navy colonel, set up his 28mm amateur motion-picture camera and tripod on the Blue Hill Country Club lawn. Richards hand-cranked his camera, recording an amateur theatrical production of *Snow White*. A graceful teenaged Snow White dressed in a flowing white gown moves back and forth across the stage; she mimics the melodramatic flourishes of Isadora Duncan. Children in cotton beards and pointy hats, carrying pick axes and shovels, perform the roles of the seven dancing dwarves returning from their labours in the mines. The base of the outdoor stage covered with cut pine boughs gives the impression of a pastoral proscenium but cannot quite obscure the cedar-shingled country club behind it. Juxtaposing the rustic and the worldly, the film is an unintended portrait of bucolic life as imagined by privileged society. Like the fairytale that it records, in which uncomplicated rural workers comfort, protect and redeem the regal but troubled Snow White, Richards' film captures a complex dialectic of urban and rural life.

Staged at a country club in a relatively remote Maine community, Richards' film is an artefact from an era when people in the United States first began documenting their families and the places where they lived, and their vacations. Richards and his family retreated from Cleveland to their summertime residence in Blue Hill. Most of these early amateur filmmakers were from upper and middle classes. Richards had the economic means both to spend his summers in Maine and to dwell in visions of rustic charm, attempting to turn those visions into film productions.[1] Richards' camera remains stationary, recording ten unblinking minutes of theatrical performance. His film documents a period of cultural transition, one where the familiarity and legacy of theatre came face to face with motion-picture technology still in its infancy. In *Snow White*, the conventions of theatre superseded the creative possibilities of motion-picture film, and his fixed camera merely records the live performance, and seems to flatten any dynamism it might have.

Richards' *Snow White* is a rare document. He was one of a few known amateur filmmakers in Blue Hill during this era. Shot on an obsolete 28mm film gauge, his *Snow White* is preserved and catalogued as one of the earliest amateur films still in existence.[2] Within a decade, other amateur filmmakers moved through this region as well as other parts of Maine and New England. The numbers of amateur filmmakers increased after Eastman Kodak's introduction of direct reversal 16mm safety film in 1923.[3] The newly formed Amateur Cinema League published the *Amateur Movie Makers* magazine in 1926, providing instructions to the burgeoning numbers of people from upper and middle classes who had begun making their own movies. In 1934, Bell and Howell introduced the 8mm camera, which still used a 16mm film stock, but allowed for doubling the use of a roll. The camera operator exposed one half of the 16mm stock, and then flipped over the spool to run the other half through the camera. More economical than its predecessor, the 8mm camera quickly became the standard among amateur filmmakers. By 1937, the Amateur Cinema League recognised 250 amateur cinema clubs across the United States (Sterling, 1937; Zimmermann, 1995).

This chapter focuses on a few of these amateur films made in New England, a tiny fragment of the thousands of reels that survive in archives and attics throughout the United States and abroad. The films discussed here were made between 1915 and 1940, and are housed at Northeast Historic Film, a regional moving image archive located in Bucksport, Maine. Northeast Historic Film was established in 1986 as a non-profit archive for amateur, industrial, and commercial films produced in New England.[4] The archive's extensive holdings include films such as Richards' *Snow White*, as well as a multitude of home movies, amateur dramas and commercial moving images produced by the region's residents, vacationing families and others who, at one time or another, filmed events and people relating to New England life.

Compared to commercially produced films, the audiences for

amateur films are small. Initially made for private use, the extent that amateur films circulated beyond small clusters of family and friends is usually unknown. In the same vein, amateur films often come to us with a minimal amount of contextual information regarding their production. That an amateur film has survived at all does not guarantee that a corpus of historical or contextual information regarding its production is available. In most cases, analysing such films requires piecing together any available information about the circumstances of their production. A great deal of ambiguity surrounds such films, and it is unlikely that most readers will have seen any of the films discussed here. At the same time, the value of amateur films far exceeds their public circulation. Initially created by amateurs, such films offer a unique testimony to the interests and practices of everyday life. They are often an index of public and private lives, images of communities circumscribed by the social relationships of their creators, and they often express elements of real life as well as life's idealisations and fantasies.

In the broadest sense, the democratisation of the movie camera made it possible to record nearly all facets of life, including many visions of rural existence. By examining a few of these amateur films, we focus on how the presence of the movie camera in various rural settings enabled people to both document and dramatise rural existence. The four films discussed below offer a curious glimpse at how the rural appears as an imaginary site, a cinematic space where depictions of rural life are a product of the filmmakers' relationship to their subjects. In each case, these relationships render the rural as a space and time that celebrates the growing forces of modern life and progress and, at times, seeks out a fantasy of the small town and the folk as a retreat from such forces. In all of these films, the movie camera records the ambivalences of these filmmakers' insider and outsider status, their simultaneous closeness and distance from their subject. This status helps to shape the filmmakers' vantage point, their portraits of the rural, and their relationship to both progress and nostalgia. Richards' *Snow White* – a film documenting summering elites staging a fairytale of royalty among the forest folk – marks both of these impulses. For the other filmmakers in this chapter – a town clerk with a 8mm camera, an itinerant filmmaker who brought an imagined Hollywood to rural communities, and two wealthy urban men who sought respite from the city – images of the rural grow from desires for documenting ordinary life and creative impulses. In all of them we find that the idea of the rural is neither an exact geography nor a precise historical moment.

The local documentarian of small-town life

Raymond O. Cotton, a grocery store owner in the small town of Hiram, Maine, was one of the many amateur filmmakers who purchased an 8mm movie camera during the mid-1930s. In addition to being a storekeeper, Cotton was also a blueberry farmer, a member of the town's volunteer fire department, and served as Town Clerk, a post he occupied for fifty years. This latter role, one where he recorded births, deaths and marriages in Hiram – a town with a population of less than 1,000 people when he made his films – provided him with the kind of knowledge that eventually allowed him to become the historian for Hiram's Historical Society.[5] Between 1935 and 1939, when Cotton was in his thirties, he used his movie camera to document a range of activities in and around his town. His filmed observations of Hiram and its people were edited together with a series of intertitles to caption particular events during this period. Cotton titled the film *Time Marches On*, and subsequently provided a voice-over narration.[6]

Time Marches On comprises a mix of events revealing Cotton's sense of civic pride, a sensitivity for the transformation of his community, the big events that punctuate the routines of everyday life, and the peculiarities of his small town. It is a fragmented and seemingly chaotic chronology of what caught his attention and what he thought was worth recording during those years. We see the 1938 Memorial Day parade, with marching band and baton twirlers pounding down Hiram's Main Street. Veterans of the First World War are among the procession, marching to remember Hiram's sons who had died in the conflict, but not yet aware of the even larger war looming. In 1937, the town had organised a volunteer fire department and Cotton filmed their annual fire drills, capturing images of men assembling fire hoses, and extinguishing a blazing home intentionally set on fire for training purposes. He documented the action of Hiram's annual 'Coon Hound Field Trial' held on 24 July 1938. As the dogs tracked the scent of a racoon across the fields and woods, Cotton ran along with them and filmed their fluid and enthusiastic intensity during the competition. For the record – which is truly the impulse at the heart of Cotton's films – the winning hound, Red Pepper, owned by Archie Turner of Auburn, Maine, was the first dog to successfully track down the treed racoon. For Red Pepper's efforts, Turner won a seventy-five-dollar prize.

In addition to annual community events, Cotton's camera focused on the particular, unique and – at times – peculiar. Earl Johnson, for instance, proudly looked into Cotton's camera, showing off a bobcat he killed in March 1938. In July, a carnival came to Hiram, and Cotton took his camera on the Ferris wheel filming the bustling scene from his swinging seat as it carried him high above the town. The following month, Cotton filmed the elimination of two dangerous railroad crossings at Smut Street and Mattox Street. Five women had been killed at Smut Street, and Cotton remembered the public works project as a 'great event' for the town because it made the roads safer. But Cotton was more impressed that a steam shovel had been used for the demolition of the intersection; such a machine had never before been seen in Hiram. A month later, he filmed the aftermath of a hurricane that had hit the area on 21 September. 'It was a wild night', remembered Cotton in his narration. The high winds had pulled trees out of the ground and knocked a barn off its foundation. Cotton followed hurricane footage with a mild attempt at levity. An intertitle that reads 'October 1938 – Dragon Captured by Jim Sargent Single Handed' is followed by an image of the smiling Jim Sargent holding a large salamander.

The images compiled by Raymond Cotton offer an idiosyncratic portrait of small-town life. His impulse toward reportage manifests his civic pride while capturing the particularities and spontaneity of life in a close-knit community. For today's viewer, Cotton's images may be a nostalgic portrait of small-town life. But the record he leaves behind suggests that he was fascinated by the town's relative sense of progress and transformation. The steam shovel that efficiently destroys Hiram's dangerous railroad crossings is a minor spectacle of advancement, and the filmic record registers a distance from cities where such industry was largely taken for granted. At the same time, it would be naive to think that Cotton, or other residents of Hiram, were not aware of the larger world beyond their small town parades, coon trials, carnivals and blueberry farms.

In its very composition, *Time Marches On* suggests how national cinema and its distribution made an impression on amateur filmmakers, such as Cotton. In both title and format, his movie resembles the *Movietone News* and the *March of Time* newsreels of his day. He was likely to have seen them, for the documentary-like stories of national and international interest were a routine part of movie-theatre exhibition in cities and small towns beginning in 1929. This kind of imitation was, in part, consistent with a broader ethic among amateur filmmakers, who had been encouraged through filmmaking guidebooks, magazine articles and camera clubs to create films that strived toward a level of 'professionalism' seen in Hollywood films (Zimmermann, 1995: 64–72). But as nationally circulating newsreels documented feats of aviation, wartime actualities, public figures and celebrities, Cotton's camera focused on the feats of local firemen and coonhounds, and looked with awe on the advancement of a steam shovel into Hiram.

To the extent the conventions of professional filmmaking influenced and shaped Cotton's vision as an amateur filmmaker, they do not diminish his status as an indigenous reporter. We cannot know if his propensity to film the subjects of his small town was a realisation that Movietone camera crews were not likely to visit Hiram. Instead, Cotton's film reveals how images and techniques spawned in places far from the Maine countryside infused the rural imagination. In part, Cotton seemed to film his friends and neighbours *as though he were from elsewhere*, as if his camera could elevate the unique and particular, and cast them into a broader visual arena of public life. The images of Earl Johnson showing off the slain bobcat, or Red Pepper wagging his tail, achieve a larger status and significance *because* Cotton films them. Documenting the particulars, he implicitly claimed the importance of the details that comprised his world. Today, the value of his surviving cinematic record extends beyond both his town and his time. As the title suggests, Cotton knew well that Hiram would change, and with his camera he sought to save some of it for himself and anyone who would see his movies. Perhaps the most tragic event in his life ended his desire to make films. While filming his wife and daughter on the banks of a rain-swollen stream in 1939, a dam broke and suddenly swept all of them away. Cotton survived, but his wife and daughter drowned. He lost his camera in the harsh waters and never bought another.[7]

Time Marches On helps us to understand how the amateur film-maker's camera penetrated the habits and local knowledge of rural life during the 1930s. Patterns of life that had been understood and negotiated only through conversation, the local paper and photo-graphs could now be understood through moving images. Functioning like a stranger, the camera allowed rural inhabitants to see themselves and their small towns from an outsider's perspec-tive. This was particularly evident in the *Movie Queen* films produced in a handful of small New England towns during the 1930s.

The *Movie Queen* comes to town

Margaret Cram, an independent itinerant filmmaker, travelled to small towns in Maine, Vermont, New Hampshire and Massachusetts during the mid-thirties. Collaborating with civic leaders in each town, Cram shot a similar fictional film that employed local citizens acting as themselves. The films were made in a matter of days and then exhibited at a local movie theatre. Cram used the same formula each time. The storyline went like this: a movie queen (a local young woman was selected for the role) returns to her home town so that the residents can celebrate her success in Hollywood. The *Movie Queen* begins as townspeople wait at the train station or ferry dock to greet the returning celebri-ty, allowing Cram to film many of the town's residents in a single scene. When the faux celebrity finally appears, she is paraded through town with much pomp and circumstance, and given a tour of the local businesses. She visits service stations, grocers, lunch counters, dry-goods stores, automobile dealerships, appliance stores and clothing shops. She is greeted by proprietors who, in most cases, welcome her with gifts from their businesses, such as a tennis racket, a tyre, a bathing suit, a bag of groceries or a ham. Amidst the close-ups of the always-thankful movie queen, Cram's camera captured the faces of business owner and employees, commercial signs, placards advertising sales, and flattering shots of refrigerators, stoves, tableware, automobiles and other merchan-dise.

Cram's films required neither rehearsal nor much aptitude for acting; nearly everyone simply played themselves. Even the movie queen needed only to convey surprise and gratitude. This rudimentary storyline was geared toward boosterism; the town congratulated itself not only for its sense of commerce and enterprise, but its willingness to participate in the creation of a relatively elaborate fiction of their lives. Despite the changing faces of movie queens and merchants, the storyline typically ended on a moment of contrived drama. A group of local men portray a villainous gang and set out to kidnap the wholesome movie queen. In an effort to parody screen gangsters of the period: the men darkened their cheeks, creating five o'clock shadows; chomped on cigars; and turned up their coat collars, doing their best to look dangerous. A stock intertitle cut into several of Cram's films identified the gang leader as 'Slarbo', otherwise known as 'Public Enemy No. 999'. In every *Movie Queen*, the gangsters first botch the kidnapping and abduct the wrong woman. When they finally seize the movie queen, a dashing young man comes to the rescue and single-handedly fights off the villains, carrying the faux celebrity to safety and the film abruptly ends.

Cram produced a *Movie Queen* film in a matter of a few days. Nearly all of the editing was done in her 16mm camera, with the exception of splicing in a few stock intertitles. The final production had the same kind of hand-held cinematography and jump cuts often seen in home movies. Upon completion, the townspeople attended a screening at the local theatre. The very production of the film was simultaneously an occasion for assembling its eventual audience. In a parade scene from the *Movie Queen* made in Lincoln, Maine, Cram's camera captures the passing sign on a decorated truck that advertises the end product of the event:

Lincoln-Hollywood
Motion Pictures
See Yourself on the Screen
1:00 on Monday Tickets 40 cents

Filming such a story required a high degree of participation and organisation among the town's citizens, and they were able to view the final product of their efforts. Cram's narrative enabled a small town to compose its own cinematic biography, a narrative blend of fact and fiction. Filmed 'on location', the *Movie Queen* provided a visual record of the town's business community, citizens and the local landmarks. But it is also an imagined community; one where all of its businesses prosper, and local girls become Hollywood celebrities, graciously returning home to be rewarded with gifts of hams, tyres, pies and parades. The story also carried a fantasy of the urban. On film, these quiet communities of commerce and agriculture had their own precarious outskirts where gangsters lurked and conspired against unsuspecting movie stars.

It is difficult to draw a line between any real or imagined sense of a community documented in these films. The parades organised for the films were pseudo-events, but they are also evidence of the town's willingness to suspend the routines of daily life, to co-ordinate the festivities, and to collaboratively submit to a collective fiction. At the same time, this fiction lent legitimacy to what was always there. *The Movie Queen*'s Hollywood success story refracted an image of community life that implicitly suggested success was found somewhere beyond the town's limits. The arrival of Margaret Cram and her 16mm camera was another instance of how ideas about life from elsewhere might temporarily penetrate rural communities. As she filmed a hybrid of fiction and reality, Cram recorded the evidence that these small towns were securely lodged in a broader vision of American enterprise. Alongside images of local dairies and coffee shops, we find the signs of businesses that marked how corporate American industry had found customers in rural communities: Ford; Chevrolet; John Deere. Automobile and farm machinery dealers such as these appear throughout these films. Images of native foodstuffs displayed in local market windows were juxtaposed with images of display windows stocked full of General Electric appliances. Cram's films did not aim to celebrate people living a quaint rural life in the thickness of tradition and homemade jam. On the contrary, like the cinematic portraits of the townspeople projected at the local theatre, *The Movie Queen* film offered the town a magnified and flattering image of itself, one based on economic viability and progress.

The community's cinematic fantasy of itself appeared on screen for a brief moment, and we can only imagine how the audience might have revelled in it. Outside the theatre, the familiar streets of Lincoln, Lubec, Middlebury or Newport reminded them of their great distance from Hollywood. Cram's camera and her *Movie Queen* script may have changed that for a few days. What transpired once the filming began suggested that the glimmer of

Hollywood wasn't so far away, that it could animate their small and ordinary lives as public visions of community pride. The town residents bought tickets to watch themselves acting on a movie set. Peering into a kind of glamorised funhouse mirror, their faces and landmarks were recognisable but unfamiliar at the same time. While a sense of community cohesiveness was surely an integral element of the *Movie Queen* experience, the outsider's camera is likely to have brought on a particular sort of self-consciousness, creating a distance between what they saw and what they thought they had known about themselves all along.

While Cram mapped a Hollywood success story on to small towns, other amateur filmmakers were happy to dispense with any pretence of the real. In the Northeast Historic Film archives, we find a variety of amateur filmmakers fabricating stories about rural communities. Alongside the documenting of numerous facets of everyday life, some amateur filmmakers drafted scripts and enlisted their friends and families to tell stories that imagined life's dramas as a set of fictions. In such films, the story is typically told with intertitles and, quite often, the narratives lean toward a comic frame while offering some kind of moral lesson.

The stranger in the small town

The small town serves as a backdrop for such lessons in Meyer Davis' thirteen-minute comedy *Miss Olympia* (1939).[8] Relying on the familiar premise of 'a stranger comes to town', *Miss Olympia* features a minor celebrity, 'Miss Olympia Swiftly', who has agreed to spend a day with the women of the 'Village Improvement Society' in the fictional town of Drinkwater Hollow. Community members are divided in their enthusiasm for the arrival of Miss Olympia. Members of the Improvement Committee are overjoyed, but the town patriarch, Hiram Dusenberry Drinkwater (played by Meyer Davis) is annoyed at the prospect of putting on airs for the celebrated visitor. His wife, head of the women's committee, reprimands him for his habit of pipe smoking because it might offend the guest.

Drinkwater Hollow may serve as an *idea* for a small town, but there are few visible traces of small-town living. The women in Drinkwater Hollow wear fashionable fur coats and hats and arrive in a speedboat to meet Miss Olympia at the ferry. Young boys in suit jackets play tennis. Teenage girls smoke cigarettes and roll their eyes when anyone mentions Miss Olympia. Drinkwater Hollow seems a place where community life is filled with the pretensions, anxieties and the kind of impression management akin to the life of high-society circles – the sort of world with which Davis was most familiar.

A pioneer of popular dance music in the United States, Davis and his multiple orchestras were a staple of upper-class social events. Davis conducted at presidential inaugural balls, scores of debutante parties and society weddings. During a career that spanned from the 1910s to the 1970s, Davis amassed a fortune, enabling him to own – at different times – vacation homes in Maine, Rhode Island and New York. Davis' brother-in-law and good friend was the renowned Parisian symphony conductor Pierre Monteux. Davis and Monteux married sisters who were born and raised in Maine, and Monteux is routinely featured in Davis' home movies and fictional films.

An avid amateur filmmaker, Davis scripted and filmed *Miss Olympia* at his summer home in Sorrento, Maine, near 'Bar Harbor'. In the film, the mountains surrounding 'Bar Harbor' appear in the distance as the villagers wait for Miss Olympia at the ferry. Miss Olympia finally arrives, but she is not what the viewer expects; she is portly and boorish. The moustachioed and flamboyant 'Duc de Lavatoires' (played by Monteux) escorts her down the gangplank to greet the Improvement Committee.

'We wonder if you would show us how to express ourselves', one committee member inquires, 'our lives are so suppressed'. A lumbering Miss Olympia leads them in some modern dance movements on a tennis court, but her talents are minimal, and one of the young women who wants to show her up, begins dancing like a 1920s flapper. Meanwhile Miss Olympia lurches across the court, losing her undergarments. Her students are unimpressed and walk away from her. Meanwhile, the Duc de Lavatoire seduces Lily Languish, the town's dance teacher, who submits to his advances.

Miss Olympia's credibility continues to spiral downward when asked to 'show some finer points in swimming'. Again, failing to impress, Miss Olympia looks fat and ungainly in her swimming attire. After struggling in the water, she washes up on the dock looking exhausted and bewildered. At this moment, another woman appears from the town's ferry. Attractive, slim, sophisticated, and apologising for her late arrival, she is the real Miss Olympia. The residents of Drinkwater Hollow realise that a charlatan has duped them. 'You imposter!' they exclaim. 'Leave this place immediately.' The counterfeit Miss Olympia jumps into the water. Wearing a life jacket and clutching an inflatable toy, she swims away while the town's women and the Duc taunt her from the dock.

Little in Drinkwater Hollow resembles any picture of rural life as we have seen it in *Time Marches On* and the *Movie Queen* films. Instead, *Miss Olympia* envisions a rural world as an enclave for urban elites, small-town playgrounds that cultivated their notions of a simple life and therapeutic retreat to nature. At the same time, rural resorts incurred divisions between the generations of families who lived there year round, and elites like Davis and Monteux who lived and worked in major cities and spent their summers in small New England towns.

Davis' understanding of the stranger who both fascinates and repels rural inhabitants may have been formed, in part, by his own circumstances. His wife Hilda and her sister Doris (who was married to Monteux) appear in *Miss Olympia*, and Davis credits them with the storyline. Hilda and Doris were from a working-class family that had lived near 'Bar Harbor'. In an unpublished memoir, Hilda remembers the division between the summer and the year-round residents. 'The natives labelled the summer people "rusticators" and "people from away" and had a feeling of dichotomy about this moneyed class', she recalled. 'While resenting their presence, they appreciated the change their wealth brought to the local economy.'[9] Hilda Davis also noted her own resentment. 'I experienced a particularly bitter sense of frustration with this seemingly social cleavage,' she writes, 'knowing that my family on both my mother's and father's sides had been early Island settlers. One grandfather had owned land which he sold for $5 an acre to the interlopers.' The young Hilda met Meyer in 'Bar Harbor' and their subsequent marriage catapulted her into high society. When they returned to Maine as summer residents, they were a curious hybrid of native and rusticator.

Davis' image of small-town life hardly extended beyond urbane stereotypes; his rural inhabitants are insular and self-conscious; they are first susceptible to and then unforgiving of a duplicitous stranger. Most significant though are the ways that *Miss Olympia* might have mirrored some of Davis' own sense of displacement in small Maine towns. As one who travelled in elite circles and entertained dignitaries, Davis surely understood social posturing and posing. He maps these very games onto Drinkwater Hollow, a place gesturing toward small-town life merely in name.

Miss Olympia becomes more complex when we consider the historical, biographical and geographical context of its production. On this level, the film is a thorny drama about insiders and outsiders, locals and strangers, and the class divisions (and potential resentments) that can grow out of such confrontations. The making of *Miss Olympia* was a way for Davis to engage his family and friends in his hobby of amateur filmmaking, but it was also an avenue for expressing the kinds of internalised contradictions and allegiances a man like Meyer Davis likely experienced during his summers in a small town. Given the biographies of its principal players, we see this story as one where a sense of displacement and belonging seem to seep into the film.

In a more general way, *Miss Olympia* captures a set of cultural and social tensions in a geography where urbane outsiders were increasingly appearing in small towns in Maine. Meyer Davis appears to be expressing some of the ambiguities of his own identity as one who was marked as being 'from away'. In Drinkwater Hollow, questions of belonging and identity – of being an insider or outsider – found easy resolution. Such answers, however, may have only seemed provisional when the final frames whipped through the projector. The film and its creation offered a respite from a more complicated landscape, one where family loyalties and local suspicions likely never found such an easy resolution.

Magically transforming the rural

Davis was not the only amateur filmmaker who made movies in which rural identity confronted issues of class and status. Hiram Percy Maxim's 19-minute silent film *Mag the Hag* (1925), for instance, is a fairytale of magical upward mobility. The film's narrative and special effects hinge upon a country girl's instantaneous transformation to city sophisticate. Maxim described *Mag the Hag* as a 'dripping melodrama'. He told the story with intertitles and featured four young women playing all of the roles.[10] The protagonist Percy Proudfoot (played by Maxim's daughter, Percy) is a wealthy and aimless dandy living on a country estate in Connecticut. An intertitle informs us that he has found 'happiness in the pure love of a simple country lass'. The barefoot and pig-tailed Peg first appears in a simple dress, sitting on a stone wall. She is shy and innocent when the self-confident Percy visits her.

Percy's love for Peg does not sit well with Elizabeth, identified in the opening credits as Percy's 'Aristicrooked Sister'. Angered by her brother's affection for Peg, Elizabeth thinks the country girl is below them. Her criticism prompts Percy to storm away in anger. During a drive in the country, he meets Mag the Hag, an old witch and the keeper of a magic talisman. Mag the Hag gives the talisman to Percy, who learns it has special powers to transform ordinary objects. Back home, he demonstrates its magic for Elizabeth. He passes the talis-man over a loaf of bread, and it becomes a squash. He transforms a stuffed bird into a live cat. In the next scene, he returns with Peg and demonstrates the talisman's powers for her and Elizabeth. His sister is enthusiastic, but the magic frightens Peg. After conferring with both women, Percy tries another experiment. This time, he slowly passes the talisman over Peg's body and head. With a dramatic snap of his fingers, Peg suddenly transforms into a sophisticate dressed in high heels, flowered dress, scarf and stylish hat. The final intertitle reads 'All Obstacles Removed at Last, Peg and Percy Find Great Happiness in Their Great Love', and the camera moves in for a close-up of Peg and Percy locked in a passionate kiss.

Mag the Hag depicts the attraction and repulsion of the rural for the urban elite. While Percy sees Peg as one of 'pure heart', that purity comes with too much social contamination for a man of his status. For their love to continue she must enter his world and be changed into a woman who, at least, can wear the accoutrements of urban sophistication. The very thing that draws him to Peg must be veiled by a new dress and hat; she must lose the pigtails and adopt a confident, glamorised posture. The image of Peg is a famil-iar and popular expression of idyllic country life; she is a divided emblem of how the rural is imagined by those who do not live there but are drawn to its symbolic value, ultimately transforming it into an image of their own desires.

It is worth noting that Hiram Percy Maxim's father, Sir Hiram Stevens Maxim, grew up on a farm in Sangerville, Maine. He received a modest public education, moved to Boston, and then to England, where he became a naturalised British subject and was

knighted by Queen Victoria in 1901. His early interest in science
set the stage for his life as an inventor. When living in England, he
became the well-known inventor of smokeless gunpowder and the
'Maxim Gun', the first portable automatic machine gun. His son,
Hiram, born in Brooklyn, New York in 1869, followed in his
father's footsteps. After attending the Massachusetts Institute of
Technology, Hiram invented the 'Maxim Silencer' that quieted
rifles and handguns.

By the time Hiram Percy Maxim made *Mag the Hag*, the Maxim
family was far removed from their rural Maine origins. Filming
during the summer of 1925, at the age of fifty-six, Maxim's social
standing was similar to the fictional Percy Proudfoot. A wealthy
inventor, in 1926 he founded the Amateur Cinema League and
published the first issue of *The Amateur Movie Maker* magazine,
where he listed *Mag the Hag* as one of several personal films he
wished to share with other amateur filmmakers. It is difficult to
know where Hiram came up with the storyline for *Mag the Hag*.
The old witch who holds the talisman is not so different from the
legendary 'Mag the Hag' in Welsh folktales who appears as a gypsy
with the power to put curses on villagers. Perhaps this story had
made its way to Hiram through his father, and his amateur film
holds the traces of that legend. More importantly, the film gives the
story – *and the context of its creation* – a modern twist. *Mag the
Hag* suggests that witches and magic still secretly thrive in the
countryside, and it is easy enough for the wealthy Percy to access
this phantasmagoric world. His for the taking, both Peg and Mag
the Hag (and the purity and the magic that are inherently theirs)
bring Percy happiness, and provide him with – at least on a superficial level – a bridge between the rural and the urban.

In the world outside the frame of his 16mm camera, Hiram Percy
Maxim had thoroughly embraced the possibilities of modern technology. In 1915, ten years before he founded the Amateur Cinema
League, he established the Amateur Radio Relay League, a network
of ham radio operators who also collapsed geography and reduced
the divide between the rural and the urban with their broadcast
signals. Dorothy Rowden, writing in a 1926 issue of *Amateur Movie
Makers*, suggested that Maxim believed 'that the day is not far
distant when amateur movie makers will be exchanging films with
the same ease and enjoyment as the amateur radio operator now
communicates with his distant friends' (Rowden cited in Kattelle,

2003: 239–43). Most of Maxim's life was devoted to a vision of progress through technology, but his film offers a nostalgic portrait of an imagined rural existence that seems barely shaken by such advances. Viewing rural life in this way, Maxim's film revives the charm and magic of a folktale. But in this story, the talisman's power for sorcery is merely an emblem for the camera's magic and its capacity to create the illusion of Peg's transformation.

It is important to note that Peg does not resist her transformation. For all of the virtues that come with the image of idyllic rural life, Peg seems happy to shed it all and wear the city like a new dress. In *Mag the Hag*, the visions of rural life and wealthy elites are extreme images, full of stereotypes about country innocence and aristocratic selfishness. Even if Maxim's story finds resolution on the side of elevated status, the subtext is that neither of these worlds can exist without the other. They are places that hold mutual, but different, promises of rescue and redemption.

Cinematic fragments of the rural

The visions of rural life in these films implicitly record the transformation, disappearance and recuperation of the rural in the face of modernisation. Raymond Cotton's *Time Marches On* may have documented daily life in a small town, but he did so as an historian, recognising and recording the significance of the present with an eye toward the future. He films the events of his town in a manner that salvages them in the flow of time and the transformations he witnessed in the years from 1934 through 1939, as if he was a reporter for some future audience. Margaret Cram's *Movie Queen* films capitalised on the desires of small rural communities to indulge in a collective fantasy of the promises of modern life. Each town had spawned a movie star, as the story goes, and the emissary from the big outside world returned to witness how her small town had kept up with the push of progress. These were small towns with electric refrigerators, auto dealerships and, of course, they were places where the myths of Hollywood had penetrated their population well enough to make up one of their own.

For Meyer Davis, the small rural town was a cinematic fiction, a place where stylish, rural inhabitants embracing narrow social codes viewed outsiders with awe and scepticism. Drinkwater Hollow, a fictional backdrop for the modest plot, becomes a more complicated place when situated in a historical context. Coming to terms with Davis' and his family's biographical backgrounds, we see *Miss Olympia* as a creative and therapeutic film. Its comic frame enabled the Davises to play with the ambiguities of their own insider/outsider status within the rural community of Sorrento. When Hiram Maxim makes *Mag the Hag*, a fairytale of cinematic magic able to render folk life in its own image and interests, the rural imagination seems a familiar and nostalgic portrait aimed to soothe urban discontent. 'The celebration of rustic felicity was never intended for rustics', notes Christopher Lasch. 'It could be savoured only by people of refinement who did not seriously propose, after all, to exchange the advantages of breeding and worldly experience for a life close to nature, no matter how lyrically they sang nature's praises' (Lasch, 1991: 84).

In Maxim's hands, the amateur movie camera could enchant the rural as a place of magic, but it also showed how that enchantment was a property of a class who could remake it according to their own desires. Conversely, in the hands of amateurs like Cotton or entrepreneurs like Cram, the camera was a device that allowed small-town inhabitants to be enchanted with themselves. Each of these views occupies the ends of a spectrum we might see as a rural imaginary, thriving on the tensions between progress and nostalgia. In these films, that tension is implicitly and explicitly manifest through stories and images, rendering a fragmented vision of rural life that ultimately escapes any aims toward containment. Instead, they show us idiosyncratic approaches to the rural. They are visions contingent upon the mobility of the camera as it found its way into the hands of people bound neither by class, community allegiance or geography. They are partial maps of places and brief moments in time that now only exist as film.

Notes

1 Richards was cranking a Pathé Kok amateur movie camera and was wealthy enough to afford the camera, film stock, processing costs and a projector; just the projector, screen and carrying case sold for approximately seventy-five dollars in 1912 (Coe, 1981).

2 F.B. Richards' 1916 *Snow White* is part of the Kitty Clements Collection at Northeast Historic Film, Bucksport, Maine. The film was preserved by the National Archives of Canada from the original 28mm nitrate camera negative.

3 A complete 16mm system of camera, projector, tripod, and screen sold for $335, and a 100-foot roll of film cost $6, including processing (Kattelle, 2000: 82–3; 2003: 238).

4 For an account of Northeast Historic Film's founding and an analysis of its relevance to the region see Jones (2003).

5 These details about Cotton's life are from a personal communication on 19 November 2004 with Hubert W. Clemons, Historian and Curator for the Hiram Historical Society, Hiram, Maine.

6 During the 1980s, Cotton had his film transferred to videotape, and narrated his recollections for *Time Marches On* into a tape recorder. His narration was added as a soundtrack to the video recording, and copies were distributed through the Hiram Historical Society. Cotton's original films are preserved in the collection at Northeast Historic Film.

7 The story of the drowning comes to us from Hubert Clemons of the Hiram Historical Society.

8 *Miss Olympia* is part of the Hilda and Meyer Davis Collection housed at Northeast Historic Film.

9 Hilda Davis, unpublished memoir, Hilda and Meyer Davis Collection files, Northeast Historic Film, Bucksport, ME, pp. 11–12.

10 For another reading of this film that focuses on the significance of the all-women cast, see Neumann (2002).

References

Coe, B. (1981), *The History of Movie Photography* (London: Ash and Grant).

Jones, J. (2003), 'From forgotten film to a film archive; the curious history of *From Stump to Ship*', *Film History: An International Journal*, 15(2): 193–202.

Kattelle, A.D. (2000), *Home Movies: A History of the American Industry, 1897–1979* (Nashua, NH: Transition).

Kattelle, A.D. (2003), 'The Amateur Cinema League and its films', *Film History: An International Journal*, 15(2): 238.

Lasch, C. (1991), *The True and Only Heaven: Progress and its Critics* (New York: W.W. Norton).

Neumann, M. (2002), 'Home movies on Freud's couch', *The Moving Image*, 2(1): 24–46.

Sterling, P. (1937), 'Sowing the 16mm field', *New York Times*: (025 July p. 3 sec. 10, C7).

Zimmermann, P. (1995), *Reel Families: A Social History of Amateur Film* (Bloomington: Indiana University Press).

14

Amber and an/other rural: film, photography and the former coalfields

Katy Bennett and Richard Lee

Set in the former coalfields of Durham, the film *Like Father* (2001) ends with a dramatic climax. An old, retired ex-miner called Arthur has kidnapped, bound and gagged the head of the local development agency and is holding him hostage on his allotment. This is a place where the old man spends much of his time and is also an area that the development agency wants cleared as part of its regeneration programme. Looking on with a mixture of horror, terror, understanding and pride are his son and grandson. Unlike other parts of the film, the concluding scene is not based on the actual experiences of the local residents involved in its production. When asked about its ending of *Like Father*, the Amber Film and Photography Collective said:

> When we'd almost finished the script, we went to see old Joe, one of the pigeon men who was one of the main influences on the character of Arthur. He was the last man on the allotments at Easington that were going to be demolished, and we asked him how we should end it and he suggested taking the council officer hostage – he wished he could have done that. (Young, 2001: 67)

When we wrote about the final scene of *Like Father* being based on fantasy in an earlier draft of this chapter, Amber drew our attention to a local event that had made headline news. In April 1992 Albert Dryden was sentenced to life imprisonment for the murder of a Derwentside council planner in a dispute over his bungalow. Dryden was fifty-one years old, a bachelor and unemployed, having been made redundant when British Steel at Consett closed eleven years previously. He had used his £13,000 redundancy money to build a bungalow on a small-holding without planning permission. When council officials arrived to demolish Dryden's bungalow in June 1991, police and the press accompanied them. Extraordinarily, the BBC filmed the murder and the reporter, himself injured by another bullet that Dryden fired, continued to talk about the unfolding drama to the camera. One of the many reports that followed the incident had the headline 'Gunman "acted out role in Western"' (*Guardian*, 1992: 8) and described how the court was told that Dryden performed as if "in a scene from a Western in which a homesteader is going to be evicted". With the cameras rolling, onlookers had watched Dryden fetch a revolver, strap a holster to his hip and calmly shoot the Council official.

Drawing upon the work of the Amber Film and Photography Collective, this chapter explores the relationship between performance, representation and identity. In particular, it looks at how the landscape of the former Durham coalfields is simultaneously identified and embodied through a focus on both its representation and some of the practices that affect its representation. The ending of *Like Father* shows how practices and representation are implicated in each other. It was a fantasy of old Joe's in the sense that is was not based on his own life. Quite possibly, though, Joe identified with the effort of Albert Dryden to defend his home from powerful law enforcers, an act in itself which could have been influenced by fantasy, films and representations of other places at other times. No one can be completely sure exactly how practices and representation mediate and affect one another, but such a space of uncertainty inspires us in this chapter.

Sitting at the heart of this chapter are the creative practices of the Amber Film and Photography Collective. In a corpus of work dealing with the impact of industrial restructuring on working-class communities in the northeast of England, Amber explores identities in the former coalfields of Durham. Amber's work is unusual in its approach to photography and filmmaking, working with residents over a long (and continuing) period of time so that their accounts and experiences inform the writing, production and direction of its material. Furthermore, they employ local people to perform in films such as *Like Father* and *The Scar* (1997). This means that the former coalfields of Durham, some of its residents and Amber are drawn into a collaboration whereby the representations, practices and performances of each affect the identification of others.

The former coalfields of Durham do not sit comfortably with idyllic representations of the countryside. Although they resonate with other visions of countryside represented in this book with their villages and empty green spaces, the devastating scale and speed of pit closures in the 1980s and 1990s mean that things are far from idyllic. The former coalfields of Durham are not a location to where people move to pursue romanticised visions of rurality that haunt television screens, but a place that harbours high levels of poverty, ill-health and economic inactivity. Easington District, where much of Amber's work is based, is the eighth most deprived local authority in England and Wales (www.neighbourhood. statistics.gov.uk). This is a landscape, though, that matters because of the practices of those who create it as they affect its regeneration, remember its past, get on with its present and fill the empty green spaces that mark the sites of former collieries with rather different meaning compared to those empty green spaces celebrated elsewhere (Rose, 2002).

Two of us write this chapter. Our common agenda is to demonstrate the interplay and mutual identification of Amber and its subjects. To do this, we present two stories, written together and separately. One of these stories is called 'Embodied landscape' and shows how Amber's work gives form to the Durham landscape, influencing how it is experienced. Important to this piece are the creative practices of Amber and its relationships with others, including people and places of East Durham, funding bodies and the Baltic arts centre. 'Embodied landscape' introduces two of Amber's projects: the film *Like Father* and a photographic exhibition called *Coalfield Stories* (exhibited 2002). The second story is called 'Landscape embodied'. Here the performances of local residents in *Like Father* are the focus to demonstrate how dynamic interconnections between an industry and landscape affect processes of identification (particularly gendered identities) as individuals negotiate the changes instigated by pit closures. The piece explores how both an industrial heritage and changing landscape mediate performances of residents (and Amber). The two stories are written side by side to demonstrate the impact of Amber's collaboration with people and landscapes on its work and how its practices simultaneously identify (itself and) the former coalfields.

Important to this chapter is a focus on the endless process of identification, in which identity is never entirely established as individuals relate to others and are subject to diverse discourses. Important to this process are performances (including practices) which have many elements to them. To start with, there is the unintentional aspect of performances, as individuals reiterate historically situated cultural practices that begin to define them (Butler, 1990; 1993). In East Durham, for example, the continuing discursive power of the mining industry, and the particular politics and patriarchy that it created, positions people and frames practices. An individual's performances, though, are not simply contained by positioning in various discourses. Subjectivity mediates discursive identification so that an individual's wishes, desires and emotions are another important aspect of performances (Hollway, 1989; Hall, 1996). Through their relationships, individuals identify with and affect emotion in others who similarly affect emotion in them. There is an inter/subjective experience of identity that mediates the grasp of discourses. Contributions to a visitors' book at the Side Gallery, for instance, show how some individuals emotionally identified with the photographs of Coalfield Stories, as its images were meaningful to them in sometimes unexpected ways. Finally, elements of performances are utterly self-conscious as individuals identify themselves in relation to others (Cohen, 1994, 2000; MacDonald, 1997). The relational character of gender construction, for example, is significant in Like Father with masculinities constructed through self-conscious performances and interactions with others (Connell, 1995; Hall, 1996; Mac an Ghaill, 1996). Inevitably, though, such self-conscious performances are never entirely disconnected from the discourses that identify (Nelson, 1999; Gregson and Rose, 2000; Nash, 2000; Crouch and Malm, 2003).

Our previous and current roles inform the writing of this chapter. Katy started work in the former coalfields of England and Wales in 1998 through a project, funded by the Joseph Rowntree Foundation, dealing with coalfields regeneration (Bennett et al., 2000). Through the project she came into contact with the work of the Amber Film and Photography Collective, which is now key to a new project exploring the relationship between identities and regeneration in the former coalfields of East Durham.[1] Richard previously worked for Durham County Council and is now a PhD researcher at Newcastle University. He and Katy met in 2003 when he was studying for an MSc degree, taking a module on which she taught. Fuelled by the work of Amber, ideas flowed, circulated, and slipped through seminars and writing on identities and the former coalfields. This chapter emerges from performances in previous and current field/work, seminars at Newcastle University, the Side Gallery, and the Amber office, cinema, website, films and photographs.

Embodied landscape

Introducing Amber

The film *Like Father* and the photographic exhibition *Coalfield Stories* are elements of a body of work that stretches back to 1969, when the Amber Film and Photography Collective formed in Newcastle with the aim of creating a film and photographic practice in relation to the working-class communities of the northeast of England (Amber, www.amber-online.com),

To be more specific about the essence of Amber is difficult. Whilst on the one hand it is a long-established organisation with a clear socio-political agenda, on the other it is not so much a thing but a process shaped by a number of key individuals (and others). These individuals work together and independently, often in a close relationship with their subjects, who in turn affect the substance of Amber. The moments when Amber takes on its clearest, sharpest form are in response to the current state of British cinema, its funding structures and practices, all of which help to define that which Amber is not.

The base of the Amber Film and Photography Collective is near the Quayside of Newcastle and Gateshead, an area that has witnessed tremendous change with the demise of the city's heavy industrial base and the closure of its ship-building yards. Once a place of immense production, the Quayside has transformed into a space of mass consumption with the development of hotels, prestigious living spaces, bars, restaurants and big corporate sites of high culture, such as the Baltic arts centre. Just as the heavy industrial character and working-class communities of the city and its region defined the ambitions of Amber, so too, in some ways, has the transformation of the Quayside.

Set a little way back from the Quayside, the Side Gallery, opened in 1977, is the easily accessible, public face of Amber. It is open most days and entrance is free to view photographic exhibitions. To describe the Side Gallery and the Baltic as two sites of cultural production that stand in opposition to one another would be too simple, yet the presence of the hegemonic cultural practices of the Baltic in some way identify the agenda of Amber as alternative and edgy (Rose, 1994). The juxtaposition of two such different galleries is meaningful to visitors to the Side Gallery, who write statements

Landscape embodied

Introducing *Like Father*

14.1 *Like Father* publicity poster

such as 'Better than the Baltic' in Amber's comments book. Members of the Amber Collective regularly exhibit their work here. *Coalfield Stories* (which included the work of Amber members) ran in 2002. Other photographers also exhibit their work in the Side Gallery, bringing to the audiences and spaces of Amber images and experiences from around the world.

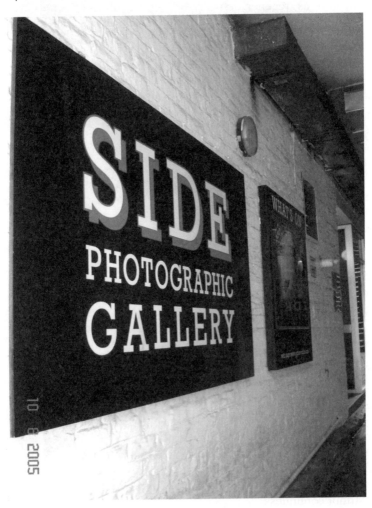

14.2 The Side Gallery

Amber's film *Like Father* focuses upon three male generations of
the Elliott family and their interwoven identity performances. It is
situated within the post-coalfield landscape of East Durham, a
landscape affecting the performances of the central characters
through its industrial legacy and uncertain future. Masculinities
embody scenes of demolition and a landscape undergoing transformation as regeneration agendas, flows of information and
institutional changes mediate space. *Like Father* is a visual and oral
narrative on a changing landscape's impact upon masculinities.

Performances in *Like Father* are conditioned by the legacy of a
mining culture and the changes that pit closures have brought to
the former coalfields. The three Elliotts at the centre of the film are
Arthur, Joe and Michael. They represent three life stages. Arthur is
a former miner in his sixties. Joe, his son, is also a former miner and
is in his thirties. Joe now works as a musical animator and community worker whilst Arthur spends much of his time at the
allotments. Michael is Joe's son and is in primary school. Besides
the male Elliotts, other prominent characters include Carol Elliott
(sewing machinist, Michael's mother and Joe's wife) and Dave
Hylton (head of a local development agency).

Important to the identification of the three male Elliotts is their
interconnection with others (including a coalfield landscape). One
of these relationships is with Amber, who is implicated in the identification of the former coalfields and those who live there. Its
subjects similarly influence the practices of Amber. To produce a
focused account of how the coalfield landscapes are embodied in
Like Father (2001), the performances of each of the three male
Elliotts will be given primacy.

'I'm Arthur Elliott, ex-miner'

Arthur embodies the coalfield landscape, which is mediated by an
assemblage of institutional relationships that frame his performances. He opposes the new hegemonic masculinity of the senior
management official represented by the character of Dave Hylton.
Dave fails to understand the pervasiveness of Arthur's coalmining
identity performance in the context of a post-coalfield landscape.
He is informed that: 'Once a pit man, always a pit man.'

Arthur continues to perform as a 'coal miner' in a coalfield landscape by moving his site of labour and socialisation from the pit to
the allotment. He produces a militant performance in this theatre of

Amber and the Durham coalfield

Much of Amber's work is about documenting the lives of working-class people in the north of England. Its projects tend to develop organically and inter-subjectively. *Like Father* (2001) explores masculinities in the shadow of colliery closures. It simultaneously details the fracturing of relations between generations of men and the bonds that draw them together. *Like Father* (2001) developed out of *The Scar* (1997) (a film that focused on women's experiences of life in the former coalfields after pit closures). Similarly, *Coalfield Stories* developed out of *Like Father*, as members of the Amber Collective were introduced to subjects and locations in the process of film-making. Using the metaphor of voyage to explain its organic way of working, Amber said:

> Every film is a voyage of discovery – that's why you make the film. It's not because you know the subject, it's because you want to know about it, you want to understand something, and that's why you set out on the voyage. The making of the film is the way of understanding it, and hopefully at the end of the day the product then gives other people some insight and understanding into that way of life. (Young, 2001: 71)

Key to Amber's practices is developing a relationship with places and people so that subjects have an impact on filmmaking and photography (Crouch and Grassick, 2005). Amber's films are pitched at the interface between documentary and drama. The precise relationship between documentary and drama is important. When asked to compare its approach to that of other film directors, Amber said:

> Loach is another person we're sometimes compared with . . . The term which covers Loach is 'documentary dramas' and what they mean is, you take a drama and make it look 'real'. We're more likely to take a documentary and convert it into 'a dramatic story'. (Young, 2001: 72)

Because the drama emerges from documenting people's lives, a script for *Like Father* (2001) did not exist before work began on the film. Instead Amber collected people's accounts of their lives and used these to develop a script. They trained three retired men to use video cameras to document their own lives, interviewed people and organised workshops for children. Also, some of the scenes in the school and club were filmed before the script was written and so his choosing, reacting to the proposed demolition of his allotment by Dave's development agency with the language of industrial action: '... we're digging in'.

Through his performances Arthur defends the landscape of his labour, once the pit and now the allotment. His coalfield landscape is one of production and he mocks the commercial aspirations of the development agency: 'The last time we had tourists round here was when the Vikings invaded.' These words demonstrate his desire to play out a performance rooted in the landscape of his industrial past and his self-conscious resistance to particular elements of economic and social change. Arthur embodies a politicised landscape which the regeneration agenda hopes to wipe out to attract corporate investment. Brian, who acts as a liaison for the developers in the allotment, walks away muttering: 'Keep the red flag flying.'

Arthur's identity performance is, in part, constructed alongside the practices of Dave, amongst others. Whilst Arthur performs the role of masculine working-class militant, defending his territorial rights to a working landscape, Dave represents an agenda seeking to remove reminders of coalmining from the landscape. His agency's promotion video refers to a: '... coastline littered with a century's colliery waste ... Our children and their grandchildren deserve a safe and better future.'

The conflict between Arthur and Dave over the future of the landscape is mediated (in the interests of the developers) by Brian. Brian, although aligned to the development agenda, is sympathetic to Arthur's connection to the coalfield landscape. He explains to Dave that: '... some of these lads have spent half their lives on the same allotment. What about compensation for the pigeon lofts?' He also explains that although the mines have been closed for over a decade, Arthur and his mates: '... are pitmen.'

Arthur's coalfield landscape is one that speaks directly to those who understand it and Amber constructs Arthur's character as a living embodiment of the traditions of the East Durham coalfield. On the one hand he selflessly embodies coalfields culture; on the other he self-consciously reacts to the attempts of others to redefine his place.

The interplay of self-conscious performance and performance as reiterative of discourse can also been seen in Arthur's interactions with his son Joe and grandson Michael. Coalmining discourse substantiates his performances when he plays the role of some of the writing process happened around these scenes (Young, 2001). Other scenes were shot once the script existed and required local people to learn lines that embodied the accounts of others' lives as well as their own. Once a film is shot it is shown to local people in familiar venues and ensuing discussion inevitably informs the organic process of Amber's work and its voyage into new issues.

In the making of *Like Father*, subjects for *Coalfield Stories* emerged, for which a similar process of work was important. Although members of the Amber Collective focus on different aspects of the Durham coalfields, linking much of their work is the time they spend with people. In a body of work called 'The Coal Coast', Sirkka-Lisa Konttinen (2003) captures the snippets of past working lives that are revealed on the East Durham beaches with the ebb and flow of tides. Despite the on-going efforts of regeneration agendas to rid the landscape of its mining heritage, she shows how the industry continues to embody the landscape. In one photograph a half-submerged miner's boot fuses with desiccated clay; in another a section of a mine ventilation duct haunts the beach (Konttinen, 2003). The body of work took years (1999–2002) to evolve, developing out of *Like Father* when she met Easington allotment holders who introduced her to the beaches of East Durham. The allotment holders were retired miners and Konttinen (2003) discovered:

> the amazing affinity these ex-miners had for the landscape, the particular details of it and the way they felt their own personal histories were so intricately bound up with those details. (www.amber-online.com)

In 'Fathers', a very different body of work for *Coalfield Stories*, Peter Fryer and Graeme Rigby worked with three men and their families over a period of two years. Reflecting on the process, Fryer (2001) wrote:

> Working that intimately and closely with a small group of people over such a long period, you begin to get a degree of openness and relaxation of trust and a mutual understanding. You don't want to force yourself down their throats and at times, it's about recognising when you're not welcome. Working together in this way is a collaboration, where everyone is able to suggest things that should be explored, and each voice is heard. This interaction informed and directed both the photography and the writing. (www.amber-online.com)

domineering family patriarch in the company of Joe. With his grandson Michael, Arthur's performance self-consciously shifts to that of an educator and guardian as he invites Michael into his world at the allotment. Arthur defends Michael's rights to the allotment and surrounding landscape against the developers whilst simultaneously making a stand of his own as he resists the performances of the developers. He rages at the security guards who chase away Michael and his friends, telling them that the kids live there, implying that it is their landscape and part of who they are.

'I'm Joe Elliott, and that's my dad you're slagging off'

Through the character of Joe Elliott, a more complex relationship with the coalfield landscape can be seen. Joe becomes aligned with the interests of the development agency when he accepts a musical commission under the direction of Dave. Joe's performances with Dave are as uneasy as those he produces with his father, Arthur. He self-consciously plays upon his coalmining culture when faced with the post-coalfield landscape in the form of regeneration, but finds it difficult to be sympathetic to the coalfield landscape held dear by Arthur. These performances are rooted in the coalfield landscape and Joe's confused relationship with it. The former coalfields speak of his, and Arthur's, shared and individual histories. For Joe to abandon it completely would be a self-conscious denial and an act of betrayal that would undermine his father's performances. Towards the film's climax Arthur asks Joe: 'How long did it take ya to count ya thirty pieces of silver?'

Joe takes money from the family home as well as the development agency. He spends money set aside by his wife Carol and rationalises it through 'his' redundancy money being used for family holidays, a caravan and so on. These claims ring hollow for Carol and she suggests that: 'It's not just about money, we never see ya, you're always at the club with ya mates.'

Joe's performances in the household embody a coalfield landscape, and are inspired by Arthur's performances years ago. But the landscape of the household has changed since those days and for Joe it is becoming as unrecognisable and contested as the post-coalfield landscape threatens to be for Arthur. The prevalence of the coalfield landscape in performances can be problematic for men in the post-coalfield landscape as they face changes in their

The continuing relationship that Amber has with the former Durham coalfields means that occasionally the lives of subjects can be traced across films and photographs. Joe Armstrong, a man in his forties who is a musician and former miner, performed a leading role in *Like Father* and his biography and experiences informed some of the script writing. He was also one of the key subjects of Richard Grassick's work 'On the Surface' for *Coalfield Stories*. In these two projects Joe banters and drinks with his mates in the club, carves out a life teaching music, running a small business and entertaining people, and spends little time at home with his family. His relationship with his wife and son is crumbling under the pressure of dealing with change. In some of Richard Grassick's most recent work, called 'Post-Industrial', there is a DVD comprising filmed interviews with former miners in Durham juxtaposed with interviews with men mostly still working in the ship-building industry in Bremerhaven (Germany). The latter group of men talk about uncertainty and insecurity as they live amongst job loss and industrial restructuring. A pace behind the Durham men, their accounts are matter of fact, their faces deadpan. Flick back to the interviews with ex-miners and the heterogeneity of life experiences since pit closures is revealed. Among these, Joe Armstrong talks to the camera about frittering away his redundancy payment, always being the entertainer to compensate for being over-weight and not spending enough time with his wife because of the draw of the club. Ever the entertainer, he laughs at himself but his voice is tinged with regret and sadness. The interview then moves forward in time and the chubby face morphs into a slimmed down version of Joe. Images appear of Joe on a treadmill and in a suit as East Durham's Life Long Learning Officer. He is no longer laughing, but serious and talking about valuing himself more. The transformation is stark and viewers are left to themselves to consider how and why the change happened. On the one hand Joe has lifted himself out of 'victim' status, on the other he has a job with precisely the Development Agency portrayed in the film. Grassick leaves us with questions regarding how the making of films and images affects processes of identification and what this means for subjects as they embody deep identity conflicts, caught between old and new landscapes (Grassick, personal communication).

households and places and interact with others and alternative masculinities. Whilst Joe persists with performances about the house that define his sense of masculinity, Carol becomes increasingly ambivalent to him as she works hard to earn money to finance the household. Joe is becoming an outsider in his own home as it becomes unfamiliar territory and he is unable to maintain a close relationship with his son Michael. Michael and Carol are brought even closer as the rift between Joe and his household develops. The tensions in his relationships with others cause Joe to question his future and self-identity. By asking him to leave, Carol undermines his coalfield performances and Michael sees his father become even more alienated from the household.

Joe's relationship with his ten-year-old son is complicated by the fact that Michael has only known the post-coalfield landscape. For Michael, there is more space for alternative performances that are not disconnected from his sense of (post) coalfield landscape but are different from those of the older generations with a working knowledge of collieries. Michael is growing up in an informational age. His proximity to information, images and symbols from indefinite sources means that his performances are explicitly mediated by the practices and flows of these.

Michael's relationship with his mother is portrayed as a close one as she provides him with the space (and props) to playfully perform alternative characters. His performances for her attention as she busies herself with work mean that Michael pushes the boundaries that condition his behaviour. Michael's mother reacts to her son's performances with amusement and encouragement (when she has time) and frustration/anger (when she is struggling to meet a deadline). Michael's father, on the other hand, ridicules his performances when he witnesses them, calling him 'Michelle' when he catches him playfully wearing a dress. Michael's performances are shown in stark contrast to those of Joe in the club entertaining audiences and drinking beer.

It is through his grandfather that Michael learns about a way of life that embodies the landscape and imbues identities. Arthur helps Michael to fill the symbols important to coalmining culture with meaning, occupying the young boy with activities that involve greyhound racing, pigeons, story telling and the allotments. Michael's sense of belonging and attachment to the landscape is played out through his relationship with his grandfather as he sides

Amber and funding

A final key aspect of Amber's work which shapes its practices and identification is its search for funding to sustain its activities. '(D)riven by cultural rather than commercial concerns, Amber has never sought to be part of the mainstream industry' (www.amber-online.com). This means that Amber has produced and distributed its films with relatively small pockets of funding, navigating changes to the structure of funding with sometimes very little money at all. Also, despite the evolving relationship between its films and photography, funding bodies rarely, if ever, have supported Amber's working practices of integrating film and photography.

Funding structures and practices have contributed to the identification of Amber in two key ways. Firstly, on the one hand institutions condition Amber's activities as they frame elements of its performances and absorb some of its energies, on the other they produce political, vocal and public responses from Amber that identify the Collective at the centre of the margin. Secondly, there have been occasions when Amber has turned down potential funding opportunities that come with conditions (and script writers), opting for smaller budgets and greater freedom that identify its agenda. Reflecting on turning down a larger budget for *Eden Valley* (1994), Amber said:

> We took (the smaller budget) with not a lot of hesitation, because we knew we wanted to make a film which accurately reflected the community we represented. As soon as you go down the other route, you're into this thing about 'How do you make a commercially successful film?' That's when they move in the big guns – you get the money, they come in. (Young, 2001: 69)

with Arthur against his father and opposes the local development agenda. Once Joe sides with his father against the bureaucrats, *Like Father* (2001) reaches its climax with the three Elliotts in the allotment bound together by the coalfield landscape.

Performances/identities

Amber's work demonstrates how it, local people and landscapes, amongst others, are drawn into a collaboration whereby the practices and performances of each affect the identification of others. To appreciate and understand the practices of Amber, the performances of others need to be considered. We hope that eyes might have occasionally glanced across the stories to appreciate the process of mutual identification whereby Amber's practices embody landscapes which mediate the performances of local people. At the same time, Amber's relationship with people and places affects its practices. It is important to recognise, however, that the performances that shape this chapter are not in isolation of others. Other performances elsewhere and at different moments mediate identities and practices. The action plans of regeneration agendas in East Durham, including the removal of allotments and clearing of beaches, and disembodied representations of the coalfields (to obtain funding and encourage corporate investment) elicit particular performances from residents and Amber alike. Similarly other representations of East Durham in films like *Billy Elliot* (a film made at a similar time to *Like Father* [2001]) affect the performances of local people and the practices of Amber, especially when they identify the Durham coalfield as a place to escape. The biographies and experiences of individuals similarly influence performances. Although members of Amber, for example, operate as a collective and usually avoid crediting individual contributors to their film work and website, the touch of individuals and the importance of their unique biographies emerges in both their own work and collaboration with others. Their relationships elsewhere (and at other times) with particular people and landscapes affect their work in the Durham coalfield. Amber's film and photographic work is impossible to understand without others.

Acknowledgements

Firstly, we would like to thank Richard Grassick and Graeme Rigby at the Amber Film and Photography Collective for helping us with this chapter and offering their thoughts and opinions on an earlier draft. Thanks also to Giles Mohan for his support and advice on our writing.

Notes

1 The research project is called *Identities and Regeneration in the Former Coalfields of East Durham* and is funded by the ESRC (RES-148-25-0025).

References

Bennett, K., Beynon, H. and R. Hudson (2000), *Coalfields Regeneration: Dealing with the Consequences of Industrial Decline* (Bristol: Policy Press).

Butler, J. (1990), *Gender Trouble: Feminism and the Subversion of Identity* (London: Routledge).

Butler, J. (1993), *Bodies that Matter: On the Discursive Limits of 'Sex'* (London: Routledge).

Cohen, A. (1994), *Self Consciousness* (London: Routledge).

Cohen, A. (2000), 'Introduction: discriminating relations – identity, boundary and authenticity', in Cohen, A. (ed.), *Signifying Identities: Anthropological Perspectives on Boundaries and Contested Values* (London: Routledge), pp. 1–13.

Connell, R.W. (1995), *Masculinities* (Cambridge: Polity Press).

Crouch, D. and Grassick, R. (2005), 'Amber Films, documentary and encounters', in Crouch, D., Jackson, R. and Thompson, F. (eds), *The Media and the Tourist Imagination'* (London, Routledge), pp. 42–59.

Crouch, D. and Malm, C. (2003), 'Landscape practice, landscape research: an essay in gentle politics', in Dorrian, M. and Rose, G. (eds), *Deterritorialisations … Revisioning: Landscape and Politics* (London and New York: Black Dog Publishing), pp. 253–63.

Gregson, N. and Rose, G. (2000), 'Taking Butler elsewhere: performativities, spatialities and subjectivities', *Environment and Planning D: Society and Space* 18: 433–52.

Guardian (1992) 'Gunman "acted out role in Western"' (28 March 1992), p. 8.

Hall, S. (1996) 'Who needs "identity"?', in Hall, S. and du Gay, P. (eds), *Questions of Cultural Identity* (London: Sage), pp. 1–17.

Hollway, W. (1989), *Subjectivity and Method in Psychology: Gender, Meaning and Science* (London: Sage).

Konttinen, S.-L. (2003), *The Coal Coast* (Newcastle: Amberside).

Mac an Ghaill, M. (1996), *Understanding Masculinities* (Buckingham: Open University Press).

Macdonald, S. (1997), 'Identity complexes in Western Europe: Social Anthropological perspectives', in Macdonald, S. (ed.), *Inside European Identities* (Oxford: Berg), pp. 1–26.

Nash, C. (2000), 'Performativity in practice: some recent work in cultural geography', *Progress in Human Geography*, 24(4): 653–64.

Nelson, L. (1999), 'Bodies (and spaces) do matter: the limits of performativity', *Gender, Place and Culture*, 6(4): 331–53.

Rose, G. (1994), 'The cultural politics of place: local representation and oppositional discourse in two films', *Transactions of the Institute of British Geographers*, 19(1): 46–60.

Rose, M. (2002), 'Landscape and labyrinths', *Geoforum*, 33(4): 455–67.

Young, N. (2001), 'Forever Amber: an interview with Ellin Hare and Muray Martin of the Amber Film Collective', *Critical Quarterly*, winter: 61–80.

Internet sources

www.amber-online.com
www.neighbourhood.statistics.gov.uk

Index